A STRATEGY FOR WINNING

In Business • In Sports
In Family • In Life

CARL MAYS

FOREWORD BY LOU HOLTZ

THE LINCOLN-BRADLEY PUBLISHING GROUP

New York

Permissions Department
The Lincoln-Bradley Publishing Group
305 Madison Avenue - Suite 1166
New York, NY 10165

Publisher's Cataloging in Publication

Mays, Carl
    A strategy for winning: in business, in sports, in family,
in life / Carl Mays; foreword by Lou Holtz. —

    p.   cm.
    ISBN 1-879111-75-6

    1. Success. 2. Self-realization. I. Title.

BJ1611.2   158
                                        90-62803

Printed on approved acid-free paper

Book Design by Rick Soldin

Front Jacket Photo by Larry Miller

2 3 4 5 6 7 8 9 10

WHAT A GROUP OF TESTIMONIALS!

These high-profile winners have read

A STRATEGY FOR WINNING

by

CARL MAYS.

Here's what they say:

"A Strategy For Winning will have a very positive impact upon me, our football team and certainly our family. I highly recommend the book." (also see foreword)

– Lou Holtz
Football Coach, Notre Dame

"Carl Mays is sending out a great message through his writing and speeches. *A Strategy For Winning* shares something that everyone wants to know and should have access to. It is very inspirational and constructive. The Lord has endowed Carl Mays with a touch of real genius. He is a superb communicator."

– Dr. Norman Vincent Peale
Clergyman/Author

"In any situation in life there are people who win and people who don't. In this book, Carl Mays has clearly outlined the reasons people win and how a person can put himself or herself in a position to do so. Reading *A Strategy For Winning* will most definitely put you in a winning frame of mind. This book is a 'Humm Baby,' and a must for the collection of anyone who wants to succeed."

– Roger Craig
Manager, San Francisco Giants

"*A Strategy For Winning* is a positive, inspirational message. It not only opened my eyes to a more uplifting outlook but also will definitely help others to continue to strive for their meaning of success. Carl shows us that when we apply ourselves to the best of our abilities, we will all be winners."

– Crystal Gayle
Entertainer

"Carl Mays has given us the 'mile markers' on how to win - and to stay on track to win again. *A Strategy For Winning* is clear and direct, with understandable logic. Winning is never easy, but Carl shows you how to get a 'second wind' in the effort. I thoroughly enjoyed and benefited from the book - and I made notes!"

– Sam Wyche
Head Coach, Cincinnati Bengals

4

"There are probably thousands of books written on 'how to' do something, but very few tell you what to do after you try to do something and don't succeed. *A Strategy For Winning* is different because it not only tells you how to do it, but also how to pick yourself up when you get knocked down. It's a wonderful book and provides an excellent game plan to finding peace, love, happiness and success in your life."

**– Dale Brown
Basketball Coach, LSU**

"*A Strategy For Winning* is a most comprehensive text on all the ways of winning. I liked it because of the many, many real life examples, and I believe everybody who reads it will enjoy and benefit from it tremendously."

**– Rich DeVos
President, Amway**

"I had heard that Carl Mays presented some valuable information in a delightful manner. Therefore, I appreciated the opportunity to read *A Strategy For Winning*. I thoroughly enjoyed it and found it to be entertaining and enlightening. I'm always interested in finding ways to improve myself and our program, and discovered Carl to have a lot of good ideas and valuable insights."

**– Terry Donahue
Football Coach, UCLA**

"A Strategy For Winning is truly a formula for success. The basics are addressed with humorous anecdotes and each chapter is written with clarity. Carl has shared the secrets of winning in all phases of life. Common sense so often is uncommon, but anyone who reads and implements Carl's strategy will have a huge head start on the competition. My only regret is that the book was not available to me when I first started coaching; had it been, I know that I would have made far fewer mistakes."

– Ara Parseghian
Sports Commentator/Former Coach

"A Strategy For Winning is great! Carl Mays provides the answers we are all looking for in the game of life. If there's one equal factor where many women are concerned, it's lack of self-confidence. To see a woman so timid and shy she could hardly talk over the phone develop in a few months into a beautiful, personable woman is really wonderful. This book can assist in such a development."

– Mary Kay Ash
Founder, Mary Kay Cosmetics

"We are entering the most competitive decade in the history of mankind and this very special book can mean the difference between victory and defeat for you."

– Og Mandino
Author/Speaker

"In its bulky, pre-book, manuscript form, I lugged *A Strategy For Winning* on and off airplanes and found myself transfixed by Carl's work, despite all the distractions. In an era of negativism, here is a great alternative! *A Strategy For Winning* organizes psychological principles, humor, the human drama and practical application for all of us who seek to lead. I think it is terrific! Now that it's in book form, I intend to read it again!"

> **– Bill Curry**
> **Football Coach, Kentucky**

"*A Strategy For Winning* is superb! This gem is for everybody, be they successful or seemingly failures. God does not make a 'nobody' - there are talents and abilities in everyone He brings into being. Carl Mays makes this very clear. Carl presents lesson after lesson from real-life experiences, and then shows how we can apply great philosophical and spiritual principles to make our lives really count."

> **– Dale Evans Rogers**
> **Actress/Author**

"Carl has made a great contribution to the understanding and implementation of self-motivation and success. With drama and humor, he pulls together many proven concepts that will work successfully in all of our lives when they are applied. I recommend it highly."

> **– Grant Teaff**
> **Football Coach, Baylor**

7

"Carl has done a masterful job which will inspire anyone who reads this book to achieve goals they never thought possible. He has addressed the fear of failure and the expectation of success in such a way that no one can miss the message. Having spent 40 years as a sports announcer and 14 years as a sports apparel retailer and franchiser with Fan Fair, I have heard many coaches, managers and business leaders hold their teams or organizations spellbound with inspirational speeches in preparation for the competition they would face. None was more inspiring than the message presented by Carl in *A Strategy For Winning.* I plan to have copies of this excellent book circulated throughout our corporation!"

– Merle Harmon
Sportscaster/Retailer

"I wrote a book called *Pray to Win*, emphasizing that God wants everyone to succeed. My book is based upon Proverbs 16:3 and upon my revelation that God *intends* for us to be successful and generous and able to have dominion over our circumstances in life. Sadly, so many of us settle for so much less. Carl Mays has experienced his own revelations - and has employed them with dramatic success. Because of this success, he's able to share with others what he has learned. Through *A Strategy For Winning*, Carl is able to help you to be successful in every area of life. I know this is how God intends it to be, and I recommend this book heartily to one and all."

– Pat Boone
Entertainer/Author

"A Strategy For Winning presents life changing principles and specific strategies to help us obtain that quantum leap that can truly change our lives for the better. The book contains a treasure of anecdotes which provide examples of procedures that have already proven to be of big help to others. The book is more than trite advice. It is real. Read it. Think about it. Apply it."

– Kyle Rote, Jr.
Superstar Athlete/Sportscaster

"Having been fortunate enough to win five NAIA National Championships in the 80's, my staff, players and I truly realize the importance of faith and creativity - two areas Carl covers so well in *A Strategy For Winning.* A person can take all nine principles dealt with in this book and build relationships, businesses, teams and even his or her life. This book also reminded me that the truth is always the truth."

– Ken Sparks
Football Coach, Carson-Newman

"A Strategy For Winning will be of value to everyone who has difficulty in prioritizing life and managing dreams. Let's face it, most of us are not well-organized. Most people tend to take things as they come rather than strategizing about which should come first, second, third . . . Unfortunately for many people, life is what happens while you are making other plans. This book will help you manage 'what happens,' and will keep you pointed toward real values and goals in your life."

– Art Linkletter
Entertainer/Author/Speaker

"In his speaking and writing, Carl Mays really does a nice job of getting his message across in an interesting and entertaining fashion. That's why I'm confident that *A Strategy For Winning* will be a winner. It is an interesting, entertaining and informative book. It is an important supplement for people in all professions to stimulate positive thinking, self-motivation, goal setting and avenues to achieve success."

– Pat Head Summitt
Women's Basketball Coach, Tennessee

"*A Strategy For Winning* should be required reading in schools all over our nation. I count it a privilege to have had the opportunity to read the pre-publication manuscript. Now that it is a book, may God speed *A Strategy For Winning* to the winning place it deserves."

– Roy Rogers
Actor/Singer

"Carl Mays has paid his dues and is an authority on the subject of winning. His varied background has produced a positive, precision blueprint for complete success. Carl has taken proven principles and presented them with a fresh, new approach. If you are interested in improving your personal skills, I recommend you read, make notes, study, reread, make more notes and restudy *A Strategy For Winning*. It will become your personal success bible and you will win big! I especially suggest you spend a lot of time with chapters seven (Set Goals) and eight (Visualize). Seven, alone, is worth much, much more than the price of the book!"

– Dr. Homer C. Rice
Director of Athletics, Georgia Tech

"Carl Mays' writing style is clear and simple. And I like that. No putting-on. No fifty-dollar words. Carl gets down to the nitty-gritty of what it takes to win in anything we do. And what he says makes a lot of sense to me. To be honest with you, I don't read many books, but I'm glad I read this one. I recommend that you read it, too. You'll be glad you did, because it's going to make a very positive difference in your life."

– Mike Snider
Entertainer

"Carl Mays deals with some important principles in *A Strategy For Winning*. He spotlights the fact that all successful people have problems to overcome, and he emphasizes that unless you accept responsibility and make a commitment, you can't win. His advice to concentrate upon what you *do* have rather than upon what you *don't* have is fundamental, but often neglected. Once we do win, Carl encourages us to 'stay hungry' in order that we might win again and reach greater heights."

– Tony La Russa
Manager, Oakland A's

"To the reader: Carl Mays welcomes your comments. The purpose of his writing and speaking is to help people to better reach their potentials, to succeed in various areas of life, to win. If *A Strategy For Winning* assists you in doing this, he would appreciate your letting him know, at P.O. Box 808 - Gatlinburg, Tennessee 37738."

– Jason Allen, Editor
The Lincoln-Bradley Publishing Group

11

DEDICATION

   . . . to all of you who have attended my keynote addresses, seminars and banquet talks through the years.

   Following my presentations, many of you have asked me, "Do you have a book about **A Strategy For Winning**?"

   My answer was always the same, "I'm working on it."

   I have a new answer now: "Here it is!"

   And as I continue my speaking, I look forward to many new listeners and many new readers for **A Strategy For Winning**.

Carl Mays

A Strategy For Winning is available at special quantity discounts for sales promotions, premiums, fund raising, educational use or other programs.

For details regarding quantity purchases, write or telephone:

Special Markets
The Lincoln-Bradley Publishing Group
305 Madison Avenue - Suite 1166
New York, NY 10165
(212) 953-1125

or

Through special arrangements with the author's organization, the same quantity discounts may be obtained by contacting:

Creative Living, Inc.
P.O. Box 808
Gatlinburg, TN 37738
1-800-245-7685

FOREWORD

Merle Harmon said, "Only one other book has grabbed me so completely, *Iacocca*." That is quite a statement. But with **A Strategy For Winning**, Carl Mays has produced quite a book.

Merle was on the road for most of three months. Constantly on the go with his Fan Fair Corporation and sports endeavors, part of his travel consisted of driving over 12,000 miles. It was during this time that he received a preview copy of **A Strategy For Winning**. He put it aside because in his words, "I don't think it is right to read a few pages of a book and then give it a review."

Then, again in his words, "One day I started to read **A Strategy For Winning**. It turned my day around. I became so engrossed that I read every page that day, taking time out only for lunch."

I can relate to Merle Harmon. When Carl sent me a pre-publication copy of the manuscript, I was extremely busy. Then I glanced at the book, got into it, and read it from cover to cover. Personally, I have no doubt that the book will have a very positive effect upon me, our football team and certainly our family.

I telephoned Carl, told him I was most impressed with the manuscript, that he had done a beautiful job, that he had written an outstanding book which would prove to be an important manual in the field of motivation, self-improvement and success.

Then I asked Carl, "What is it you want me to do?"

Carl paused before replying, "Well, Lou, just share with the people how you feel about the book, about the principles and philosophy it contains and the way they are presented." I was honored and humbled when he went on to say, "I think it is very important that a known winner such as yourself recommend the book."

I do recommend **A Strategy For Winning**. Highly. Carl has a natural way with words and a great philosophy of life. The book is enjoyable, very uplifting, upbeat, very inspirational, motivational. At the same time, it provides a lot of thought, yet it is easy to read.

Carl Mays is a very talented individual. It is easy to see why he received the National Faith and Freedom Award from W. Clement Stone, founder of *Success* magazine and chairman of the Religious Heritage of America foundation. This honor is bestowed upon a communicator who upholds the highest ideals of America and makes a positive impact on both the local and national levels.

It is also easy to understand why he received the Distinguished Alumnus Award from his alma mater in Kentucky, Murray State University. Of the more than 40,000 graduates from this institution, only 62 have been honored in this manner.

I recommend Carl's book to anyone who has a burning desire to succeed and improve his or her life in all areas. If you do not have a burning desire, this book can light your fire.

A Strategy For Winning is for adults and young people alike. It is for male and female, regardless of race or background. No matter who you are or where you come from, you either get better or worse in this world. You don't stay the same. If you really want to change your life for the better, regardless of where you are now, I strongly suggest you read this book - several times.

If anything will change you from where you are now to where you're going to be five years from now, it's the people you meet and the books you read. Because of this, I say, "Read **A Strategy For Winning** and through it meet Carl Mays."

Lou Holtz
Head Football Coach
University of Notre Dame

ACKNOWLEDGEMENTS

When success occurs, there are usually many people working together to make it happen. As I emphasize in Chapter Nine *(Enjoy, Like And Appreciate Others)*: "Winners work together. Winners support one another and believe in one another. Winners are interested in getting the job done together."

And one winner who was vital to this book project is my friend and associate Steve Williford. I mention Steve a couple of times in the text, but he deserves much more than just a couple of mentions. He deserves a special acknowledgement for the encouragement and assistance he gave to me during the two years we worked together on the manuscript. Without Steve - and his trusty computer - I don't think you would be reading **A Strategy For Winning** at this moment.

My wife Jean has been an important part of my life and my work. She helped me as I wrote this book, but she also helped me prior to the writing, as together we have lived many of the real-life examples shared in these pages. She has been a great wife, co-worker, friend and companion.

My son Carl II has been an inspiration to me; evidence of that is found throughout the book. He has helped me to live out the principles recorded here.

The workers who have staffed our *Creative Living* offices have made important contributions to my career and to this book. These co-workers include: Linda Easterly, Ardelle Rich, Diane Ray, Deanna Becker, Eddie Maynard, Barbara Funderburg, Melissa Billings and

Jean Berry. Ray Considine offered advice on the book as he helped me transpose it into a video and an audio series.

Bill and Barbara McGill, Ed and Barbara Whaley, Bud Lawson and Carol Snyder are special to me. They helped me to establish *Creative Living* back in 1973. And if there were not a *Creative Living*, there would not be **A Strategy For Winning**.

Football coach Benny Hammonds and I have been close for many years. We have helped each other. He has allowed me complete freedom to be creative and to experiment with new ideas. In turn, I have helped him to win. I appreciate Benny, his assistant Mike Helton and their entire staff.

Jason Allen, my editor at Lincoln-Bradley, answered the numerous questions I asked and he worked with me to improve the manuscript greatly. I also appreciate editor Trish Todd who counseled me. And I thank editor Alison Acker who offered me some sound advice. Literary agent Howard Morhaim made it possible for me to form a successful union with The Lincoln-Bradley Publishing Group.

I'm grateful to Lou Holtz for writing the Foreword. He is such a fine gentleman, the epitome of a winner who exhibits intelligence, creativity, wit , high morals and persistence.

And I appreciate all the high-profile winners who read preview copies of the book and were kind enough to supply testimonials.

Thank you everyone - those whom I have mentioned and those whom I have not. You all are a part of **A Strategy For Winning**.

– CM

CONTENTS

Introduction: What This Book Can Do For You 24

This is a how-to book. It shows you how to be more efficient, productive, creative and successful. It deals with winning in business, sports, family and life.

Chapter One: How To Win 33

We all have things that we can do well. We all have abilities that we can tap, powers that we can use. But sometimes we don't know how or where to begin. That's where **A Strategy For Winning** comes in.

Chapter Two: Accept Yourself And Your Worth 53

A good self-image is the highest human value. It is the first step in **A Strategy For Winning**. Your self-image determines how you will live your life. It determines how you will perform as a professional, a husband, a wife, a parent, a student, an athlete and a member of society.

Chapter Three: Develop And Maintain A Positive Attitude 81

Problems can bring out the worst or the best in you. You can fold under the pressure or you can tap powerful resources that are already within you.

Chapter Four: Be Creative 103

True creativity involves taking an idea, an object, a method, a group of people - something that's been around awhile - standing back, looking at it with a new perspective and giving it a different twist.

Chapter Five: Don't Fear Failure 127

There's a big difference between temporary failure and total defeat. Don't miss smelling the flowers for fear you may get stung by a bee!

Chapter Six: Clarify Your Values - Act Rather Than React 153

When you adhere to a set system of values, you will discover more productivity, harmony, fulfillment and profitability in all areas of life.

Chapter Seven: Set Goals 178

The one purpose of goal-setting is to help you accomplish what you want to accomplish. Setting, planning and working toward goals will lead you to the winner's circle.

Chapter Eight: Visualize

Visualization is seeing things happen before they actually happen, then doing what needs to be done to make them happen. It is "mental engineering" at its best.

Chapter Nine: Enjoy, Like And Appreciate Others

Through the years, I've noticed that so many corporations, sports teams and communities with talented individuals have never become winning groups because they can't live together, work together or win together.

Chapter Ten: Do It Now!

Go for it! To reach your goals in life, you have to take the offensive. You can't sit back and wait for things to happen. You have to make them happen.

INTRODUCTION: WHAT THIS BOOK CAN DO FOR YOU

Anyone Can Be A Winner

Anyone can be a winner. But it's amazing how few people take advantage of their opportunities to succeed. Too many people are overcome by the obstacles they encounter day-in and day-out. Too many people are defeated by the troubles and problems that are a part of life. Too many people let temporary failure become total defeat. This doesn't have to happen to you. You can succeed in school, in your career, in athletics, in your family and in all aspects of life.

In chapter one, *How To Win*, I present some personal experiences and some experiences of others who have *won* in certain areas of life. Then, I outline the nine principles that can lead you to *win* in *all* areas of life. Chapters two through ten cover the principles in depth.

At no time in this book do I want it to appear as if I am bragging about my accomplishments. As a matter of fact, only after the urging of friends and co-workers did I revise the original manuscript to add numerous personal examples, which they felt would add greatly to the book's validity. Nor am I over-emphasizing the accomplishments of anyone else. I'm merely sharing bona-fide examples of how the principles described in this book have led me and have led others to experience success as we have applied the principles to our lives. Some of the people I have used as examples may not have experienced success in all areas of life, but you can learn by examining the areas in which they have succeeded.

This book is not based upon theory. It is based upon *real stuff.* It does not deal with what *could* happen to people who apply the principles. It deals with what *has* happened to people who have applied the principles and what *can* happen to you when you apply all nine principles.

I'm no philosopher sitting in an ivory tower. I'm "out there amongst 'em." And even though along the way I have experienced my share of temporary failure, I have experienced success in school, athletics, career, family and community involvement. Examples to support these claims are found throughout the book. And, importantly, there are plenty of examples of others who have succeeded by applying the same principles I have applied. You can do the same. There is no "if," "and" or "but" about it. You can do the same.

Anyone can win. Let me tell you about some people I have met recently who would really like to win.

The Hooker

Minneapolis. It was late in the evening and I had taken a cab from the airport to the hotel where I was speaking the next day. I paid the fare and the cab drove away.

"Wannta' have some fun?" a melodious voice pierced the night.

I turned toward the voice.

An attractive young lady was sitting in a late model car, parked about 25 feet from where I stood. A hooker.

"Wannta' have some fun?" she asked again, smiling.

I returned her smile and walked over to the car. I shook my head and said, "No thank you." Then I paused and told her, "You know, there's more to life than this." She had a questioning look on her face. I took a copy of my newsletter, *Creative Living Today*, from my briefcase and handed it to her. "I'm in town to speak to a business group about the principles of *winning*," I continued. "This material supports what I am going to speak on. I think you might enjoy it."

She glanced at the newsletter, then looked back at me with an expression of disbelief. She didn't say a word. This particular issue had some tips on appreciating your own self-worth, advice on goal-setting and a few pointers on getting along with other people. It also had some suggestions on professional selling.

When thinking about it later, I hoped she would not misapply that part!

I walked away and went into the hotel, pausing at the door to glance back at her. With a strange look on her face, she drove off into the night.

I don't know if I had any effect on her or not. Maybe she read the newsletter; maybe she didn't. I haven't heard from her. She hasn't become a subscriber to *Creative Living Today*. Maybe she'll get ahold of this book. Maybe she'll realize the principles it contains are not just for business people and athletes, not just for students and parents, but also for hookers.

A Strategy For Winning is for anyone who wants to be a real winner in life.

The Would-Be Robber

Miami. I stepped onto the hotel elevator and a young man got on behind me. I had spoken at a banquet that evening and was dressed in a tailored tuxedo. The young man wasn't too neatly attired. I pushed the button for the seventh floor. He didn't push one.

We arrived at the seventh floor and he followed me off the elevator. I turned down the corridor to the left and he was right behind me. I have traveled much and have been to many places, but this was the first time I ever felt I was going to be robbed. There was no way I was going to lead him to my room.

So, I stopped in the hallway, turned toward him and said, "The others are coming up on the elevator at any moment now. We're supposed to have a reception in my room." We weren't, but it sure sounded good at the time.

He looked at me nervously, then glanced back toward the elevator. I took a business card from my jacket. "Here," I said as I handed it to him. "I'm a speaker and writer. I talk about *winning*."

He glanced at the card and continued to hold it. He had not reached for a knife or gun yet, if he had one.

"You may have all types of problems," I said. "Or, you may have just a few. But be on the lookout for a new book by me. It'll be in the bookstores. It's called **A Strategy For Winning**."

I stared at him and smiled. He looked bewildered.

"**A Strategy For Winning**," I repeated. I felt sweat dripping from my armpits and running down my sides. "Can you remember that?"

The elevator bell sounded. It startled us both and he jerked around to look. "You haven't done anything," I assured him. Nodding toward the nearby exit sign, I added, "Why not take the stairs and get out of here?"

He looked at me briefly, then quickly ran toward the stairway and was gone. The elevator doors opened. It was empty. I went to my room, bolted the door and chained it.

That young man would love to be a winner. He would love to be able to apply the principles of **A Strategy For Winning** to his life, to achieve happiness, to have a worthwhile life, to realize financial success without even considering robbery. He can do it. Just like I can. Just like you can.

The Gambler

Las Vegas. I arrived early in the afternoon, prior to presenting a convention keynote address the next day. Walking through the combination hotel lobby/casino, I stopped at the roulette table to witness some heavy action.

I watched a man lose $30,000 in 15 minutes.

He turned his head toward me and caught me looking at him. "I'll get it back," he said.

He liked to talk as much as he liked to gamble. He told me of his various gambling experiences and of his apparently bottomless financial reserves.

He said he was a landowner and had interests in several businesses passed along to him by his father. The free drinks the young hostess kept offering him probably caused him to talk more than he intended.

He asked me to join in and suggested how I could beat the wheel. I told him that I was just watching, was in town to speak at a national insurance company's annual convention. He asked what I was talking about and I told him *winning*. This caught his attention.

"No," I explained to him. "I don't talk about winning at roulette or twenty-one like some of those books in the gift shops. I talk about winning in life, in careers, in athletics."

He looked at me, sort of stuck out his bottom lip, tucked his chin and nodded his head, as if to say, "Oh yeah - *that* type of winning."

In parting, I cordially handed him one of my business cards, saying essentially the same thing I had said to the would-be robber, "Keep an eye open for my upcoming book, **A Strategy For Winning**. I guarantee you, you will enjoy it and get something out of it."

"Okay," he replied as he turned back toward the roulette table and placed several hundred dollars on three or four different red numbers, plus several hundred on the *even* position. I watched the wheel roll and the little ball pop into the black 17. His money was raked off. "Can't win 'em all," he philosophized.

I've got a feeling this compulsive gambler would really like to win at something larger and more important than the roulette table.

But let me tell you about some other people - people that you and I might more easily identify with.

The People Of Steamboat Springs

I was sitting on the terrace of the Dos Amigos Cafe in Steamboat Springs, Colorado. It was a beautiful June evening in this ski resort village. The Rocky Mountains were green, much like the Great Smoky Mountains where I live. And the people in Steamboat Springs were much like the people back in Gatlinburg. They were also like those I meet weekly in my travels. They want to enjoy life, to be happy. They want to contribute, to succeed. They want to win. Just like you.

I spoke about *winning* at a national conference for business people earlier that day. Then I enjoyed the evening, dining alone, before I flew out the next morning for another engagement. My efficient and friendly waitress was rather talkative. By her name tag, similar to those worn by all Steamboat Springs employees, I saw she was from San Diego. She had lived in Steamboat Springs two years, had fallen in love with snow-skiing, but misses the California beaches. She has two jobs, the other one at a gift shop. Her goal is to save enough money to open her own gift and crafts shop someday.

The young man who drove the van from the airport to the hotel when I arrived in Steamboat Springs also has high aspirations. From Ohio, he came west to attend the University of Colorado and to be on the school's ski team. He has hopes of competing for the U.S. in the Winter Olympics. A political science major specializing in foreign diplomacy, he works at the hotel and practices on the slopes when he can.

A young lady from Boston who works at the hotel's registration desk was very interested in the fact that I'm a professional writer and speaker. She noticed on my room reservation card that I was presenting the conference's keynote address. "That's exactly what I want to do," she told me after I briefly explained my work to her. Early childhood education is her area of interest. She wants to write books for and about children, and wants to speak on the subject of childhood psychology.

Another young lady working at the front desk with the aspiring writer/speaker is from Tokyo. She is a business major in college and wants to manage a small American corporation of some type. The writer/speaker-to-be has been talking to her about becoming her business manager and their working together as a team. "Do you have a business manager?" they asked me. When I replied in the affirmative, I almost had to present a *How To Become A Professional Writer and Speaker* seminar right there in the lobby.

A young man working as a desk clerk with these two energetic ladies is from New Jersey. He, too, is a business major, but doesn't know what he wants to do after he obtains his degree.

The bellman who finally rescued me and assisted me to my room was actually born and reared in Steamboat Springs. He told me he really enjoys resort work, and it shows. He intends to remain in the hotel industry.

These four people, like the waitress and the van driver, want to enjoy life, to be happy. They want to contribute, to succeed. They want to win. Just like you.

Don't we all? The desire to win is universal.

The People In The Airport

Often, as I sit in airports I study people and wonder who is currently losing and who is currently winning in life. I wonder what they have done and what they are going to do. Their expressions often reveal answers to such questions. I see happiness and sadness on faces. I see failures and successes. I see some people who are obviously winning and some who are apparently losing.

In the Denver airport, on my way to Steamboat Springs, a serious-looking man in his blue business suit (you see a lot of blue suits in airports) was in sharp contrast to a young lady in her "Michigan" sweatshirt. She looked like she didn't have a care in the world - footloose and fancy free. But you never know, do you? Then, there was the young mother trying to corral her three small children, growing more harried by the moment. The fact that the flight was delayed and the plane was overbooked didn't help any. A frail, elderly woman in a wheelchair took all of this in, and I just wondered what she was thinking as she watched the action around her.

The businessman, the college student, the young mother with her children and the elderly woman are all just like the people in Steamboat Springs. They want to enjoy life, to be happy. They want to contribute, to succeed. They want to win. Just like you.

What About You?

Currently, you may be *winning* in many areas of life. If so, this book can be used as a springboard to even greater achievement. You may be *winning* in a few areas of life. Should this be the case, carefully study and apply the principles that you may be leaving out. See how they can broaden your success. Or, you may not be *winning* in any area of life. Should this be the case, turn to chapter one to see how you can get on the path toward experiencing a happy, satisfying and worthwhile life.

One Final Thing. . .

One final thing, though, before you begin: Don't let anyone else read your book.

Why would I make such a request? Because, I want you to make your book as personal as possible. Underline the things that apply to you the most. Write in the margins. Make comments, give personal examples, ask questions. Live with your book. Please don't make it just a *one-time-through-without-a-pen-or-pencil* experience.

Over the years, I have discovered that the books that have meant the most to me are the ones in which I have written almost as much as the authors. Often, when I have been introduced to a book at a library, I have purchased my own copy for future readings and have begun my writing in it the second time though. And it's dangerous for me to borrow a book from a friend. Invariably, I have to shell-out money to replace it.

Make **A Strategy For Winning** yours. Personalize, personalize, personalize. That's how you will receive the greatest benefit. It's a simple book presented in a simple style. But it's real. And it's full of practical, useable ideas that you can apply daily to all of your endeavors. If you want to pass along its contents to others, you can suggest to friends, family members and associates that they purchase their own. Or, you might give copies to them as special gifts. But live with yours. Make it a part of your life and it will become a part of yours.

You will develop your own workable **Strategy For Winning**.

– CM

Chapter 1

HOW TO WIN

Through experience, study, work and help from other people, I have developed **A Strategy For Winning** that has led me to personal success. This "strategy" has also allowed me to assist other individuals and organizations in being successful. Without any hesitation or reservation, I make this promise to you on page one, paragraph one: This "strategy" can revolutionize your life.

As I write this book, I have just completed working on a program designed for a professional football team. This program shares the same material I've had the opportunity to use with business groups, sports teams and individuals across the nation. It's the same thing I want to share with you.

This is a how-to book. It contains material I have used in hundreds of speeches and seminars in the past dozen years. It's material that I've used in my life to set and reach my goals and to help others do the same. As we go along, I'll share some specific examples with you. The book will show you how to be more efficient, productive, creative and successful. This book can guide you toward true happiness.

If you have a strong desire to be successful as a professional, as an entrepreneur, as an athlete or coach, as a student or as a family member, **A Strategy For Winning** is for you.

Let me tell you what **A Strategy For Winning** can do:

From $500 To $9,000,000

I invested $500 to start a Convention Hotel Sales Organization "on the side." Ten years later, as **A Strategy For Winning** principles developed, our organization had generated over 150,000 room nights, resulting in a gross income of over $9,000,000 in room revenue alone. And on top of that, our organization helped hundreds of groups and thousands of people have great conferences and conventions. Last year, I leased my mailing list, contacts and expertise for $250,000, plus an on-going monthly fee for consultation.

From 150 To 8,000

A national organization asked me to assist them in establishing a convention program. The first year, we had 150 people in attendance. Five years later, as **A Strategy For Winning** principles developed, we had to place the convention in three different locations, housing over 5,000 at one location and over 3,000 at the other two locations.

Sales Increase

A sales group that applied **A Strategy For Winning** increased their sales by 300% the first year we began the program. The second year produced an additional increase of 60%, followed by increases of 55% and 90% the third and fourth years.

Football Team Improves

Over the past nine years, I've worked on a weekly basis with a football team. In the nine years prior to our sessions, the team's record was 43 wins and 47 losses. Since installing **A Strategy For Winning**, their record has been 83 wins and seven losses, with four undefeated seasons.

From Football To Career

A young man who was a member of the football team I have been working with for nine years told me he was going to apply **A Strategy For Winning** principles to a professional sales career. I kept track of him. Within two years after his graduation, he was his company's top salesperson. Within four years, he was a regional sales manager. Within six years, his region led the entire company in sales. His comments: "**A Strategy For Winning** works in football, in sales, in life."

Student's Goals Lead To The Top

I sat down and talked with my son Carl Mays II, a high school freshman at the time, who was serious about succeeding in life. We discussed **A Strategy For Winning** principles and I continued to work with him throughout the next four years as he set goals and devised plans and deadlines.

Like me, Carl II was just an average middle-class person from a small town in Tennessee. No privileged background. But the great thing about **A Strategy For Winning** is that you don't have to be born a genius or with a silver spoon in your mouth. As a matter of fact, **A Strategy For Winning** works best for average people who want to reach the top in school, athletics, careers and all of life.

Carl II graduated as valedictorian of his senior class, captain of his football team, president of the student council, state scholar-athlete of the year, national winner of two oratorical contests and, among other achievements, represented Tennessee at Boys' Nation in Washington, D.C.

He applied to, was actively recruited by and gained invitations to attend Princeton, Harvard, Yale, Cornell, Vanderbilt and several other prestigious universities - with accompanying scholarships. He chose Princeton, where he played football and graduated with a degree in aerospace and mechanical engineering. He is now a research and development engineer with one of the top aerospace corporations in the world.

A Strategy For Winning Works!

Let me tell you why it works. **A Strategy For Winning** is not a magic formula. It is no potion that you drink, no pill that you take or wish that you make. Rather, it challenges you to use your mind as it should be used. You've probably heard the expression, "mentally tough." Well, **A Strategy For Winning** helps you become mentally tough. It equips you to do the things you already have the power to do.

We all have things that we can do well. We all have abilities that we can tap, powers that we can use. But sometimes we don't know how or where to begin. Sometimes we're like the young men invited by a rich man to a party for his beautiful daughter.

The rich father gathered the young men around a swimming pool filled with alligators. He promised his daughter in marriage, a sports car, two oil wells and a top position in his company to anyone who had the courage and skill to swim across the pool.

Immediately, a young man splashed in and swam like blazes to the other side. The crowd went wild, clapping and cheering as the hero made it across. The rich father ran to his side, congratulated him, then asked, "Which prize do you want first?"

"First," the young man sputtered, "I want the name of the guy who pushed me into the pool!"

At times, we all need a push. Maybe not into a pool of alligators, but a push in the right direction, a push onto the winning path. Or, if you are already on the winning path, you might need a push to help you reach even greater heights. You'd be amazed at how much you are capable of achieving in every area of your life.

That's what we're going to be looking at in this book: How to discover the winning path and how to use your abilities to get you to the end of the path to your goals. It is possible to achieve your goals if you're mentally tough.

Bruce Jenner: Decathlon Champion

Bruce Jenner, winner of the Decathlon Gold Medal in the 1976 Olympics, said that he played a lot of different sports in high school, but was never very good at any of them. So, what transformed Jenner from a mediocre athlete into the best in the world?

According to Jenner, his greatest asset was not his physical ability but his mental ability. He said, "I honestly felt I was mentally tougher than the guys I competed against in the Olympics, especially in terms of coming up with a good performance in pressure situations." And Jenner believes that the key ingredients in an athlete's make-up are: "Their personalities, their intelligence and the way they attack the game."

Sports psychologists agree with Jenner. That "certain something" that lifts some athletes above others seems to be more mental than physical. In fact, sports experts question the concept of the "natural athlete." True, some athletes are bigger, stronger and faster than others, but these bigger, stronger, faster athletes don't always end up winners. Bruce Jenner is a good example.

And there are many other well-known athletes whose mental toughness helps them win over physically superior opponents. These successes support the fact that sports experts are finding more and more evidence that being a real winner may well have more to do with what's inside an athlete's head than with his or her physical ability. We can learn a great deal from such athletes and apply their winning principles not only to our own athletic endeavors but also to our lives as professionals, entrepreneurs, students and family members.

Buster Douglas: From Just Another Boxer To Champion

James "Buster" Douglas went from being just another boxer to heavyweight champion on February 11, 1990. It was a shocking upset when he defeated Mike Tyson. Shocking, because Douglas never before even demonstrated a strong passion for boxing. More than once, his management team complained that he just didn't have his heart in it. He had lost matches he should have won. People talked about his potential, but they also talked about his not being mentally tough. And, because of his lack of mental toughness, he never reached the physical toughness of which he was capable.

That changed as he began to prepare for the bout with Tyson and caught a vision of the boxer he could become. He began to believe in himself and to believe that he could, indeed, become heavyweight champion. His mental toughness grew as he studied videotapes of Tyson in action, picking out the defending champion's weaknesses and determining how he could use his strengths to meet those weaknesses head-on. With a new enthusiasm, he began to work himself into the best physical condition he had ever experienced and his confidence increased.

Where previous challengers might have seen an invulnerable champion, Douglas saw a boxer with glaring flaws. He and his management team devised a specific battle plan and Douglas knew he could make it happen. On that Sunday, at the site of the bout in Tokyo, he executed the plan perfectly. When asked about the tremendous upset, Douglas' manager, John Johnson, said, "I had never seen him so confident and so focused."

Larry Bird: Basketball Great

You've heard sportscasters say that the great Boston Celtic forward Larry Bird was not fast, was not strong and could not jump. Yet, experts and fans alike consider him one of the greatest players who ever put on a basketball uniform. What made him great? Ask his coaches and teammates, as well as his opponents. They'll tell you that it was his determination, his will power, his mental attitude that he took into each practice and each game.

Determination. Will power. Mental attitude. Mental Toughness.

Mary Lou Retton: Perfect 10

How many of us remember the four foot, nine and a half inch tall, 16 year-old Mary Lou Retton in the 1984 Olympics? Standing at the end of the runway, needing a perfect 10 in the vault to win the all-around gold medal in women's gymnastics, she suddenly turned toward the television camera and smiled one of her winning smiles to 80 million viewers around the world. When she was later asked what she was thinking at that moment, she replied, "I was thinking: Watch this. I'm going to do it."

And she did. A perfect 10. Mental Toughness.

Carl Joseph: Handicapped?

Carl Joseph, a high school defensive nose tackle in Madison, Florida, tackled the fullback on the first play, the tailback on the second play and destroyed the receiver of a screen pass on the third play. Three straight tackles. Someone might say, "That's pretty good." But it's more than pretty good when you consider that Carl Joseph was born with only one leg. He can slam dunk a basketball, too - with either hand. He threw the discus and the shot put and even won the high school high jump competition.

Mental Toughness.

Raymond Berry: A Study In Determination

Raymond Berry, National Football League player and coach, as a child was physically handicapped. As a young man he was left with a weak back, one leg shorter than the other and poor vision. Despite these handicaps, he went to college at Southern Methodist University and wanted to make the football team. Through persistence, hard work and constant training, he made the squad.

Later, he wanted to play professional football, but was passed over by most pro teams and was not drafted until the 20th round by the Baltimore Colts. Not too many people expected him to make the team, much less become a starter.

Berry wore a harness on his back, mud cleats on one foot and regular cleats on the other to balance his uneven stride, and was probably the first player in the league to use contact lenses to see the ball. He continually practiced running pass pattern after pass pattern as a wide receiver. He worked on the fundamentals and his techniques. He perfected everything he did. He became an expert at blocking, faking and catching passes from every conceivable angle.

On the days when the Colts were not practicing, he would go to a nearby high school and get the students to throw passes to him so he could continue to perfect his patterns. When the team was traveling, he would often carry a football, to keep his hands accustomed to the feel.

Berry became the leading pass receiver in the NFL and helped take his team to the NFL Championship two years in a row. He was the favorite target of quarterback Johnny Unitas.

How did Berry become such an outstanding player? Was it because of his superior physical abilities? How did he achieve such high marks? Was it because he was born with inherent physical abilities that most people don't have?

The answer is: He acquired an unbeatable mental attitude. And, he did something that an unbeatable mental attitude leads people to do. He practiced, practiced, practiced!

Practice improves our skills. Practice improves our confidence. Whether you are interested in playing football, selling a product or service, designing a lunar module or performing brain surgery, it is through practice that you program yourself to win.

Mental toughness led Bruce Jenner to practice eight hours a day for four years in preparation for the decathlon.

It led Buster Douglas to increase his poundage from 180 to 400 on the bench press as he entered a special weight-lifting program in preparing for his bout with Mike Tyson.

It led Larry Bird to spend hours alone in the gym.

It led Mary Lou Retton to spend her childhood arising at six a.m. and practicing all day, everyday.

It led Carl Joseph to overcompensate for a missing leg by giving 220% instead of 110%.

It led Raymond Berry to practice everyday, with or without the team.

A Lesson From Dave Thomas

Dave Thomas worked in a restaurant in Knoxville, Tennessee, about 40 miles from the town in which I live, Gatlinburg. Later, Dave went to work for Colonel Harlan Sanders and the Kentucky Fried Chicken chain. A hard worker who was known for his ability to think, Dave did a good job. Eventually, his boss sent him to see what could be done with four small restaurants that were failing in Columbus, Ohio.

Dave combined his mental abilities with his hard work to turn around the restaurants. He then took his profits and opened up a small hamburger restaurant. His unbeatable mental attitude and his continued hard work led to success at the restaurant he named after his daughter, *Wendy*.

Today, the Wendy's chain consists of over 3,500 restaurants and is consistently rated among those at the top of the highly competitive fast-food business. And, Dave Thomas has been presented the prestigious Horatio Alger Award, given to distinguished Americans who have risen from poverty to positions of honor and influence.

Dave Thomas does not even know where he was born, nor does he know who his parents were. He was an orphan who lived a while with foster parents before going out into the world on his own. His first full-time job was as a restaurant busboy. Dave's mental toughness and hard work led him to the top. He became an example of the type of American who constantly improves the American economy and represents what the American free enterprise system is all about.

The Difference Is Mental

I was flying to a speaking engagement to talk to a corporation about the unleashed power of our minds. Looking at a newspaper, I discovered some new ammunition.

An article told how the NFL's Houston Oilers currently had six wins and only one loss, pointing out that they already had more wins in the '87 season than in the entire '86 season. The article described how fourth quarter rallies in their last two games led to victories and, of course, bolstered the Oilers' confidence tremendously.

Their coach at the time, Jerry Glanville, said the major difference between the first place team and the last place team in the NFL is mental. He claimed 1987 to be the first year his team could put anything together mentally. He said that the winning mental attitude showed up in pre-season practice and grew week-by-week as they prepared for each game.

It happens in the mind before it happens in the body. When we program ourselves to win, we discover the desire and methods to make it happen. We taste the sweetness of success as we reach our goals.

In a later chapter we'll look in-depth at goals - their setting, planning, working toward and achieving. For now, however, let me say that when we set our goals, we must be careful to make them realistic. They must be goals that we actually can achieve. The big question is: "Can you do the things you need to do in order to accomplish the goals you have formed in your mind?" If the answer is "yes," then go for it. Don't let anything or anyone hold you back.

Be Realistic

But be fair to yourself. Be realistic.

I could tell a group of high school football players that they could beat the Chicago Bears next week. We could talk about programming our minds and we could practice to perfection. But we'd get killed, because a high school team couldn't block, tackle or outrun professional athletes.

Too often, I see young men and women who want to start out on top in the business world. Not only are they usually not capable of doing so, but it is normally the worst thing that could happen to them. Just like a magnificent sky scraper needs a strong foundation, so do we - no matter what we're involved in.

A Lesson In Reality

Regularly, following speaking engagements, people approach me and declare, "I want to be a professional speaker. What must I do?" Further discussion with them reveals that they want to begin by demanding a fee of at least $1,000 per engagement. They then explain that they know it will take a couple of years for them to receive what I receive, but that they are willing to work and sacrifice. Let me tell you about work and sacrifice.

Early in my career, I spoke not for fees but for honorariums. One weekend, I spoke to a group for one and a half hours on Friday evening, one and a half hours on Saturday morning, one and a half hours on Saturday evening and closed out the conference with one and a half hours on Sunday morning.

The participants were very receptive and responsive and the group's leader was elated over the positive outcome of our time together. He thanked me profusely and handed me a sealed envelope containing the honorarium check. I graciously thanked him and placed the envelope in my pocket, anxiously looking forward to reaching my car, driving away and ripping it open to discover the check that would take care of some bills.

Alone at last, I eagerly inspected my reward for six hours of speaking, which of course had been preceded by multiple hours of preparation. You can imagine my reaction to the check which had imprinted on it "PAY TO THE ORDER OF CARL MAYS - $35.00."

That is the day I made the decision to begin speaking for set fees rather than honorariums, which quite often were less than honorable!

When some people learn that I now receive several thousand dollars for a speaking engagement, they immediately think of how easy it must be to pull in such fees. When I tell them the best way to begin is to speak for free at civic clubs, churches, schools and other such organizations in order to hone their skills as I did, they appear to be offended.

It is important to believe in what you're doing. It's important to have faith in your abilities. But, you must also be realistic. You must consider who you are, what strengths you have and what you are capable of achieving. If your goals are realistic and if you use your resources wisely, then you can reach your goals.

Taking into consideration what we have and then wisely developing and using it can be illustrated by a couple of cartoons that are favorites of mine.

The Saga Of Broom Hilda

In one cartoon, Broom Hilda, the little green witch, is standing on the edge of a cliff. Across the way, with a deep canyon separating them, Gaylord, the buzzard, is standing near the edge of another cliff. Gaylord yells to Broom Hilda, "Come over here with me!"

Broom Hilda looks down at the canyon, then looks at Gaylord and replies, "I can't jump that far!" Gaylord says, "You're defeating yourself with negative thinking. I'm writing a book on the power of positive thought, in which I can prove you can do anything if you have the correct attitude!"

Broom Hilda just stands there, eyes wide, taking all of this in. Gaylord continues, "Tell yourself you can do it - and do it!" Now Broom Hilda is really psyched-up. She says, "Okay - here I come!" She rares back, kicks up her leg and leaps. She goes down, down, down. . .

Gaylord steps to the edge of the cliff and looks at Broom Hilda falling, becoming a mere dot in the canyon below. Then, as he turns to walk away, he says, "You know, I think I'll add a chapter on building up your leg muscles."

This is an important thought. If someone sets a goal to be the Number One salesperson in an organization, but never puts in the hours needed to learn how to be a true professional, I doubt that he or she will ever reach the top.

A person may have the goal of being a professional speaker. But if he or she doesn't work hard on the content, practice on the delivery for hours, hone his or her skills presenting free speeches and learn from seasoned professionals, the goal will never be achieved, even if the ability is there.

A young man might dream of being the starting tailback for his football team. But if he doesn't attend practices and work hard while he's there, if he doesn't lift weights and run sprints during the off-season, he is just fooling himself.

We should not imagine that we can achieve a goal, even one within the scope of our abilities, without hard work. The mind is a wonderful, powerful tool. One person with the proper attitude can turn around an entire organization in a very positive way. But we must be aware of our abilities, then create realistic goals and determine the means that are available to help us best reach those goals. Which, talking about available means, brings us to the second cartoon:

The Eagle And The Rabbit

An eagle and a rabbit were standing at the edge of a deep gorge. The eagle flew to the other side, then turned and called to the rabbit, "Come on over! The view is better and there's plenty of food."

The rabbit thought to himself, "I have strong legs to help me leap and large ears to use as wings." So he took a running start and sprang into the air, only to fall to the bottom of the gorge.

The eagle looked down at the rabbit and called, "Perhaps you should have used the bridge!"

If you are currently in a negative situation - if things are not going great for you, not even going fairly well - you can turn them around. Most sudden changes are mental, not physical. Athletes don't grow stronger and become faster overnight. Fortunately, however, much of any game and much of life itself is still played in the mind. There, miracles are possible, if you wisely use the means available to you - if you take what you have, where you are, and get the most out of it.

A Great Salesman - What A Turnaround!

Lewis Delaney was the sales manager of a large company in Chicago that employed over 500 salespeople. He told of a salesman in the group by the name of Tim. He said that Tim was a complete failure as a salesman, the lowest person in sales production in the entire organization, and they were about to fire him. Delaney said he hated to have to do it. Everyone liked Tim. He was good-natured, friendly, easy to get along with, but a poor salesman. And then, all of a sudden, something happened.

Tim began to produce. Within a period of one year, he went from the very bottom to the top third in sales. By the end of the second year, he was the Number One producer in the company. At the annual convention that year, they presented an award to Tim. He was called up out of the audience and the company's president said, "Tim, you're wonderful. You're a great salesman. You're the top person." Then the president paused and said, "But Tim, you've got us all mystified. A couple of years ago, you were a complete failure. And now, look at what you've accomplished. How did you do it? Would you tell us?"

Tim wasn't much of a public speaker and replied, "I don't know, sir, exactly what to say."

The president persisted, "Tim, there must be some reason."

Tim paused, then said, "Well, okay. . . I like all the folks here, and I think you'll understand." He caught his breath and continued: "I knew I was a failure. And one night I said to myself, 'I don't want to be this way anymore.' And I did some thinking. And while I was thinking, I happened to notice the Bible on the bookshelf. I hadn't read it in years. I got it out and looked at it.

"Then I opened up the Bible and came to a place where it said I could become a different person. So I decided to change. The next morning, I went downtown and bought myself a complete new outfit. New underwear, new socks, new shoes, new shirt, new suit, new tie, everything. I know clothes don't really make the person, but they're the symbol of the person. And I wanted to be new inside and out.

"Then, I went home and took a shower. I rubbed my skin until it was like a new born baby's. Then, I shampooed my head, scrubbing like never before, to get all of those old, failing thoughts out of there. I then went to work with the knowledge that I had become a new man and was ready to lead a new life."

Lewis Delaney said there was complete silence for a few seconds, then over 500 salespeople rose as one, clapping, cheering and stomping their feet. Tears ran down the faces of many. A man they knew as a failure had found himself and had become a new man.

Many times, when I share ideas about winning with various groups in various parts of the nation, I'll see people nod their heads and get expressions on their faces that say, "Yes, I know what you're talking about."

Then the question is, "What are you going to do about it?" We must recognize that the amount of knowledge we have about a subject is not as important as how efficiently we use it. I've heard it put this way: "Happy are those who dream dreams and are willing to pay the price to make them come true."

How Are You Farming?

A young man recently graduated from college and got his first job as an assistant county farm agent. After watching a farmer at work in a large field, he introduced himself and said, "I've been watching you for about 30 minutes, and I've seen a lot of things you could change to get a better yield from your crop."

The old farmer cocked his head to one side, spit out some tobacco juice and said, "Son, I ain't farmin' now half as well as I know how."

This could be the case with a lot of us. Reaching your potential does not always mean obtaining more knowledge. You probably know more now than you practice. The real key is *what you do with what you've got*.

And that raises some questions: What can you do to develop the potential that is inside you? What can you concentrate on? How can you bring out your winning qualities?

These are the questions that are going to be answered in this book. **A Strategy For Winning** will be clearly developed in the chapters that follow. You will discover what turns losers into winners and raises winners to even greater heights of achievement.

Here are the principles to be covered:

Principle One: Accept Yourself And Your Worth.

A lady said to her friend, "I hear your son is on the football team. What position does he play?" The mother, not knowing much about football, answered, "I believe he's one of the drawbacks."

Don't see yourself as a drawback. Don't be overly self-critical. Keep in mind that nobody's perfect. Often, we compare ourselves to someone who does something better than we do. But we overlook the things we do better than someone else. Don't ruin your uniqueness by trying to be like someone else. And remember, the more you are like yourself, the less you are like anyone else.

Most people are not coming close to accomplishing what they have the ability to accomplish. So many people live so far below the level on which they could be living that when they release their real selves it is almost like becoming transfigured. Accepting yourself and recognizing your worth is the beginning of true success in life.

In chapter two we will look at how you can better accept yourself and how you can better determine and recognize your worth.

Principle Two: Develop And Maintain A Positive Attitude.

An optimistic coach told his team, "We are undefeated, untied and unscored upon. And now we're ready for our first game!" Great attitude!

Mahatma Ghandi said:

> *If I believe I cannot do something, it makes me incapable of doing it. But when I believe I can, then I acquire the ability to do it, even if I did not have the ability in the beginning.*

You shouldn't close your eyes to problems and obstacles; you should be realistic. But at the same time, look for ways to win rather than excuses for losing. We'll examine how you can develop and maintain that type of attitude.

Principle Three: Be Creative.

A minister asked a professional football coach, "Don't you know it's a sin to play ball on Sunday?" The coach replied, "The way we play, it is."

Now, that's a creative answer! But we're going to go deeper into creativity and see how creativity leads people to the winner's circle.

Creativity is vital.

It often means the difference between failing and succeeding. I'll offer certain suggestions and guidelines to help you develop more creativity.

Principle Four: Don't Fear Failure.

A doctor had some water pipe problems at his home one Saturday morning and called a plumber. The plumber arrived, solved the problems within 15 minutes and presented a bill for

$150. The doctor was dumbfounded. "Why, I don't even charge that much!" he exclaimed.

"No," the plumber replied. "And I didn't either when I was a doctor."

If you can't make a go of it trying one thing, then try something else!

Don't fear failure as you search for success in all areas of life. Most successful people have experienced failures, have learned from these failures and have grown stronger. We will see how various people turned failure into success and how you can do the same. People who resist all forms of failure rarely succeed. People whose main purpose in life is to play it safe rarely expand.

Remember, *there's a big difference between temporary failure and total defeat*. Temporary failure *can* lead to total success.

Principle Five: Clarify Your Values - Act Rather Than React.

Two men were hiking in the woods when they saw a bear in the distance coming toward them. One of the men quickly pulled his tennis shoes from his back pack and began putting them on. The other man looked at him and said, "You know you can't outrun that bear!" The first man replied, "I don't have to. I just have to outrun you."

Do you know what you would do should certain situations arise? Do you have a game plan?

Many people never take a position, never clarify their values. Like water in a bucket, they slosh from side to side. A real key to developing **A Strategy For Winning** is understanding your value system. In chapter six, we'll examine the types of values real winners have and look at criteria for determining such values.

Principle Six: Set Goals.

A father was worried about the date his daughter was preparing for. "Are you sure he's a good driver?" he asked.

"Oh yes, Daddy, he has to be," she answered. "If he gets arrested one more time, he'll lose his license."

Unfortunately, many of us have goals about as lofty as the daughter's date: Just trying to get by while avoiding calamity. The date's goal was not to lose his license. But what are your goals? Where are you now? Where do you want to be? What will it take to get you there?

Don't set goals so high they can never be reached. That's frustrating. But don't set them so low they can be reached too easily. That's no challenge. We'll inspect how to set goals, how to plan for them and how to reach them. Such action will lead you to levels that previously you only dreamed of.

Principle Seven: Visualize.

Visualization may be the best kept secret of winners.

If you want to drive someone crazy, send a telegram and on the top put "Page Two." Obviously, the question: "What was on page one and where is it?"

That's visualization, but not quite the type you'll learn from me. We'll look at something with greater depth and purpose.

Visualization is one of the most life-changing concepts I can share with you.

Year-in and year-out, individuals tell me that this principle has turned their lives around in a very positive way.

In golf, for example, a novice thinks, "I hope the ball gets to the green." The champion, however, actually sees the flight of the ball and where it will land on the green before it's ever hit.

I'll show you how to visualize and how to use visualization to be more productive in both everyday achievements and major goals.

It works. I guarantee it.

Principle Eight: Enjoy, Like And Appreciate Others.

The mother yelled upstairs to her teenage daughter, "If you don't turn down that tape player, I'll go insane!" The girl yelled back, "Too late, Mom. I turned it off an hour ago!"

How do you get along with others? Help other people to be successful and you will be very successful. To be a winner, help others to be winners. If you help others to get the best from themselves, you will get the best from yourself.

Sometimes people are so preoccupied with their own problems and projects, they fail to enjoy and appreciate others. There's a skill to this process. In chapter nine, I'll teach you how to attain and use it.

Principle Nine: Do It Now!

Some people say: "Don't put off 'til tomorrow what you can do next week!"

We'll look at reasons why we procrastinate and steps to overcome procrastination. The sooner you attack any problem, with as much energy as possible, the more likely that problem will be resolved. The longer it hangs on, the more likely it is to grow out of hand. Procrastination is a major problem in all fields of endeavor and helps to explain business reversals, upsets in sports and breakdowns in families.

There you have it - a preview of what is to come in the chapters ahead: The nine principles in **A Strategy For Winning**.

But, before I share with you some ideas and examples about the first principle, consider this:

View From Afar

As I was flying into Columbus, Ohio, for a speaking engagement, the young lady sitting next to me was on her way back home from Florida. She had driven from Columbus to Florida with her parents, but they remained while she returned to her job. This was her first plane trip.

"It's beautiful down there," she said, looking out the window as we approached the airport. She had been on stand-by in Atlanta and was elated when she had received a window seat in the first-class section. She had enjoyed the refreshing snack and the constant attention of the flight attendant, but now she was experiencing the high point of her trip. She was seeing her hometown of Columbus as she had never seen it before.

I looked out the window and nodded my head in response to her statement. "Yes," I agreed. "It is a beautiful sight."

"I never thought of Columbus being this pretty," she continued, then paused. "But, I've never seen it from afar like this."

The definite patterns and the clean lines of the landscape were impressive. But you really had to be able to view it from a distance to appreciate it. I understood what she was experiencing. She had always been so close to Columbus that she could never really see it. Sort of like not being able to see the forest for the trees.

Sometimes it helps tremendously to be able to step back and view something - or somebody - from afar. This is what I ask you to do as you read, study and apply **A Strategy For Winning**. See yourself as objectively as possible. That way, you can get a better overview of yourself. You can see your personal worth that transcends your involvement with people and events. Become a spectator looking at you, then you can become a better participant in life, using your potentials and realizing your value.

And, realizing your value is what chapter two is all about. . .

Chapter 2

ACCEPT YOURSELF AND YOUR WORTH

Good News And Bad News

One day, two elderly men were talking about their favorite sport, baseball.

"I wonder if there'll be baseball in heaven?" Ed asked.

"Of course there will," Joe responded, "or it wouldn't be heaven."

Not long after that, Ed passed away. Then, one night while Joe was sleeping, Ed appeared in all his radiant glory in a bright light at the foot of Joe's bed. Joe was badly shaken.

"Calm down, Joe," Ed reassured his friend. "Everything's going to be alright. I just came back to visit and to bring some good news and some bad news."

"What's the good news?" Joe asked.

"The good news is, there *is* baseball in heaven."

"That's great!" Joe responded. Then he paused and slowly asked, "Now, what's the bad news?"

"Well, Joe, the bad news is, you're pitching this coming Saturday."

That's the way it often is. We have some good news and some bad news. And, the good news I share with you is, YOU

ARE SOMEBODY. You are important. You have certain unique abilities and talents. You have a lot going for you. The bad news is, many people don't realize what they have and never come close to using their abilities and talents.

The Stone Cutter

An old Chinese fable tells of a stone cutter who was dissatisfied with his position in life. One day, while passing a wealthy merchant's home, he saw many fine possessions and important visitors. The stone cutter thought, "How powerful that merchant must be," and he wished that he could be the merchant.

To his surprise, he suddenly became the merchant. He enjoyed his power and luxuries, until one day he noticed a high official accompanied by soldiers. Everyone, no matter how rich, bowed to this official. "How powerful he must be. I wish I were he," the merchant said.

Lo and behold, he became the official. He was carried around everywhere in his embroidered chair and was feared by everyone.

One hot summer day, however, the official felt dreadfully uncomfortable. He looked up at the sun beaming down on the earth and thought, "How powerful the sun is. I wish I were the sun."

And suddenly he became the sun.

He beamed down fiercely on the earth, on the fields and on the people, until one day a storm cloud moved between the earth and himself, blocking his light. "How powerful that cloud is," he thought. "I wish I were a cloud."

And he became a storm cloud that flooded the earth and wreaked havoc, until he realized that he was not in control of himself. He was being pushed by the wind. So, he wished again and became the wind. He blew hard and ripped the tiles off of houses and uprooted trees, until he came upon something he could not budge, no matter how much energy he used nor how hard he blew.

It was a huge, towering stone. He thought, "How powerful that stone is. Oh, how I wish I were that stone." He became the stone.

There he stood, more powerful that anything on earth - or so he thought. Suddenly, he heard a hammer pounding a chisel into his solid rock and felt himself being changed. "What could be more powerful than I am?" he thought. He looked down. At his base was a stone cutter.

To some people, the grass is always greener on the other side of the fence or in another part of the country. Other jobs or careers always seem more attractive. Some people spend so much time thinking about how they would like to be someone else, to do something else, to live somewhere else. These same people spend little time thinking about who they are, what they are doing, where they are living. They're so busy thinking about what they don't have, they don't have time to consider and appreciate what they *do* have.

Comparison is damaging to self-esteem. Don't do it. Don't compare yourself to others and don't compare your situation to other situations. Instead, compare yourself to yourself. The real challenge is to be the best *you* possible. The real challenge - and the real reward - is to take what you have, where you are and get most out of it.

It is as Walt Disney said, "The more you are like yourself, the less you are like anyone else. This is what makes you unique." The problem is, we have very few originals and many copies.

I'm O.K. - You're O.K.

A few years ago, Thomas Harris, author of the popular book, *I'm O.K., You're O.K.*, described four types of people in our society.

I'm O.K. - You're Not O.K.

First, there is the person who says, "I'm okay, but you're not." This person thinks he or she is God's gift to the world, with potential and abilities that most people only wish they had. This person thinks that he or she is a winner and everyone else is a loser.

This person can turn any conversation towards himself or herself. Although initially exciting and fun, this person's selfishness eventually becomes apparent. This person is a user and a manipulator. You'll find this person has few long-term friends.

I'm Not O.K. - You're O.K.

This type thinks that other people have potential and abilities, but that he or she was left out. This person views other people as winners while thinking, "I'm a loser. And if you like me, you either don't know the real me, or there must be something wrong with *you*, too!" Although willing to give others the benefit of the doubt, this individual refuses to be as generous to himself or herself.

I'm Not O.K. - You're Not O.K.

This third type of person thinks everyone is a loser. According to this person's thinking, nothing nor no one is worth anything. This person wants to drop out of life and encourages others to do the same. This person is no fun to be with and essentially dies years before being placed in the grave.

I'm O.K. - You're O.K.

The fourth type of person believes, "I have unique potential and abilities, and you do, too. I respect myself and respect you, despite our differences. I'm a winner and you're a winner. I can get it together and you can get it together. And, if we can get it together, together, we can accomplish anything!"

At this moment, which of the four types are *you*?

A good self-image is the highest human value. It is the first step in **A Strategy For Winning**. Your self-image determines how you will live your life. It determines how you will perform as an athlete, a student, a professional, a husband, a wife, a parent and a member of society. Individuals, corporations, families, schools, teams and communities win when they see the positive abilities in themselves and others.

As a professional writer, speaker and consultant, I feel a responsibility to help people see and appreciate who they really are.

To me, it is a rewarding challenge to lead people to look inward, and to assist them in seeing their strengths and weaknesses. Then, I can guide and encourage them to wisely use their strengths and to improve in the areas in which they are weak.

Many people go through life with wrong beliefs about themselves. Their self-esteem is out of whack. Sometimes, like the "I'm O.K. - You're Not O.K." personality, they blow themselves out of proportion with undue pride. Then, like the "I'm Not O.K. - You're O.K." personality, they sell themselves short with undue self-criticism. Others, like the "I'm Not O.K. - You're Not O.K." personality, sell *everyone* short. True winners have developed the balanced "I'm O.K. - You're O.K." attitude.

What Am I Bid For This Fine Piece?

In the Great Smoky Mountains area where I live, we have a large number of auctions. We have a lot of estate sales at which antique furniture, jewelry and other items are auctioned off. The auctioneer will point to an item or hold it up and ask, "What am I bid for this fine piece?"

The bidding begins as the potential buyers evaluate the items and place values on each one. It is the responsibility of the auctioneer to help the buyer to realize the true value of the piece to be sold.

Like the auctioneer, I want to help you to realize *your* true value. Value and esteem are interchangeable. You need to be aware of your value in order to hold yourself in proper esteem.

We also have numerous garage sales in our area. At these events, you can find a lot of junk. But you can also find some beautiful, once-expensive items, now selling at unbelievable, dirt-cheap prices. Like the self-esteem of many people, the value of these items is out of whack.

I think too many people are viewing themselves as garage sale items. You may be such a person. Think about it.

Are you under-rating yourself and belittling your abilities? Are you limiting yourself in your own eyes? Are you holding too small a picture of your talents? Have you been convinced and conditioned to hold a low opinion of yourself?

We all struggle in a world of problems, but if you see yourself as able to meet these challenges, the way you handle them will be different. The whole business of finding success is to *make the most of who you are, with what you have, where you are*.

However, there are obstacles to attaining a good self-image. And, there are other people who, for various reasons, want to keep us from reaching our potential.

The Peanuts Parable: Look At My Hands!

Several years ago, I had the privilege of being on a conference program at which Charles Schulz also spoke. I heard Schulz, creator of the comic strip, *Peanuts*, tell his audience that the original idea for *Peanuts* came to him when he was just a small boy. One day, he walked into his elementary school, and a little black-haired girl came up to him, looked him in the eyes and said, "I'm having a birthday party Saturday, ha, ha, and you're not invited." The little girl became Lucy and *Peanuts* was born.

And *Peanuts* has some excellent examples of obstacles we encounter. One of my favorite examples involves Lucy and her younger brother, Linus, who constantly hangs onto his security blanket.

In this cartoon, Linus is in the kitchen, eating a jelly sandwich. As he finishes the sandwich, it seems like for the first time in his life, he notices the hand that held the sandwich. He begins to admire the hand. Then, without realizing it, he drops his security blanket and admires the other hand. He tells himself that with these hands he could be anything: a captain of industry, a great leader, a pro athlete, a surgeon, a renowned novelist - even the President!

Excited about his hands and the potential they hold, he runs into the next room where Lucy is watching television and shouts, "Lucy! Lucy! Look at my hands!"

Lucy looks at his hands, then looks into his eyes and says, "They've got jelly on them."

Has anybody told you lately that you have jelly on your hands? Has someone told you that you don't have the potential to do something you want to do? Has someone suggested that you should settle for less than what you really want? Too often, we tend to live up to the highest level of others' lowest expectations.

Three Sad Stories

A young lady with very low self-esteem sat in my office. Her eyes were red and swollen from crying and lack of sleep. Her husband had done an excellent job in convincing her that she was, in his words, "a worthless bitch!"

In another consultation session, I listened to a man in his 40's who had been unhappy in his job for the past 12 years. But now he wanted to pursue his dream of getting into a career he could, in his words, "really sink my teeth into." He had studied and planned for this career change, but his wife had told him that he was unstable, that he shouldn't risk his future and the future of her and their children. "Grow-up, and for once in your life try to act your age," she had admonished him. "You're not a kid anymore."

Still another of my sessions was with a graduating high school senior who had aspirations of going to college. He would be the first in his family to take such a step. As a matter of fact, none of his relatives had ever sought formal education beyond high school. The young man's dream was fading, however, because his parents had almost convinced him that he was "not cut-out for college."

These three sad, but true, episodes represent a small fraction of similar happenings occurring daily. People are getting distorted pictures of themselves and are accepting the distortions as truths. They are questioning their worth and are developing low self-esteem.

One's basic picture of himself or herself develops during childhood. Your feelings of who you are are shaped by parents, close relatives and friends. As you grow older, these basic feelings are reinforced or changed by other contacts with people.

Sing Your Song!

Some people become winners with a lot of help from good,

positive, uplifting "contacts." Other people become winners in spite of bad, negative, debasing "contacts." Throughout this book, I will challenge you to associate with high quality people. I will emphasize the importance of reading, seeing, hearing and experiencing positive things. But this is not always possible. So, in the end, you must take control of your life and not let other people or other things control it.

We often see ourselves negatively because we live in a negative society. Look at the lead stories on the TV news programs: deaths, murders, scandals. A few bits of good news are usually tucked in, on down the line. What makes headlines in the newspapers? Just recently, a bold, across-the-entire-front-page headline told of a college athlete's involvement with drugs. Way back in the paper was a small story about another college athlete who had saved the lives of two children while sacrificing his own. Much ado was made of the drug-related incident and it has remained in the news. The heroics of the life-saving athlete almost went unnoticed.

Individually, we average hearing seven criticisms to every one compliment. And most of us remember the negative comments far longer than the positive statements. Most of our limitations are self-imposed, as we often see ourselves through the eyes of people who discourage us rather than encourage us. That is why Oliver Wendell Holmes said, *"Most of us die with our music still in us."*

I challenge you to release your music.

I challenge you to sing your song!

How can you do it? How can you overcome obstacles constructed by others and by yourself? How can you realize your value and accept your worth? How can you use your abilities and reach your potential?

How To Sing!

Step One: Know Yourself

First, you must know yourself. You must know what you are like, what your strengths and weaknesses are.

When I begin to work with a corporation or athletic team on a continuing basis, I have the members list their strengths and weaknesses as individuals and as a group. Then, I ask the members and managers or coaches to share their lists with one another. Sometimes the realities are surprising to the participants. The members and the managers or coaches often view strengths and weaknesses differently. What they discover through this interchange helps develop winners.

You can go through the same process. Divide a piece of paper with a straight line. On one side, list strong points; on the other, weak points. You can construct several lists. See yourself in various roles: as a parent, a professional, a student, an athlete, a family member . . .

Athletes list items such as physical quickness, mental quickness, foot speed, upper body strength, lower body strength, adaptability and attitude as either strengths or weaknesses. Salespeople list items such as organization, pleasing personality, enthusiasm, patience, technical knowledge and perseverance as either having or not having. Managers may list people skills, motivational ability, consistency and loyalty to employees as assets or liabilities.

You are trying to discover what kind of person you are. You are putting on paper who you are. It's important that you know your good side and your bad side, your positives and your negatives, your pluses and your minuses. How well you know yourself will determine how well you'll be able to set, plan and reach your goals.

Strengths

Among your strengths, include things you feel you do well or that other people have praised, along with things that give you self-satisfaction. Consider intangibles like strong values or how you feel about yourself. Also include good work attitudes and a willingness to take a calculated risk. In short, list any attribute you can think of that appears to you to be a strength. Think of activities you really like to do - that you can work on all day and, yet, it seems like only an hour has passed.

Weaknesses

Among your weaknesses might be:

things you feel you don't do well,

things deservedly criticized by other people,

things that offer you no self-satisfaction.

List things you don't enjoy doing. You know, things that seem to make time crawl by when you've only been working on them for a short period of time. Maybe you have some negative personal habits such as lack of discipline or lack of concentration. Or, maybe you procrastinate, putting off doing things you know you should do. Maybe you are lazy or indifferent in certain areas.

Study Information

Once you have your information in front of you, spend time studying it. Concentrate on how your strong points can be used most effectively. Consider how they can be used to strengthen your weak points. Many people never take advantage of what they have. They waste their strengths and overlook their weaknesses.

This technique works not only with individuals, but also with departments, companies, teams, organizations and families. The people who work together, like a well-oiled machine, coordinating their strengths and understanding their weaknesses, are the people who will win.

Teamwork Through Compensations

It is not always the sports team with the individual all-stars that wins. More than likely, it is the group with the real "teamwork" concept that gets the job done. A wise coach takes stock of what he has and develops and adjusts his or her plans accordingly. As one football coach once said of another coach he greatly admired: "He can take his and beat yours or he can take yours and beat his."

Many years have passed and I have experienced much since my high school days (which seem like another lifetime). But through college, graduate school, work toward my doctorate and four distinct careers, I have kept in mind something that my senior English teacher scribbled in my yearbook. And I thank her for it.

Among other things, she wrote, "I hope you see daffodils and rainbows on the way . . ." Then in closing, she penned the words I have remembered and have called upon through the years. Her greatest gift to this parting student was, ". . . and always remember there are 'compensations.' "

That closing remark captured my attention the first time I read it, but it took me a while to fully comprehend it. Philosophers helped me to understand: Feltham wrote that all of creation is kept in order by discord; Hume said that all advantages come with their disadvantages, that a universal compensation prevails in all conditions of being and existence; Giles made it simple by claiming that if the poor man cannot always get food, the rich man cannot always digest it.

Author/speaker James Dobson more recently said, "It will always hurt to be laughed at, snubbed, ignored or attacked by others. But I would remind you that the human personality grows through adversity, provided it is not crushed in the process." Then, Dobson claimed that the way to overcome such adversity is through developing a tool called "compensation." He suggested that a person counterbalances his weaknesses by capitalizing on his strengths. The person compensates.

Like a smart coach taking advantage of the individual strengths of his players to develop a strong team, you can use the strengths within you to develop a stronger person. You are your own coach. You have within you your own team. Parts of you are strong in certain areas and other parts need help from those areas of strength. When you really get to know yourself, you act as the coach who brings all the players within you together to reach victory.

After you have taken inventory of yourself and have a better understanding of who you are, then you can move to the second step in "accepting yourself and your worth." This second step is a natural outgrowth of the first.

Step Two: Develop Good Habits

Work on yourself so you can develop good habits. Through habits, we program ourselves to be winners or losers. If our habits are not good, we beat ourselves. If our habits are good, we can be winners.

The Black Snake Parable

A man vacationing in the mountains returned to his hotel from a walk in the woods. His clothes were torn; his face and arms were scratched and bruised; he looked terrible. The hotel desk clerk stared at him and asked, "What in the world happened to you?"

"A big black snake chased me," the tourist replied.

"But a black snake isn't poisonous," the clerk pointed out.

"Listen," the vacationer said, "it doesn't have to be poisonous if it can make me jump off an 80 foot cliff!"

So it is with our habits. No one or nothing outside of us has to defeat us when we defeat ourselves. I've often told sports teams that more games are lost than won. Most contests are determined by mistakes made by the losers. Missed free throws, off-sides penalties, errors, busted plays, *mental mistakes* - all these things can kill us. So it is in business. More groups defeat themselves than are defeated by competitors. The same applies to our personal lives. Good habits, however, can prevent many mistakes and prevent us from defeating ourselves.

For example, it's amazing how much more we can accomplish in a day if we get up 30 minutes earlier than usual. But, we must develop the habit of getting up earlier before we can benefit from it.

The first morning that alarm goes off 30 minutes early, we struggle to cooperate. As a matter of fact, we may even reach out and backhand the clock for waking us up! The next morning, it's still not easy. The following morning is not much different. However, as the days continue, getting up earlier becomes a little easier. Finally, after about three weeks, it seems the normal thing to do.

It takes about 21 days to form most habits. After this amount of time, we get to the place where the thing we have been practicing and working on actually becomes a part of us. And, if we don't do it, we don't feel right. In your profession, education, sport and personal life, you can consciously choose to replace bad habits with good ones.

Habit-Forming Formula

I believe the only way to get rid of a bad habit is to replace it with a good habit. Rather than concentrating upon what you are not going to do, concentrate on what you are going to do.

For example, if you have a bad habit of being late for meetings, concentrate upon being on time rather than concentrating upon not being late. Making a determined effort "not to do something" reinforces it instead of preventing it.

To form the habits I want to form, I use mental imagery. I create a "picture in my mind" of the desired end-result and then concentrate upon what needs to be done in order for the "picture" to come to life. For example, when you are tempted to eat improperly, you can flash a "picture" in your mind of what you ideally want to look like. This will reinforce good eating habits. Although we'll talk about *visualization* in another chapter, the very act of picturing yourself reaching your goal is a good habit to replace negative ones.

The bottom line is, are you forming habits consistent with the person you want to be? Our habits determine our physical, mental, emotional and spiritual successes. Our habits lead to wins or losses. We are the sum result of our habits.

In my office and in the meeting rooms and locker rooms of groups to whom I have spoken is posted the sign: *Winners Develop The Habit Of Doing Things That Losers Don't Like To Do* .

Stop That!

People frequently use "bad habits" as an excuse to rationalize bad behavior. "You'll have to excuse me," someone will say. "I'm sorry, but it's just a bad habit."

65

Realizing how people use "bad habits" as a crutch, a clinical psychologist of my acquaintance developed a unique therapy with some psychological inpatients. When a patient begins to exhibit bad behavior, the psychologist abruptly says, "Stop that! When you're in my office, I don't want to see you do that anymore."

Regardless of how that might work in a psychologist's office, I think it's another method for us to deal with many of our habits. Simply say to yourself, "Stop that!" After a few days, many habits will begin to fade as you replace them with good habits.

On your lists of strengths and weaknesses, you will see evidence of good habits and bad habits. Take full advantage of your good habits and work to replace your bad habits with something positive. Developing positive habits can be the turning point of your life. Such action leads to personal power. It is **A Strategy For Winning**.

Step Three: Take Care Of Yourself

The third step in the development of a concept of self-worth is to take care of yourself physically, mentally, emotionally and spiritually. Too often, we fall into routines rather than choose a program that can help us grow. The better you take care of yourself, the more you will like yourself. And, the more you like yourself, the better you will take care of yourself. It's a positive circle.

Proper exercising and eating are two areas people often have trouble with, like the football player who approached his coach and said, "I've got to do something. My stomach's getting so big I can't even look down and see my big toe."

The coach glanced at the boy and said, "You need to diet."

"What?" the player asked.

"Diet," the coach repeated.

"Oh," the player replied. Then, after he thought for a moment, he asked the coach, "What color?"

Now that football player has a problem - and so does the coach! (Okay, so does that joke!) Not only does it appear that the player needs to get his act together physically, but it seems he may need some mental work, also. And, I'm sure he would benefit from some emotional and spiritual exercises.

Just as you seek advice from coaches, business owners, doctors, professors, family members and self-help books, also keep a close relationship with guidance counselors, ministers or other spiritual leaders. Don't be one-dimensional. Wisely combining your physical, mental, emotional and spiritual abilities leads to real winning.

In conference workshops, people have asked me to give examples of how I hone my abilities in these areas. Likewise, a couple of co-workers have suggested that I offer some hints on how I work to improve myself physically, mentally, emotionally and spiritually. So, let me open-up and share in a very personal way.

Physical Care

I make it a point to do some type of physical exercising everyday. When at home, 10 minutes of calisthenics followed by walking for about 30 minutes to an hour up and down the mountain road on which I live seems to get the job done.

On speaking trips and tours, I can do the same calisthenics and walk inside or outside, according to the prevailing weather.

People ask me how I can keep trim with all the traveling I do and banquets I attend. My answer in part is, I never eat all that I could eat and pace myself, thinking of upcoming meals as I sit down to the one at hand. And, importantly, I always keep a mental image of the person I want to be - the type of person appealing to myself and others - the type of person who can motivate himself before he tries to motivate others. Walt Disney said, "People look at you and me to see what they are supposed to be. And, if we don't disappoint them, maybe, just maybe, they won't disappoint us."

The importance of taking care of ourselves is underscored by the fact that more and more major corporations are installing exercise facilities and offering special meals for employees. Some even have periods set aside for special exercise classes.

As I travel across the nation, very seldom do I ever visit a hotel that does not have an exercise room and/or a walking or jogging track. Special, health-conscious meals are listed on most hotel and restaurant menus now.

It's not always easy to do the things we need to do in order to take care of ourselves physically. Often, it's downright hard. But as Cher said in her television ads, "If you could get a good body by taking a pill, every person would have one."

Mental Care

Mentally, I challenge myself to read at least one book and several magazines weekly. As I have told corporations and teams, "When you're through improving, you're through."

I am constantly impressed by the people I come in contact with who have sacrificed to go back to school to obtain a degree which seemed far beyond their reach.

I know a man in his 30's who could not read, but spent hours, months and years to finally gain a high school diploma.

A divorcee with three children worked as both a hotel maid and as a waitress to have the money to attend evening school and acquired her college degree.

What possibilities we have! Most people never come close to developing and applying the mental capacities that are theirs. I challenge you to never stop growing mentally - to break beyond the fact that about 90% of the average person's mind is never used.

Emotional And Spiritual Care

To help myself emotionally and spiritually, I have been teaching a Sunday School class since 1977, and have been a leader in the Fellowship of Christian Athletes since 1980. I have discovered that the more I study and prepare to help others to gain emotional and spiritual maturity, I gain so much more. It is my belief that one never really learns until he or she begins to teach.

Of course, before you can teach, you have to spend time as a student. You certainly don't want to be involved in a situation of the blind leading the blind.

In the mid-60's, when I was engaged in radio and TV work, I chose to attend a seminary to study theology, psychology and communications in a disciplined atmosphere. I was searching for personal and spiritual growth which I, in turn, could use in my work and share with others. The benefits I received meant much more to me than the Masters degree diploma I was presented.

However, you don't have to "go back to school" in order to find sources of emotional and spiritual help. Books, tapes and magazines are available, as well as community support groups that promote such growth. The means are there. The challenge is to find them, use them and apply them. Become a student and grow into a teacher.

My first after-college job was that of a teacher and coach. I learned more that first year of teaching than I had in the four previous years as a student. Later, while I obtained my graduate degrees, I continued to teach. Looking back on it now, I realize how much the simultaneous teaching complemented the studying. There's something about preparing to present something to someone else that overshadows studying for personal knowledge.

If you attend a church or synagogue or other place for spiritual growth, let me suggest that you become more actively involved if you are not already. Some people attend spiritual services or classes all their lives as spectators only. Take it from me: Participants gain more - and teachers gain the most.

A Tragic Lesson From Elvis

In my brief Rock 'n Roll career of the 60's, I met some interesting people (what an understatement!). One such person was the *King* himself, Elvis. And the thing I remember most about him involved the circumstances of our introduction.

Elvis had rented a skating rink for his entourage and himself for an after-midnight party. Dewey Phillips, the Memphis D.J. who first played an Elvis record on the radio, had invited me to attend the event with him. Elvis was dating Anita Wood at the time, a young lady I had known for several years and with whom I had double-dated during her "pre-Elvis" days.

When Dewey and I arrived, he paused just inside the door to speak with friends. Anita saw us come in and waved to me, so I left Dewey with his cohorts and walked over to the edge of the skating floor to meet Anita as she skated toward me. We hadn't seen each other in a while, so we hugged, exchanged some greetings and began to catch-up with each other's activities. All the time, I couldn't help but notice that Elvis had stopped to look. Then he skated over, frowned toward me and asked Anita, "Who's this?" It wasn't what you'd call a friendly greeting.

Anita introduced us, then explained the relationship she and I shared. Elvis nodded toward me before grabbing her around the waist and saying, "Let's go." They skated away. Anita was embarrassed, evidenced by the look in her eyes as she glanced back toward me.

Elvis was jealous!

I guess I should have felt flattered. Instead, I was surprised and disappointed. I was surprised that he would feel threatened by anyone, especially a young unknown such as myself. I was disappointed that he wasn't the warm and cordial person of whom I had heard and greatly admired.

Later, Anita apologized and told me that it was a combination of things that had caused him to act like that. She explained that he and Dewey had been on the "outs" and he had seen me come in with Dewey. Also, he wasn't feeling well and was facing some deadlines on some important decisions he had to make. Still, even though I now remember Elvis as a great entertainer and later found him to be more friendly, the thing I remember most about him are those few moments when the person who seemingly had the world by the tail showed some insecurity and some unbecoming reactions to an admirer.

By the way, in one of my scrapbooks, I have a *WHBQ Radio Official Big 56 Survey* printed in Memphis on July 5, 1963. *Sukiyaki* by Kyu Sakamoto was number one that week; *Surfin' U.S.A.* by the Beach Boys was number 10; *Those Lazy, Hazy, Crazy Days of Summer* by Nat King Cole was 24; *STEADY* by Carl Mays was 39; *Still* by Anita Wood was 47; and *Devil in Disguise* by Elvis had just been released and had come on the chart at number 55.

I have shown this chart to friends and have kiddingly said, "Look. . . I was above Elvis!" But all kidding aside, whenever I look at that survey chart containing the names of Anita, Elvis and myself, I re-live that evening at the skating rink, the evening when it hit me like the proverbial ton of bricks that the person who I thought was on top of the world suffered insecurity like most everyone else.

Such insecurity, increased by unbelievable pressures that only he could understand, played no small part in Elvis' early death. He did not take care of himself. He abused his body and his mind. He struggled physically, mentally, emotionally and spiritually. Plus, he believed strongly that he was destined to die at a young age, like his mother. Such a destined type of feeling will be covered in the next chapter.

The bottom line here: take care of yourself. Take advantage of the *positive* circle to which I referred earlier. The more you develop a well-rounded self-esteem, the less likely you will be to "let yourself go" in any area. The more you work to improve yourself, the more positive and energetic your self-esteem will grow. Anyone is open to low self-esteem, no matter what he or she has accomplished in certain areas of life. Often, people may be giants in one area of their lives and midgets in other areas.

If you take care of yourself, the goals you set and work toward will be less difficult to reach. I'll offer some in-depth advice on goal-setting in chapter seven. But for now, let me share something with you that is of extreme importance in accepting yourself and your worth.

What Are You Shooting For?

Driving through a small town, I saw some graffiti on a window of a vacant store which caught my eye: "A Big Shot is a Little Shot who kept on shooting." I like that. The "Big Shot" advice reminds us that it's imagination, dedication and just plain old hard work that eventually pays successful dividends.

But many people are not experiencing true satisfaction in life because they lack *shooting power*. If one shoots too low, he may find that his life is unfulfilling, even though he may be reaching his goals.

I think we should pause at times to evaluate where we are in life, where we've been and where we're going. If your plans and dreams are too small or too restricted, it's more than likely that you're not experiencing what you have the potential to experience.

Setting and reaching big goals does not necessarily mean obtaining money and "things." It seems our society has always been attracted to the "rags to riches" stories of people who began with a few pennies and turned the pennies into fortunes. Such people should be commended for their imaginations and hard work, and I have used several as positive examples in this book. But we should not set them up as the epitome of what happiness and enjoyment are all about.

I personally know some low-goal-oriented people who are financially rich. Had they shot higher, they may not have been rich now, but they would have more fulfillment in life. I personally know some low-goal-oriented people who are financially poor. Had they shot higher, they probably would not be poor now, and their lives would be more satisfying.

How big and well-rounded are your thoughts? If you have big, well-rounded thoughts, you have to grow as a person in order for these thoughts to become realities. If you have small, restricted thoughts, you will remain small and restricted.

"Thinking Big" applies to all aspects of life in which you are involved. Pity the poor man who is big in business and little in family. Consider the miserable woman who is large socially and small spiritually. Think of the "successful" corporate employee who dreads or hates what he/she does. Or, what about the unfortunate person who is really into spiritual matters, but disassociates such matters from relationships with other people. There are distorted "big and little" people throughout our society - people who are lopsided and, thus, unable to experience the fulfillment which could be theirs.

If you pause to evaluate the size and scope of your dreams and aspirations in the various areas of life and find yourself lacking, you should be challenged to grow. Be happy where you are as you set your sights on higher, broader levels. That does not mean you should be satisfied with where you are. Rather, it means that you should enjoy each level to the fullest "on your way up." Your eventual happiness will be multiplied tremendously if you make the best of the climb and enjoy the struggle.

Step Four: Accept Compliments Gracefully

The next step in appreciating yourself and realizing your potential is to accept compliments gracefully. You can tell a lot about a person's self-esteem by the way he or she accepts a compliment.

A couple of years ago, the college team I was pulling for in a close football game lost by three points. I went into the locker room after the game and told a young man on the losing team that he had played a good game, which, indeed, he had. His reply to me, however, was, "We stunk. We couldn't get the job done."

His reaction was similar to that of a young lady when I told her that she was wearing a pretty dress. She responded with, "Aw, it's just an 'el cheapo' I found in the bargain basement."

Thank-You

People who react to sincere compliments by trying to run down themselves or belittle the compliments reveal low self-esteem. The best way in the world to respond to a compliment is to say, "Thank you. I appreciate that very much." This says that you have done your homework, you have produced and that you appreciate someone else recognizing what you have done. Such action reinforces the receiver as well as the giver of the compliment.

Show Confidence

Consider the example of the teenage boy asking a girl out for a date. He picks up the phone and nervously dials the number. When she answers, he says, "Hello, Jenny, this is Pete. You wouldn't want to go out with me, would you?"

To which she replies, "No."

Click.

The teenaged Pete is like the salesperson who approaches the potential customer with the question, "You wouldn't want to buy this, would you?"

A sales manager in working with his salesman heard him say, "I don't know if I can sell this product to the customer." The manager told the young man, "Son, you must be more confident, more positive, more decisive."

"Okay," the salesman responded. "Then I *know* I can't sell this product to the customer." This salesman has a problem - and so does his sales manager! They're in about the same predicament as the overweight football player and his coach that I mentioned earlier.

We have to give ourselves the benefit of the doubt before anyone else will. And then, when we receive a compliment we must have the self-esteem and confidence to acknowledge the remark and thank the person making it.

Compliment Others

Look for things to compliment in others. The self-confident person is able to transcend personal problems to let others know they're okay. You'll not only lift their spirits and pick up their day, but you'll receive more compliments yourself!

By accepting and giving compliments gracefully, you'll develop the "I'm O.K. - You're O.K." attitude. You won't be like Bob who told Sam, "I passed by Jim in the front yard the other day and he didn't say a word to me, I guess he thinks I'm not on his level anymore."

"Why that no good, flea-bitten, conceited, lame-brain!" Sam sputtered. "Of course you're on his level!"

Watch how you word your compliments!

Be aware, also, that some people are wary of compliments. These people think others are trying to manipulate them by "buttering them up." You can help yourself and others by being as sincere as possible with what you say and by accepting compliments as being sincere until proven differently.

Step Five: Keep On Growing

Never stop growing as an individual. Be willing to learn. Be attentive to what is happening around you. Ask yourself what you need to do in order to grow professionally and personally.

Are You Still Improving - Or, Are You *Still*?

The importance of knowing our strengths and weaknesses as mentioned earlier is spotlighted here. Just as we need to know these points prior to beginning a task, we need to be aware of them when the task is completed. How did you do? What were your strengths? How could you improve?

Recently, I was introduced to Priority Management's *Time Text*. This system's purpose is to assist people in making the most of their time. Interestingly, one aspect of the planner booklet asks the user to grade himself or herself at the end of a project, listing strengths and areas in which improvement is needed. Continued growth not only leads to successes in what we are doing, but also helps us to be more productive.

In every board room, class room, locker room and family room, these words should be posted: *When A Person Stops Improving, A Person Stops*. Or, as I said earlier, "When you're through improving, you're through."

Be Coachable

One of the greatest things a coach can say about an athlete is that he or she is "coachable." Managers are anxious to find employees who want to grow in an organization. Teachers love to see students who strive for higher grades. Corporation presidents listen to junior officers who want to rise to the top. Stay hungry. Never be satisfied with less than your best.

When I was a running back in football, I had a coach who seemed to stay on my back constantly. If I gained five yards, the coach would say, "Mays, you should have gained 10." If I gained 10, I'd hear, "Mays, you should have gained 20." If I gained 20, the words were, "Mays, you should have broken it all the way for a touchdown. You had a hole big enough to drive a truck through!"

One day, the coach saw that his pushing was beginning to get to me. That's when he pulled me aside and said, "Mays, if I didn't think you could do better, I wouldn't stay on your back all the time. If I didn't think you had potential, I would leave you alone and concentrate on someone else."

Often we need to thank the people who push us and who want us to do better, who help us continue to grow.

The Winner She Could Become

I advertised for an employee to fill a newly created position in my organization and received 52 applications. The applicants were narrowed down to 12, then six.

The young lady I finally chose was not necessarily the most talented, nor did she have the most experience. At the time, she was far from what one would call a "winner." However, I saw potential in her and I saw in her the "winner" she could become. And, importantly, even though she had experienced quite a lot of failure at a relatively young age, I believed she was coachable. She has been with me for several years now and has become a very important person to me. She has developed into the winner I knew she could become and has helped me to grow as a winner.

Get A Little Better Each Week

I've often encouraged my 83-7 football team to get a little better each week as the season progresses. *Peaking* at the right time is important in sports and in all of life, Some teams *peak* too soon and then remain on that level or fall back. Some teams never *peak*. Others are like a yo-yo, inconsistent, up and down.

The strength of the opposition shouldn't determine your growth and improvement. But some teams don't have the discipline to continue to improve when playing an opponent that doesn't require their best effort. However, the performance in the more difficult games later on will be determined by how you play in the less demanding games along the way.

A Springboard Engagement

You've probably heard the expression, "There are no little jobs, only little people." Always do the best you can do and always try to do it better than the time before.

Several years ago, I accepted a 15-minute speaking engagement for a university commencement program. The fee was relatively small and the presentation was relatively short, but I worked on it with the same care and fervor I would for a major address for a major fee.

The response to the brief presentation was very positive. And, in the audience was a graduate's uncle who just happened to be an executive with an insurance company. He contacted me the following week to speak to his organization. This led to other engagements.

To date, the best I can figure, that 15-minute graduation address has earned me well over $100,000.

Get a little better each week. Don't let up - or let down - whichever term you might use. Because when you do, you are going to lose something.

I think this is a good slogan to display in a prominent place on your wall:

> *The Ladder Of Success Is An Extension Ladder.*
> *Once You've Climbed As High As You Think You Can Go,*
> *You Can Extend Yourself And Go A Little Higher.*

Step Six: Practice Humility

As we continue to grow, however, we need to practice humility. Don't be like the All-Pro defensive end confronted by the flight attendant on an airplane. "You'll have to buckle your seatbelt, sir," she said.

The football player winked and answered, "Superman don't need no seatbelt."

She looked back at him and said, "Superman don't need no airplane."

77

Some people require a larger dose of humility than other people do - like that football player - and the motorcycle gang that pulled into a truck stop.

All 12 of the cyclists got off of their motorcycles and went inside. There was only one other customer in the restaurant at the time, a truck driver, sitting at a booth, finishing his meal. The gang looked around, smiled at one another with cocky grins, then pranced over to where the man sat. One bumped the truck driver's shoulder, another put out a cigarette on his plate and several more joined in the taunting.

The truck driver just looked at them, stood up, went over to pay for his meal, then walked out.

The gang really started laughing now, thoroughly enjoying themselves. The leader turned toward the cashier who had been watching it all and said, "I thought truck drivers were supposed to be tough. That one sure ain't much of a man!"

"No," the cashier replied as he looked out the window. "He's not much of a truck driver, either. He just backed over 12 motorcycles."

Keep things in perspective. Know when to speak up and know when to shut up.

Unhappiness Caused By Attitudes

Many people who lack humility are often those who never seem to get the job done, who never really enjoy life, who are preoccupied with themselves. They show little consideration for the feelings of others. They show little sensitivity or tact. They tend to dominate conversations with the word, "I."

Such people need to realize that their unhappiness is caused by their attitudes toward themselves and others. When a person has a low self-image, he or she tends not to practice humility. This person spends a lot of time cutting other people down in order to lower them to his or her own level.

There are two ways a person can grow in his or her mind. First, the person can seem to appear larger by making other people appear smaller. Secondly, the person can actually grow by concentrating upon what he or she has and by helping others to grow, too.

Right Estimate

There's been a lot of discussion as to what humility is. It is not thinking less of yourself than you really are; nor is it thinking more of yourself than your really are. True humility is having a right estimate of yourself.

Apart from those people who seem to have no humility at all, there are many who appear to have an overdose of humility. They grovel or belittle themselves. They underestimate themselves and sell themselves short. As I mentioned earlier, they see themselves as "garage sale" items.

You can fit comfortably in-between the underdose and overdose people. You can gain a realistic estimate of yourself if you do your homework on listing and studying your strengths and weaknesses. If you know who you are, where you are now and where you want to go, your self-appraisal will have a clearer focus. You'll know your capabilities and limitations. You'll understand what you can and can't change. What you can, you will. What you can't, you'll adjust accordingly. If you are a winner, you won't waste your energy butting your head against an immovable wall. But you won't quit striving for your goal just because the going gets a little rough.

Reach down inside of yourself and find your best.

Let The "Big Me" Sing

Around the turn of the century, the great Italian operatic singer, Enrico Caruso, was stricken with stage fright a few minutes before he was due to sing to a packed concert hall. His throat was paralyzed by spasms and perspiration poured down his face. He said to himself, "They'll laugh at me. I can't sing." Then, he shouted aloud, not caring who backstage could hear, "The little me wants to strangle the big me within!"

Then, in a louder voice, he shouted, "Get out of here! The big me wants to sing! Get out! Get out, little me! The big me is going to sing!"

Caruso did sing that day, and he received a thunderous ovation for a flawless performance.

Nine times out of ten, the only thing standing between you and success is yourself. Get rid of the "little me" and let the "big me" sing! You can do it if you have the right attitude. And, the "right" attitude is what the next chapter is all about. . .

Chapter 3

DEVELOP AND MAINTAIN A POSITIVE ATTITUDE

After playing all day, a small child came into the house and shouted, "Mom, if I fell out of a tree, would you rather I broke my leg or tore my pants?"

"What a silly question," his mother answered. "I'd rather you tore your pants."

"Well, I've got good news for you Mom. That's exactly what happened!"

The little boy had a positive attitude, and positive attitudes lead people to the winner's circle in all areas of life. The boy's attitude didn't prevent him from having a problem - after all, he did fall from a tree and he did tear his pants. But his attitude made the situation better. A negative attitude or reaction could have made the situation worse.

We all experience problems or troubles in life. But more important than our troubles is how we react to them. People who have positive attitudes still face disappointments, frustrations and pressures. It's the reaction that's different. Problems can cause unhappiness, can defeat you, if you allow them to. On the other hand, you can make problems work for you and use them to achieve happiness and success.

81

A motto that you might consider placing on your wall or in your wallet is: *When Problems Arise, Some People Break. Other People Break Records* .

As you commit this motto to memory, keep in mind that problems can bring out the worst or the best in you. You can fold under the pressure or you can tap powerful resources that are already within you. In fact, even though you can't appreciate it at the time, a problem can be good for you. It can help you to become the person you have the potential to become.

Betty's Story

Betty was married to a man who proved to be a cruel, shiftless alcoholic that refused to admit his condition or seek help. He would beat Betty and their four children. Debts accumulated. Often there was no food in the house. Then, when the oldest child was seven, the husband deserted Betty and the children. She had no money, no credit and no job training. Adding to her desperate situation, she had to undergo surgery shortly after her husband left.

In less than six months, the youngest child became ill and died. Betty located her husband and telegraphed the news to him. His telegraphed reply was, "Terrible shock. Sorry to hear the news." That was the extent of his reaction.

The man's heartlessness so challenged Betty that she resolved to rear the children and carve a place for herself. She toiled at any work available, then acquired two regular jobs while she resumed her education and sought additional training. All the time, she raised her children with high moral values. Not once did she say or do anything to turn them against their departed father.

While keeping the home together and making it a happy one, she became an outstanding businessperson. Her desire, dedication and determination was highlighted when she was honored with her city's "Business Woman of the Year" award.

Betty was interviewed by the media when the award was presented to her. In reaction to questions about her accomplishments she responded, "Any person can wring happiness out of life if she or he is worthy of happiness."

Standing beside Betty, beaming with pride, was a man she had recently met, fallen in love with and married. A journalist asked him what it was that lifted Betty from the bottom to the top. He replied, "Well, she was able to put things into perspective - with a great sense of humor and an unbreakable, positive attitude . . ."

The late Charles F. Kettering, distinguished research scientist for General Motors, always kept this plaque on his wall:

> *Do not bring me your successes;*
> *they weaken me.*
>
> *Bring me your problems;*
> *they strengthen me.*

The Lady And The Tiger

Ed and Joe were enjoying themselves at the circus when they came to a cage containing a ferocious-looking tiger. The two men stared at the beast as he growled and bared his teeth. At that moment, a beautiful young lady approached the cage, wearing a very brief, sequined outfit and a silver cape. She stepped up to the cage door, unbuttoned the cape and dropped it to the ground. Then, she opened the door and stepped inside.

Ed and Joe looked at one another. They couldn't believe it. Then, they watched as the tiger stared at the young lady and prepared to pounce. Suddenly, however, the young lady pointed her finger at the tiger and said, "Sit!" The tiger very meekly sat. "Crawl!" she commanded. The tiger slowly crawled toward her.

Ed and Joe continued to watch closely, awed by what they were seeing. The young lady extended her hand toward the tiger and he licked her hand like a kitten. She bent over and the tiger licked her on the cheek.

Ed turned to Joe and exclaimed, "Man! What courage! I wouldn't do that for anything in the world!"

"I would," said Joe.

"You're crazy!" Ed told him. "You wouldn't dare do that!"

"Of course I would," Joe replied. "You get that tiger out of there and I'll show you."

Attitudes Are More Important Than Facts

Attitudes are more important than facts. Ed looked at the event and saw a ferocious tiger. Joe saw a beautiful young lady.

I challenge you to have a positive attitude, to become an optimist. Don't close your eyes to reality; see the bad as well as the good. But, at the same time, be an optimist. This is vital to your success and everyday happiness.

As I'm sure you have heard, an optimist will look at a half-filled glass of water and say, "Great. That glass is half full." A pessimist will look at the same glass and complain, "It's almost gone. It's half empty."

An optimist will get up in the morning, go over to the window, pull back the drapes, look out the window and say, "Good morning, Lord!" A pessimist looks out the same window and says, "Good Lord, morning!"

An optimist thinks this is the best of all possible worlds. A pessimist is afraid he's right.

You know the type of people I'm talking about. They're always saying, "We can't do this. It's never been done that way. We can't win. It will never happen." They look like they eat pickles three meals a day - the type of people where the whole room seems to brighten up when they leave.

I challenge you to be a positive, uplifting, optimistic person, enthusiastic about what you can do and how you're going to do it.

Excellent Customer Service

Every now and then, my wife Jean will accompany me on one of my speaking engagements and we'll turn it into sort of a mini-vacation. This was the case a while back when I had an engagement in Eugene, Oregon. We flew to Portland, rented a car, drove down to Eugene, where we spent Wednesday evening and I led in a full-day seminar on Thursday. After staying Thursday evening in Eugene, we arose bright and early on Friday morning and drove to the coast.

Beginning in Florence, Oregon, we motored all the way up Highway 101 to Seaside, Oregon. It was a beautiful weekend in April and a beautiful drive as the highway paralled the ocean.

During the trip, I noticed we needed some gas as we came to a small town named Waldport. Seeing a clean-looking service station, I pulled in front of the gas pump, started to get out and get some gas, when it seemed like from out of nowhere there appeared a young lady. Wearing a crisp uniform, bow tie and cap, she came to my window and asked, "May I fill it up, please?"

"Yes," I replied, "please do."

She removed the hose from the pump, inserted it into the gas tank, then proceeded to clean the front windshield, headlights, outside mirrors, side windows, back windows and checked the pressure in the tires. She then asked, "May I check under the hood?"

"Yes," I replied, "please do."

She lifted the hood, inspected a few things, brought the oil dipstick to my window and showed me the oil mark as she said, "It's a little low. You don't need to add any right now, but I would keep an eye on it."

"Thank you very much," I said.

She replaced the measuring stick, checked a couple of other things, closed the hood, removed a rag from her back pocket and wiped away her fingerprints. Returning to my window, she said, "The water in your battery is fine, all your belts are in good shape and you have good treads on your tires."

"Thank you very much," I said. She turned to remove the hose from the car. My wife and I looked at each other in amazement over the uncommonly excellent service we were receiving.

Having replaced the hose, she returned to my window and I handed her my credit card. "If you'll hand me that litter bag, I'll empty it on the way back to the station," she offered. She left with the credit card and bag. My wife and I shared amazed looks again.

Soon, she was back with the credit card voucher and new litter bag. After signing the voucher, I told the young lady, "I want to thank you for this excellent service."

"Sir," she responded, "I want to thank *you* for coming in and doing business with us, and if you're ever in this area again, I invite you to come back."

What a great attitude! And, that attitude was reflected in the way she looked, the way she walked, the way she spoke and the way she did her job. She was uplifting and enthusiastic. She made me glad to be around her.

Too often, however, we encounter people who are just the opposite.

The Other Extreme: Are We Crazy Or What?

Recently, I had four speaking engagements in four days, in different parts of the country. Going to the last of the four engagements, I arrived rather late at an airport in the eastern part of the Midwest. I quickly caught a taxi to the hotel where I was speaking at 8:30 the next morning. I had a little trouble checking-in because the front desk clerk could not locate my confirmed reservation. Finally, however, I did get to my room.

As I rushed to get to bed and picked up my travel clock to set the alarm, the question of what time zone I was in popped into my mind. I looked around the room, but didn't see another clock. So, I called down to the front desk.

The phone rang about a dozen times. Then someone picked up the receiver on the other end and said, "Yes?" The tone was curt.

I asked, "Could you please tell me if we're on central time or eastern time here?"

The young lady's voice came back, "I don't know."

There was silence on the line.

Then I explained, "I believe you might have misunderstood my question. What I want to know is, in this city, are we in the eastern time zone or are we in the central time zone?"

She quickly replied, "I don't know. I've only lived here for a few weeks." Then she hung up the phone.

Well, I brushed away my fatigue, grew a little wiser and dialed the front desk again. And again it rang about a dozen times. The young lady picked up the receiver and gave me her "Yes?"

I was brief and to the point. "What time is it, please?"

She didn't say a word, placed the receiver on the desk and was gone for several minutes. Finally, she returned to the phone, blurted out the time and hung up before I could even thank her.

Sitting on the edge of my bed, I asked myself, "Are we crazy or what? Here is a multi-million dollar hotel with a multi-million dollar marketing campaign and then they place someone like this as a high contact person to represent them."

Maybe someone had given her a hard time. I don't know. There was a man working at the front desk when I had checked-in. And, even though he was having some problems, he remained courteous. I should be thankful she wasn't on duty when I arrived!

We perform to the lowest level of our expectations. So do others. And that's why customer service is in the sad shape it's in. Many front-line employees have a low self-expectation rate. Yet, as my experiences and your experiences show, more sales are lost or won by the lowest paid employee than can ever be affected by the highest paid executive.

Stanley Marcus said, "Why do you think you have to have so many department stores in a mall these days? It is because each of them does such a poor selling job that they survive by taking up each other's unsatisfied customers."

Fred Smith, founder and Chairman of Federal Express Corporation defines customer service as this:

> *Let's suppose a courier is having a bad day and isn't as responsive to a customer's needs as he or she should have been.*

87

It's easy for the courier to think, 'No big deal. The worst that can happen is that we'll lose one package out of a million in business.'

But let's suppose that customer does four packages a day, five days a week, 50 weeks out of the year at $25 dollars a package. And let's say that customer should average at least 10 years with us. Now instead of losing one package worth of business, that courier lost us over a quarter of a million dollars. That's the cost of poor customer service.

Recently in Philadelphia, a man parked in a parking lot adjoining the branch office of a bank in which he had some accounts. After cashing a check, he asked the teller to validate his parking ticket so he wouldn't have to pay a dollar.

The teller refused, insisting that cashing a check was not significant enough business to merit free parking. When the customer requested to speak to the manager, the manager supported the teller's stand. So, the customer wrote a few more checks - withdrawing over $1,000,000 from the bank.

Some people expect the worst, think the worst, act the worst, attract the worst.

Once, when I was in a football locker room prior to a big game, I overheard a running back say, "Man, we're going to get clobbered." The game was close, but his team did lose - mainly because of his poor performance.

We program ourselves to be winners or losers. The writer of the Book of Proverbs hit it right on the head when he wrote, "As a person thinks, so is he."

People Are Drawn To Winners

In the late 60's, I was a city-wide youth director in New Orleans, working with schools, sports teams and churches. I started a monthly youth rally that was based upon a positive, optimistic, "You Can Do It" attitude.

Utilizing college and professional athletes, contemporary music, drama and films, I would not allow anyone to present any "this is what you can't do" messages. The emphasis by me and by others was always, "Look at the tremendous possibilities you have - and take advantage of your opportunities."

At our first monthly rally we had about 150 people present. Three years later, at the last rally prior to my leaving New Orleans, we had to rent a special building to house the 5,000 young people who came to be challenged, inspired and encouraged.

People of all ages *want* to win. They want to be around others who will tell them they *can* win. They will flock to hear someone tell them *how* to win.

A Lesson From Tommy John

Tommy John is a winner. He was a winner when he pitched for the Los Angeles Dodgers and a winner with the New York Yankees. It was my good fortune to speak on a program in which Tommy John was also speaking. Listen to his story:

He was one of the greatest pitchers in baseball with the Dodgers, performing at the top of his game. Then, one night while pitching against the Expos in Montreal, he experienced a sudden, excruciating pain in his pitching arm. The doctors discovered that Tommy had torn a ligament in his arm and had separated the muscles. His hand was already beginning to draw up because the nerves leading to the hand were dead. "You will never pitch again," the doctors told him.

For two years the hand continued to deteriorate. Scar tissue grew over the nerves and the hand became paralyzed, taking the form of a monkey claw. Everyone, including Tommy, knew that his baseball career was finished.

Then, one day Tommy heard a dynamic speaker talk about the power of belief. The speaker got through to Tommy as he enthusiastically declared that the impossible becomes possible when we have enough faith and our minds are filled with an unbeatable attitude.

Tommy began to work daily. His goal was to pitch again. At first he could not even grasp the ball. Using tape, he would attach it to his palm and then push it toward home plate. He suffered pain as he struggled. His former teammates suffered, too.

They suffered for him, watching him torture himself, hoping that he would give up and not continue the self-punishment.

A year later, Tommy John won 20 games for the Los Angeles Dodgers!

What Is Your Problem?

We all have problems. We all have mountains to climb. You will not come in contact with one person who does not have problems. But the important question here is, "What is *your* problem?" And, an even more important question is, "How can you overcome it?"

You can overcome it with a dynamic, positive attitude. Amazing things can happen. As my friend and mentor Dr. Norman Vincent Peale has claimed so many times: "Your mind is the most powerful magnet in the world. It draws out of life what you think and makes you what you become."

So how can you develop and maintain a positive attitude?

How To Have A Positive Attitude

Step One: Expect To Win

Facing life is sometimes like buying a used car. You may get a lemon, but the challenge is to make lemonade and enjoy it. Don't look for failure. Don't look for all the reasons why something won't work or why you are going to fail.

You've probably heard the story of Babe Ruth taking two strikes then pointing his bat to the place where he would hit a home run to win the game for the Yankees.

After the game, a young reporter asked the Yankee slugger, "How would you have felt if you hadn't hit that home run, if you had made an out instead?"

The Babe looked at the young man and said, "Son, that never even entered my mind."

He didn't think about striking out, grounding out or flying out. He didn't even think about hitting a single, double or triple.

His mind was on the home run and the exact location he was going to hit it.

But, how many people see all the ways that they can fail rather than concentrating on how they can succeed? How many people are like the character in the "Li'l Abner" cartoons who always had a black cloud over his head? Wherever he went, there was trouble for him and for the people with whom he associated.

Like the cartoon character, some people view themselves as losers and they become losers to others. Winners dwell on reward and move toward it; losers dwell on failure and move toward that.

Toward Our Focus

If I placed on the floor a wooden board measuring 30 feet in length and six inches in width, and on one end of the board I placed a $100 bill, would you walk from one end of the board to the other to pick it up and put it in you pocket? Of course.

What if we raised the board about 20 stories, placing the ends on two separate buildings? Again, I put the $100 bill on one end, placing a brick on it so that the wind doesn't blow it away. You know, it gets drafty up there. Then, suppose I told you, "If you will walk from one end of the board to the other and pick up that bill, it's yours." Would you do it? Probably not.

In the first example, when the board was on the floor, you had your eyes and mind on the goal of getting the money. You didn't even think of falling off. In the second example, you saw the pitfalls, the penalties of failure rather than the rewards of success. You thought about the possibility of falling 20 stories. When you lose sight of what you can gain, what happens? You begin to see what you can lose. The muscles tighten and the mind doesn't function as easily.

More than likely, you would fall from 20 stories up. We tend to follow our thoughts.

Life is often like walking a board 20 stories high. Your challenge is to see the positive outcome you're going to achieve. Don't constantly focus upon the mistakes you might make. You can't grow stronger by thinking about how weak you are. You can't become faster by thinking about how slowly you run. You can't develop your talents by thinking about talents you don't have. You can't acquire more money by concentrating on poverty. You can't become a thankful person by bitterly complaining about injustice. "As a person thinks, so is he."

To develop a positive attitude, focus on succeeding, not failing.

In the first chapter, I told you about a football team I've worked with for nine years. In the nine years prior to our **Strategy For Winning** programs, their record was 43 and 47. Their record of the past nine years is 83 and seven.

During our first year, the team was approaching its fourth game of the season undefeated. They were going to play a team whom they had never beaten. This time they were excited; they were prepared to beat them. But when the game ended, our team had lost again.

The next week I asked the players, "When you went out on that field, how many of you hoped you would win?" All of them raised their hands.

"How many of you wished so hard and wanted it so badly that you could almost taste it?" All hands went up.

Then I said, "I just have one more question. When you walked out onto that field for the kickoff, how many of you *expected* to win the game and would have been very surprised if you didn't?" Not one hand was raised.

Programming Ourselves

This is the case a lot of times. We hope something will happen; we wish it would happen; but, deep inside we don't expect it to happen. Expectations make all the difference in the world as we program ourselves.

We must expect to succeed. This is where the subconscious mind is effective. The subconscious mind knows what we really feel about something. You can probably remember a circumstance in which you might have told people one thing, but deep inside, you expected another. Through our true expectations, we program ourselves to win or lose, to be optimistic or pessimistic, to enjoy life and its richness or complain about its problems.

Did you realize that about 90% of our mind is subconscious? It stores everything we see, hear, read or think, and everything that goes into our subconscious mind is accepted as truth. For example, if you believe there is no way in the world for you to be happy, the subconscious mind will work to make sure that you're not happy.

If you believe there is no way in the world for you to accomplish a task in a given period of time, you won't. If you believe you are going to fail, your subconscious mind will work 24 hours a day to help you fail. We program ourselves to lose or succeed.

Step Two: Release Your Potential

I'm not a medical doctor nor a trained biologist. However, my research on the power of the mind and my continuous study of the subconscious, teamed with personal experience and my work with sports teams and business groups, have led me to discover that certain chemicals are released into the body according to the set of the mind. For example, a positive mind set releases fluids that give us the power to accomplish what ordinarily we could not accomplish. Conversely, a negative mind set releases fluids that take away a portion of the power we already possess.

Mental Becomes Physical

Therefore, mental power actually takes on a physical aspect. That's why negative, depressed attitudes can actually bring on "colds," while optimistic, upbeat attitudes can strengthen the immune system and, thus, prevent the common cold.

The combination of the mental and physical strengths released through positive, expectant attitudes leads to upsets in sports, in business and in all of life. In chapter one, I shared Ghandi's words:

> If I believe I cannot do something, it makes me incapable of doing it. But when I believe I can, then I acquire the ability to do it, even if I did not have the ability in the beginning.

Henry Ford II put it another way when he said:

If you decide that you can or can't do something, you will usually be right.

I know someone who, in elementary school, could do nothing right. He failed at everything he did. At a very early age, he programmed himself to believe that he was a failure. Then a teacher came into his life who told him, "You can do it!" His life transformed into a life of "can" instead of "can't." He went on to a life of leadership and achievement. What changed his course in life? His ability, with the help of others along the way, to program positive expectations, altered his life.

Dr. Maxwell Maltz, author of *Psycho-Cybernetics*, tells of a young man under hypnosis who was told to hold out his hand. The hypnotist touched one of the man's fingers with his own finger and told the young man it was a red hot poker.

The young man yanked his hand back and yelled. Shortly thereafter a blister appeared on his finger. Through the power of suggestion planted in the subconscious mind, a blister was formed!

Of course, the mind is also very powerful in healing the body. Sugar pills have long been a mystery to the medical community. They contain no medicine of any kind that could actually cure a patient, and yet they can help some people improve their health.

When the Royal Canadian Navy tested a new drug for seasickness, they divided the seamen into three groups: One group received the seasickness pills; the second group received sugar pills; and the last group received no pills.

As you might imagine, Group Three reported 30% of the men became seasick. Group One, who had the real medicine, reported 13% seasick. How do you think Group Two, the group with the sugar pills, fared? They, too, reported that only 13% of their group became seasick.

It's interesting that Groups One and Two responded alike to the pills they were given, even though one group had no medical reason to prevent them from being seasick. But the members of

Group Two believed they were taking medicine and expected not to be sick. There is no doubt, the mind affects the body.

Norman Cousins' Story

In *Anatomy of An Illness*, the story of Norman Cousins' successful fight against a crippling disease, Cousins emphasized that studies show that up to 90% of patients who reach out for medical help are suffering from self-limiting disorders well within the range of the body's own healing powers.

In 1964, Cousins contracted a disease that doctors believed to be incurable. One doctor, however, accepted the challenge to work with Cousins to overcome the odds. Together, they proved what powerful weapons positive emotions can be in the war against disease. They proved how your mind can cure your body.

Cousins, well-known editor of the *Saturday Review*, waited until 1979 before he wrote in detail about his successful "mind over body" experience.

Why did he wait 15 years to publish the book? Because, in his words, "I was fearful of creating false hope in others. . ." And, he was afraid that people might accuse him of a "voodoo" or "anti-medicine" philosophy. However, when more and more people learned of his experience and journalists wrote about it, he was compelled to share what became a best-seller.

Cousins claims that a doctor knows it is the prescription slip itself, even more than what is written on it, that is often the vital ingredient for enabling a patient to get rid of whatever is ailing him. According to Cousins, drugs are not always necessary. Belief in recovery always is.

The Doctor Within

Dr. Albert Schweitzer, known for his humanitarian work in Africa, said that an African witch doctor succeeds for the same reason other doctors succeed. That is, the patient carries his own "doctor" inside him. The patient comes to a doctor not knowing that truth. Doctors, he said, are at their best when they give the "doctor" who resides within each patient a chance to go to work.

Psychosomatic Iliness

It has been estimated that approximately 10 to 25 percent of all illnesses is strictly physical. But approximately 75 to 90 percent is psychosomatic. *Psycho* means mind. *Soma* means body. *Psychosomatic* then refers to the mental thoughts affecting the physical body.

A number of years ago, some psychology students devised an experiment, using one of their friends as a guinea pig, to see if false suggestions could cause reactions in the body. On the day of the scheme, as the young man left the dorm, a friend greeted him with, "Good morning, John! How are you doing today? You look a little pale." A second friend shortly thereafter met him and said, "John, are you feeling okay? You look sick!" A third friend greeted John and said, "You shouldn't be out of bed!" Before the young man could get to class, he turned around, went back to his dormitory and fell into bed. He was sick.

"As a person thinks, so is he".

So far, I've suggested two ways to develop a positive attitude:

(1) Expect to Win.

(2) Release Your Potential.

Step Three: Say, "I Deserve The Best."

Now you need to tell yourself that you deserve the best. Some individuals, some groups, some companies, some teams don't believe they can be champions. They think the idea of reaching for the top is for others. Let me give an example. Let's suppose you saw an ad for a job in the paper. It was exactly the type job you'd been looking for. The question is, how do you react? Is your reaction like this? "I'd love to have a job like that but there are many others who are looking for such a job. I'd never have a chance, so why bother?"

I went to speak to a football team and discovered that one of the players had brought a pet hamster to keep in the locker room. The smell was terrible, but the hamster got used to it! Not only did the team's dressing room stink, but so did their attitude and playing. So we got to work.

I think the reason that many teams or businesses, don't make it to the top is because they think reaching the top requires some special person from a superior planet. Such groups need to have their attitudes adjusted.

One thing I try to emphasize to sports teams is, "Hey, you've got just as much right to be winners as anybody else in the world." Being the best is not reserved for someone else.

Destined To Win

No one is *destined* to win. No one is *meant* to succeed. No one is *meant* to fail. If a team believes it can win, it programs itself to win. When it programs itself to win, it expects to win. Then, it begins to feel it is *destined* to win. And, other teams, fans and sports writers also begin to feel the team is *destined* to win. This is the basis of the home court or home field advantage talked about in sports. Some teams and their followers have established a tradition that they can't lose at home and they seldom lose. The difference between winning and losing often is determined by what we think we deserve.

Only One You

In the history of the world, there has been only one you. There will never be anyone else like you. If you don't develop what you have, the world will never experience an individual who can do exactly what you can do the way you do it - in sports, in career, in family, in school, in society. The victories, the completeness, the success, the lifestyle that you can achieve is only for you. It's not for anyone else. And you deserve to be the best that you can possibly be.

Build Your Own House

I heard a story about a very rich man who went to a carpenter and said, "I'd like for you to build a house for me. I'll be away for quite a while and you should have plenty of time to finish it during my absence. He gave the carpenter a large sum of money and left. The carpenter worked on the house everyday for four months. When the rich man came back and looked at the house, he nodded his approval because the carpenter had done excellent work without anyone looking over his shoulder. The rich man tossed the carpenter the keys and said, "Here, it's yours." Then he walked away.

Suppose the carpenter had cut corners? Suppose he had used inferior products and had done very shoddy work in places that could not have been easily detected? Suppose he had tried to salt away some of the money, pretending he had used it all? In the end, he would have been the big loser. And from then on, he would constantly have to struggle with the thought, "Why didn't I do the best I could do? Now I have to live with this inferior product."

You deserve the best by being the best. The reason you should excel is not to impress anyone else or try to manipulate someone else. The reason you should do your best is to constantly improve yourself. You've got a right to be the best you can be. And just like the carpenter, the real winner is you.

Step Four: Cultivate Gratitude

To develop a positive attitude, you must also cultivate gratitude. There is no such thing as a self-made person. Each of us needs help along the way to success. It's sort of like the small young man who graduated from West Point and assumed his first command - the roughest, toughest platoon in the army.

He assembled the group and said, "Men there are two questions we must settle immediately. First, is there anyone in this outfit who thinks he can whip me?" No one responded. He asked again. Finally, the regimental heavyweight champion, standing six feet, seven inches and weighing two hundred and seventy four pounds said, "Sir, I believe I can whip you."

"Good," responded the Lieutenant. "You're my First Sergeant. Now for the second question. Does anyone here think he can whip my First Sergeant?" Smart young man!

Champion Water-Wrestler

That lieutenant reminds me of when I was just a kid and loved to water-wrestle at the local swimming pool in my hometown of Humboldt, Tennessee. As the youngest and smallest boy in our group, I always made it a point to acquire Doug Atkins as my partner.

You see, Doug was then an All-American football player at the University of Tennessee. Standing 6'9" and weighing about 300 pounds, he recently was voted the best player in the Southeastern Conference during the past 25 years, and made the NFL Hall of Fame playing for the Chicago Bears.

When Doug came home during the summer and visited the pool, it was his shoulders I would ride on as we defeated everyone who opposed us. Heck, to be honest with you, there was no way anyone could whip us. Doug held my legs so tightly that no one could ever pull me off. And if the battle became a deadlock, he would just wade out to the deeper water and the opponents would have to give up - or drown!

Doug helped me to be a winner in water-wrestling. At the time, I was extremely thankful to him for it. And now I am thankful for people who have helped me to become a winner in other, more important areas.

Someone In Your Corner

Be thankful for the people who help you to grow, who help you to become what you have the potential to become. You may not always agree with them. You may not always see eye-to-eye on everything, but it's great to know you have someone in your corner pulling for you, ready to help you when you fall and ready to cheer for you when you succeed.

Winners create winners. I'll talk about this concept more in a later chapter. Let me say now, however, that you should feel extremely fortunate to have someone who will stand with you and support you during the hard times as well as the good.

Almost anyone will stick by you when things are alright; cherish the one who stays with you and says, "I believe in you - right or wrong - I believe in you."

Pay Forward

Wallene Dockery is a friend, fellow writer and speaker. Wallene's husband, Rex Dockery, former head football coach at Memphis State University, was killed in a plane crash one winter night in Tennessee. During the weeks and months afterwards, hundreds of people sent cards and performed acts of kindness to Wallene and her sons. Wallene made the statement, "I can never pay back the good deeds we've received. I can only pay forward, doing the same kindness to others."

True Gratitude

I think that's true gratitude and would encourage us to take it to heart. Have an attitude of gratitude. Realize that you are not self-sufficient. Don't be afraid to say, "thank you," and don't do good deeds looking for a "thank you."

Keep It Simple

Some psychologists and psychiatrists may look upon this chapter and this entire book as being "too simple." But I think too many people make the process of winning too complex. Time and again as I have spoken to groups, people have come by following my presentation to say, "You make it simple enough for anyone to understand." And I'm always happy to hear that I am communicating. What good is it to study and experience something if you can't simplify it for communication purposes? Heck, I have to simplify it so that I can understand it!

I can relate to Ken Stabler who was being interviewed when he was quarterback for the NFL Superbowl Champion Oakland Raiders. The journalist was a fan of the late author Jack London. He quoted a passage from one of London's books to Stabler, saying:

> *I would rather be ashes than dust!*
>
> *I would rather that any spark should*
>
> *burn out in a brilliant blaze than*
>
> *it should be stifled by dry rot.*

I would rather be a superb meteor,
every atom of me in magnificent
glow than a sleepy, permanent planet.
The proper function of
man is to be alive, not to just exist.
I shall not waste my days.
Rather I shall use my time!

The journalist paused to let these inspiring words of wisdom soak in. Then he asked Stabler, "What does that mean to you?"

Without hesitation, Stabler replied, "Throw deep!"

Go for it all! That's what I challenge you to do! But before you can do it, you've got to believe you can do it. And what you believe will determine to a large degree what you will accomplish.

Magical Thinking

Other psychologists and psychiatrists may accuse me of "magical thinking." This is a term applied to a mental disorder of people who believe that thoughts cause events to occur. For example, a little boy may grow jealous of a new baby in the family and think, "I wish the baby would die." Later, the little boy may develop guilt feelings and suffer anxiety, fearing the baby may die because he wished it.

Some people do not grow out of "magical thinking" and carry it into adulthood. Suppose the little boy above wished as he did and then the baby became sick? Or, suppose for some reason the baby did die? The little boy may suffer severe mental damage.

But, no, I'm not involved with neurotic "magical thinking." At the same time, I do know that the mind is a powerful instrument and that our thoughts chart our lives. "What the mind can conceive and believe, it can achieve," is more than just a rhythmic sentence. It is pure gold.

As I write these words, Irving "Magic" Johnson has just been voted the Most Valuable Player in the National Basketball Association. He is known as the most commanding player in the game today. Let me share with you Magic's "magical thinking":

> *I get on the fast break and I just get crazy. That's when I'm at my highest point. My eyes light up, and I feel crazy down to my knees. When I'm on a fast break, and there's a defender in front of me, I am charged up for anything because I know it's two-point time and nothing is going to stop me from making it all the way!*

We should all get so crazy! We should all get so involved in what we're doing. We should all feel the magic of knowing that there is nothing that is going to stop us from doing what we know we can do!

But Magic Johnson is known not only for drive, determination and belief in himself, he is also known for his creativity. And, creativity is the subject of chapter four. . .

Chapter 4

BE CREATIVE

A sports reporter asked a minister, "What would God do if two tennis players prayed for victory with exactly the same fervor?"

"Well," the minister's eyes twinkled, "I imagine that God would sit back and enjoy a whale of a game!"

Any hard fought athletic contest is a great thing to watch. Vic Braden sees it from this perspective: "There's nothing boring about winning. In 40 years of tennis, I've yet to hear anyone say, 'Nuts! I won again.' "

But to *continue* to win you need more than the self-esteem and positive attitude I wrote about earlier. You need creativity.

Maybe you've been led to believe that creativity is bringing something into existence that never existed before. Well, every now and then that happens. But nine times out of ten, or 99 times out of a 100, true creativity involves taking an idea, an object, a method, a group of people - something that's been around awhile - standing back, looking at it with a new perspective and giving it a different twist.

Doing A Common Thing Uncommonly Well

I believe that true creativity is doing a common thing uncommonly well.

When you think about it, that's how a lot of athletes win. By performing the everyday, every-game basics with flawless consistency. Think of some sports greats. What did they do uncommonly well? Larry Bird (basketball) - jump shots; Katarina Witt (skating) - double jumps on ice; Jose Canseco (baseball) - watching the ball all the way to the plate; Steffi Graf (tennis) - her serve; Stefan Edberg (tennis) - his return of serve; Tom Kite (golf) - driving accuracy; Joe Montana (football) - passing accuracy; Wayne Gretzky (hockey) - stick accuracy; Florence Griffith Joyner (track) - start-up motion.

Doing things uncommonly well is how a lot of businesses got started. Kemmons Wilson saw the need for roadside motels with consistent cleanliness that would become taken for granted. He called them Holiday Inns. Sam Walton wanted to build stores that would provide everyday household items at low prices, sold by friendly employees he called associates. The result: Wal-Mart. Fred Smith saw the need for dependable next day delivery of high priority goods. . . Federal Express was born. Dave Longaberger wanted to make a basket durable enough to be passed from one generation to the next; over two million Longaberger Baskets are now sold annually. When you're able to do a common thing uncommonly well, the word gets out. The gigantic ultra-successful McDonald's fast food chain began as one common hamburger stand.

A Lesson From Mary Kay

In 1987, when the Religious Heritage of America presented me with the *National Faith and Freedom Award*, Mary Kay Ash received the recognition of *Churchwoman of the Year*. I considered it a great honor to be linked with her by way of the awards.

I also considered it a privilege to share dinner with Mary Kay one evening during the three-day awards event. That evening, I learned how she turned a $5,000 nest egg into the multi-million dollar Fortune 500 company, Mary Kay Cosmetics.

"We were well aware of the risks when we started our business," she said. All the money she had went into the investment. Her son Richard, a life insurance agent at the time, took a 50% salary cut to work with his mother and with what many people called a "crazy" idea. A few months later, her son Ben joined the organization, taking a 66% cut in salary.

Mary Kay and her family took some great risks, but the emphasis was placed upon doing a common thing uncommonly well. They didn't have to give up what they were doing and start on this new adventure but they chose to do so. When they did put all their eggs in one basket, however, they promised themselves they would be the best they could be. They knew there were many cosmetics companies and many direct sales organizations, but they also knew there were many who were not doing a common thing uncommonly well.

"If a man is called to be a streetsweeper," Martin Luther King, Jr. said, "he should sweep streets even as Michelangelo painted, or Beethoven composed music, or Shakespeare wrote poetry. He should sweep streets so well that all the hosts of heaven and earth will pause to say, 'Here lived a great streetsweeper who did his job well.' "

The exciting thing about developing a skill is that you don't have to wait to get a license or a degree to start. You can begin right now, where you are, with what you have. Take one common thing and start getting better at it. For example, what is more common today than answering a telephone? But how many people do it uncommonly well? I had to interview over three dozen applicants on the phone before I could find a receptionist who could answer the phone and talk on it uncommonly well!

Shooting a free throw in basketball is pretty common, isn't it? How many players have developed their skills to do it uncommonly well? More close games are lost by missed free throws than any other single cause! If I were a coach in the NBA, there would be a clause in my players' contracts that they would not get their full salaries unless they hit at least 75% of their free throws during the season and the playoffs. And 75% is not great!

Become great at something. Do a common thing uncommonly well. It could be typing. It could be painting or building furniture or playing a musical instrument. It could be gardening. It could be making-up a bed, cleaning or cooking. In the resort city of Gatlinburg, we have dozens of hotels and motels, restaurants all over the place and gift shops galore. Show me someone who will work to become the best maid in the world, one whose hotel rooms when cleaned-up are a work of art; show me a cook who turns people on with common dishes prepared uncommonly well and a waiter or waitress who is the epitome of professional service; show me a clerk who deals with customers like it is the most important thing in the world to him or to her. . . and I will show you someone whom people will clamor to hire, to treat wonderfully and to pay highly!

Become great at something. It could be writing letters or visiting patients in the hospital. It could be speaking in public, selling, negotiating. Consider your interests, talents and abilities. The possibilities are endless!

But so many people are not willing to be creative with the abilities they have. Instead, they wish for abilities or characteristics they don't have.

Some people say, "If only I'd had this opportunity; if only I'd had that opportunity. If only I'd been born earlier; if only I'd been born later; if only I hadn't been born!" Other people complain, "If only I were taller; if only I were shorter. If only I had straight hair; if only I had curly hair; if only I had hair!"

It's like the lumberman who was about five foot, two inches tall and weighed 120 pounds, who walked up to his six foot, four inch, 250 pound friend and said, "Man, if I were as big and strong as you are, I'd go into the mountains, I'd grab me the biggest bear I could find, and I'd tear him limb from limb."

The big man looked down at the smaller man and smiled, "Well, they got a lot of little bears in them woods!"

Milk It

We must be willing to get the most out of what we have. I

like to say, "Milking it for all it's worth." We must be willing to use our abilities creatively.

Psychiatrists, philosophers and sociologists are studying the concept of winning in all areas of life, and they agree that everyone can be a winner. At one of my recent speaking engagements, several speakers were asked to focus our talks on "Winning." Marie Kiesel, professor of humanities at Roosevelt University in Chicago said, "Talent and success are not synonymous." She emphasized that success comes with hard work, planning and goal setting.

Denis Waitley, author of *The Psychology of Winning*, followed Ms. Kiesel by saying, "Success is not reserved for the talented. It is not in the high I.Q. Not in the gifted birth. Not in the best equipment. Not even in ability. Success is almost totally dependent upon drive, focus and persistence."

My emphasis at the convention was: "To win, you take what you have, where you are, and get the most out of it. You *milk* it for all it's worth. You do a common thing uncommonly well. And, all the time, you keep remembering that winners look for ways to win while losers look for excuses for losing."

However, some people continue to look for excuses for why they are failing, like the elderly man in the hospital who has been married 45 years. His wife is sitting next to his bed. He turned toward her and said, "You know, Martha, I've been thinking," and she said, "Yes."

He said, "You know, we've been married 45 years now," and she answered, "Yes."

He said, "You remember that first year we were married? We had a bad crop and lost half the farm, and there you were, right by my side." She responded, "Yes."

He said, "That second year, we had another bad crop and lost the other half of the farm. And there you were, right by my side." She nodded, "Yes."

He said, "Then we started five businesses and all five of them failed. And there you were, right by my side." She agreed, "Yes."

He said, "And then we had ten kids. All of them wanted to go to college, no hope of a scholarship. And there you were, right by my side." And she said, "Yes."

He said, "Now here I am in the hospital. The doctors tell me I'm terminally ill. They don't expect me to walk out of here alive. And here you are, right by my side." And she said, "Yes."

He said, "You know, Martha, I've been thinking . . . you're bad luck!"

That's the way some people are, always looking for someone else or something else to blame. They think their failures are caused by somebody or something outside rather than somebody or something *within*.

What You Do With What You've Got

Several years ago when my son was in elementary school, there was a feature length Walt Disney film on television. As I walked into the den where he was watching TV, there was a little deer on the screen, standing in the forest. As the deer stood there in the middle of a clearing, a porcupine walked by. The little deer looked at the porcupine and said, "Boy! I wish I had quills like that porcupine so I could protect myself."

A few moments later, a big bear came walking by. The little deer looked at the bear and said, "Boy! I wish I could be big and strong like that bear."

A few moments later, along came a fox. The little deer looked at the fox and said, "Boy! I wish I could be sly and cunning like that fox."

The little deer's father had been standing nearby, hearing the comments. He took just about all he could take, walked over to his son, looked down at him and said, "Son, the important thing is what you do with what you've got."

My son turned around to me and said, "That's right, huh, Dad?" I said, "That's right, son. It's taking what you have, where you are and getting the most out of it."

The Creative Farmer

One day a man from the city was driving in the country. He stopped to admire the beauty of the hills and fields. When a farmer came by, the man from the city called to him, "You and the Lord certainly have a beautiful farm here."

The farmer answered, "Yeah, but you should have seen it when the Lord had it by himself."

Now that farmer had some spunk! He recognized the potential, used his creative ability, used the materials at hand, and now there's a farm where there wasn't one before.

You, too, have potential. You, too, have creative ability. Now it's up to you to take it and go with it. You are born with creative potential, but you must learn to use it.

"But," you ask, "how can I learn to be more creative?" Well, let me suggest some steps that you can concentrate upon day-in and day-out to increase your creativity. And, as I suggest these steps, please keep in mind that creativity, more than anything else, is problem-solving. The most creative ideas have been born and the most creative moves have been made in response to problems that have arisen.

Step One: Admit And Define The Problem

It's impossible to change a circumstance unless you first see the need for change. So, begin by admitting and identifying the problem.

A Lesson From Dorothea Brande

A number of years ago, a lady by the name of Dorothea Brande wrote and spoke on the subject of *Wake Up and Live!* She claimed she came across a formula that revolutionized her life. But, she said that before she could "wake up and live," she had to *admit* that she was a failure.

She admitted that she was not doing a tenth of what could be expected of her. She said she had an interesting job, lived not too dull a life - yet, what she was doing in life was a substitute for what she really wanted to do.

In admitting and defining her problem, Dorothea claimed that most of us live far below the possible level for our lives. And when we are set free from the things which hamper us so that we can merely approach the potentials in ourselves, we seem to be entirely transfigured. According to her, it is in comparison with the halting, tentative hesitant lives we let ourselves live that the full, normal life that is ours by right seems to partake of the definitely supernormal.

A Lesson From A Young Engineer

We are a solution-oriented society, and a lot of times we want to solve something before we know what the problem is. Let me give you an example. Residents in a new high rise apartment building complained that the elevators were too slow. The owners consulted the engineers. One young engineer, known for his ingenuity, observed the residents using the elevators for several days. It finally hit him what needed to be done. Sure enough, people were soon saying, "These elevators are much faster now."

What did he do? The young man did not speed up the elevators at all. Rather, he put mirrors on each floor outside the elevators. He watched men adjust their ties and women check their make-up and the men watch the women check their make-up! The problem wasn't that the elevators were too slow, but that passengers had nothing to do while waiting for them.

Not long ago, I had a speaking engagement at a large hotel in Dallas, Texas. I got on the elevator on the 16th floor. There was one gentleman who was already on the elevator. We nodded and started down. On the way, he said, "You know, this is the fastest elevator I've ever been on."

I said, "Is that right?"

"Yes," he said.

I said, "Let me ask you a couple of questions. Number one, did you notice on the outside of each elevator on each floor, they have two mirrors?"

He said, "Well, now that you mention it, they do."

"Did you also notice," I asked, "that all four walls in the elevator, including this shiny brass door, consist of mirrors?"

"That's right," he agreed

"What were you doing before I got on?" I asked.

"Looking at myself."

"These elevators are not all that fast," I concluded. "It's just that we have something to do while we're waiting." I'm glad I'd heard the story about the young engineer. He would have been proud. I'm sure the man I met in the elevator couldn't wait to spring those questions on a fellow guest on the way back up!

So, the first step to being more creative is to admit there is a problem and to find out what the problem is.

Step Two: Gather Resources

The second step to being more creative is to look at what others have done with similar problems. Gather resources, observe others, study people's habits and analyze situations and solutions.

In football, coaches and players watch game films to discover tendencies, weaknesses and strengths of themselves and opponents.

If we decide to build a house, what do we do? First, we look at what others have done. We look at the roof lines, at the window treatment, at the type of materials used and, of course, the floor plan. We walk through new houses and look at model houses in magazines. We talk to others who have built houses and learn from their successes and mistakes. Then we take what we like, add our own ideas and build our house.

Earlier in this chapter, I mentioned an acquaintance, Dave Longaberger, founder of Longaberger Baskets. He recently built an 8,500 square foot house with no blueprints. As the workers built each room, they'd ask, "What do you want us to build now, Dave?" He might say the dining room or a bedroom or a recreation room, and finally he decided the house was complete. That's the exception to the rule, and most people don't yet have a million dollars to experiment with!

A Lesson From Suzette Haden Elgin

Unlike Dave Longaberger and his house building experience, Suzette Haden Elgin, author of the best-selling book, *The Gentle Art of Verbal Self-Defense*, uses researched data to bring in phenomenal mail order sales. When many companies are pleased with one percent responses to direct mail offers, elated over two percent responses and ecstatic over three percent responses, Suzette is experiencing an 80% response to her offers!

Suzette has not tried to re-invent the wheel. Rather, she has built upon what she has learned from others' successes and failures, as well as her own. She and I spent an entire day together during a recent conference in Tulsa, Oklahoma, and I learned a lot from this creative lady!

According to Suzette, "I had a book published by a good publishing company. I knew it was a good book, and I thought I had accomplished something. But to my amazement that book went *nowhere!* And soon the publisher, unable to sell the minimum 1,000 copies a year that they felt had to be sold, let it go out of print and gave me back the right to the book. . . Today, *The Gentle Art Of Verbal Self-Defense* has sold over 400,000 copies in a hardcover reprint edition, and is showing no sign of slowing down; it rarely sells less than 1,000 copies a week."

In your job, in school, in your family situations, gather your resources to meet your problems or objectives. Discover what is available to you to help you do what needs to be done.

Informal Learning

At conferences or conventions, it is good to have informative seminars and speakers, but one of the greatest aspects is the *informal learning* that occurs. As participants share meals or just sit around and talk, good things happen.

One participant may tell of a problem he is experiencing in his work. Someone else may respond, "I had a problem similar to that. Let me tell you what I did to solve it." Then, someone may say, "We had a very similar problem, too, but we approached it from a different direction."

Yogi Berra said, "You can see a lot by looking." You can also hear a lot by listening. You can learn a lot through others' experiences. Don't try to re-invent the wheel when you can ride on the experiences of others.

A Lesson From Philip Goldberg

Philip Goldberg, speaker on creativity and author of *The Intuitive Edge*, suggests that in order to gather data that will lead to more creativity:

(1) *Look at the problem from as many different angles as possible. The problem should be defined in such a way to be manageable, neither too narrow nor too broad to work with.*

(2) *Write down all your thoughts and feelings about the situation. The more you can immerse yourself in the problem, the more material you will have to work with.*

(3) *Take in different types of information, even though some of it may seem irrelevant at the time. Apart from relevant information, you may walk through a new part of town, watch a TV show you've never watched before, browse in a section of the library where you usually don't go or start up a conversation with a stranger.*

(4) *Practice brainstorming. To brainstorm, write down any and all possible solutions to your problem. The real trick to brainstorming is that you write down whatever comes to mind regardless of how silly, useless or meaningless it may seem.*

Step Three: Consider Various Possibilities

The third step to becoming more creative is to consider your options. Just because you've found one solution doesn't make it the best solution. If you were on the tenth floor of a burning building, one solution to avoid burning is to jump out the window with no net below. The question is, is it your best move? Of course not. So, I suggest taking time to look at your options before setting a course of action. I realize this is hard for many of us to do. There are certain people, perhaps you, who have the philosophy of "ready, fire, aim." It's the idea that doing is better than sitting, so "let's do something, even if it's wrong!"

On the other hand, there are those who sit and sit and sit, thinking if they wait long enough, things will take care of themselves. Well, that's true enough, but things have a way of not turning out the way we want them to when we just wait for something good to happen. *Considering possibilities* is designed to make the best use of your time and energy. In basketball, for example, there may be several defenses you could use against a team. The best teams take time to analyze their opponents' strengths and weaknesses and design a game plan accordingly.

As I mentioned in chapter two, one of the greatest things a coach can say about an athlete is that he or she is coachable. As an athlete, and a player in all aspects of life, you must be able to adapt. Remember, creativity is not necessarily related to how much you know or how much education you have. The important concept is how you think about things and whether you can see them in different ways and from various viewpoints.

There are many ways to handle a problem. In basketball, one defense may be ineffective, while a combination of defenses may stop an opposing team or player. Or, a certain offensive play may not be working. If so, look at the play from your opponent's point of view. What is he or she doing to stop you? Are you doing exactly what the opponent expects you to do? If you are, a change on your part can lead to success.

A Lesson From Ken Olsen

My introduction to Ken Olsen came when he was nominated *Business and Professional Man of the Year* by Religious Heritage of America. Quite an honor to come from an organization chaired by the renowned businessman W. Clement Stone. But an honor well deserved.

Fortune magazine, in its October 27, 1986 issue, labeled Ken Olsen "the most successful entrepreneur in the history of American business." In presenting the reasons for choosing Olsen over other business giants, *Fortune* emphasized how he founded Digital Equipment Corporation and took it from nothing to $7.6 billion in annual revenues by *trying a different approach*. According to *Fortune*, he "changed the way people use computers."

Before Olsen and DEC, all computers were large mainframes housed in special centers, handled only by experts and used to process large batches of data. Today, my seven year-old niece has a computer in her bedroom.

By taking a different approach, DEC laid the groundwork in the personal computer revolution. DEC's small, rugged, inexpensive machines let individuals apply computing to an endless variety of everyday tasks in homes, schools and offices.

As a result of Olsen's innovative approach, *Fortune* touted DEC as "the hottest computer company around." It introduced more than a dozen major products in the past two years and scored back-to-back revenue gains of 20% when most of the industry was in a slowdown.

Olsen picked up his first formal training in electrical engineering after joining the Navy. Later, as a graduate researcher for M.I.T., he spent a year at IBM. IBM was trying to leap ahead of Univac, which had jumped into computers first. Following his work and observations at IBM, Olsen told his M.I.T. supervisor, "I can beat these guys at their own game."

The creative graduate student knew what he was talking about. On the day of *Fortune's* prestigious recognition, DEC was worth $11.5 billion in the stock market, and Olsen's two percent share would fetch over $230 million.

Creativity involves taking what you have, where you are, and getting the most out of it.

Like the Silicon Valley garage startups (such as Apple) that would follow 20 years later, DEC began with scraps - $70,000 in venture capital, some lawn furniture, an old roll-top desk and space rented in the defunct mill that still serves as headquarters

Nobel Prize winning physician Albert Szent-Gyorgyi said, "Discovery consists of looking at the same thing as everyone else and thinking something different." That's what Ken Olsen did.

Your ability to change your point of view can be a door to creativity. And this spark of creativity can be the winning edge in athletic competition, in business or in life. It can lead to a sale in business or a block in football, a management strategy or a fast break in basketball, a greater profit margin to a corporation or an overhead smash in tennis.

A Lesson From Yardwork

A client contacted me recently and wanted me to present a banquet address at their annual meeting. He said he really liked the motivation, the humor, the anecdotes and the simplicity of what I did. But, he said that the one thing that stuck in his mind about me was "my saying." I inquired to which of my lofty philosophical maxims he was referring. He answered:

"Cows never stay milked and grass never stays mowed."

We have to consider the various possibilities and search for different ways to do things because nothing stays the same.

One Saturday, my wife Jean and I decided to do some work in our yard. Beginning at about 9:00 a.m., we mowed and pruned and raked until noon. After a quick lunch, we continued until 5:00 p.m. Following a brief dinner, we went back out, finally concluding about 9:00 p.m.

The yard looked great. The grass was like golf greens, the flowers were magnificent, the fruit trees glistened. . . As Jean and I inspected our handiwork, I remember turning toward her and saying, "You know, I wish I could get some type of spray and spray it on everything to keep it just like it is right now."

But cows never stay milked and grass never stays mowed.

Just when we get things the way we want them, it's time to start again. That's why we had better keep on the cutting edge and not get caught in a rut. That's why we should not only realize there are various ways to get things done, but we had better know about these ways!

In his book, *A Whack On The Side Of The Head: How to Unlock Your Mind for Motivation*, Dr. Roger von Oech said, "It's no longer possible to solve today's problems with yesterday's solutions. Over and over again people are finding out that what worked two years ago won't work next week. This gives them a choice. They can either bemoan the fact that things aren't as easy as they used to be, or they can use their creative abilities to find new answers, new solutions and new ideas."

Step Four: Mull It Over

But, suppose you have no solution in mind? What should you do? Relax and let your subconscious mind take over.

Let the ideas incubate. Sleep on the problem. Unless there is an emergency or crisis, don't rush into a solution. Most problems didn't develop overnight, so why try to fix them overnight?

Remember, the subconscious mind continues to store everything we read, see, hear or experience. Every now and then, the subconscious produces solutions - like ideas popping into our minds. Actually, nothing just "pops" into our minds; but the subconscious draws from all our experiences and knowledge to offer a possible answer. And we may be surprised at how simple and creative an answer can be.

A Lesson From Grandfather

A man preparing for a trip to the supermarket was asked by his little grandson if he could go. The man's wife warned him that the little boy would "get into everything."

The man took his grandson, however, and the boy kept his hands in his pockets the entire time. Upon checking-out, a clerk commented to the boy about his good behavior.

"Had to," the boy replied. "My grandfather took away my belt!"

A creative solution to a perplexing problem!

A Lesson From Dr. Joseph Murphy

Dr. Joseph Murphy, lecturer and author of many books, including *The Power of the Subconscious Mind*, suggests that when you have a difficult decision to make, or when there appears to be no solution to your problem, begin to think positively and constructively about it.

117

He suggests that you relax your mind and body. Or, as we are sometimes prone to say, "just cool it." Then, focus your thoughts on the solution to your problem. In a comfortable, relaxed mood, try to solve it with your conscious mind.

Think about how happy you will be when the perfect solution comes along. Let your mind seek the solution and feel the joy that will come when the solution is found. Then, drop off to sleep, or at least doze.

When you awaken, and you do not have the answer, get busy doing something else. Probably, when you are preoccupied with something else, the answer will come into your mind like toast pops out of a toaster.

You have received guidance and inspiration from your subconscious mind. You have thought about it, you have mulled it over and you have been rewarded.

There are many different problems in life - in school, in the office, at home, on the athletic field or court - and there are many possible answers to those problems. This leads to the last two steps.

Step Five: Choose The Best Solution

After you've let your mind work on the problem, choose what you consider to be the best solution. Weigh the pros and cons. Decide which solution will really do what you want it to.

This is not always easy. Choosing from a dessert tray is not easy either - and choosing not to choose from a dessert tray is even more difficult!

A Lesson From A Friend

My friend, Al Headrick, a very creative person himself, invented a new way to process data. A large corporation offered to pay him over $100,000 for the idea, but he chose to accept no advance money, holding out for an on-going royalty instead. At this writing, he has received over $150,000 from this one source - and royalties are still coming in.

Think about your choices. Don't always choose the most convenient, the surest, the fastest or the most obvious. But, do choose what you personally consider to be the best.

A Lesson From The Clown

In my musical drama, *The Clown*, which I'm happy to say has now been produced in over 2,500 American communities and six foreign countries, there is a scene in which the Clown steps forward to address the audience, saying:

> . . . *the important thing is not the problems we face. The important thing is how we face them - how we respond when problems arise.*

The Clown is then supported by a companion who says:

Choices! That's what life is all about.

Creativity is not a matter of chance - it's a matter of choices. Success isn't something you hope happens. It is high achievement accomplished by consistent daily preparation and commitment to a goal with a daily plan of action, action that is determined by the choices we make.

Be wise when you make your choices, keeping in mind that losers tend to gravitate toward other losers because they love to remind each other that true success cannot be achieved.

On the other hand, if you can surround yourself with real winners - or be fortunate enough to have at least one real winner in your corner - a winner can help you redirect your thinking and set you on a winning path toward success.

And, by "success," I mean that a person becomes a whole, well-organized, well-integrated individual, in control of life's circumstances, carrying on his or her profession with skill and an adequate amount of perfection - and enjoying it.

Step Six: Try It Out

After you have chosen what you consider to be the "best" possibility, then test it. Try it out. Don't fear failure (a concept I will develop more fully in the next chapter). Keep in mind that if you have developed various possibilities, then you can always try Plan B or C or D - or you might modify or improve upon Plan A.

A Lesson From Thomas Edison

A young reporter once asked Thomas Edison, "Mr. Edison, you've tried over 8,000 filaments for the light bulb. Aren't you getting discouraged?"

Edison answered, "Son, now I'm getting excited because I know over 8,000 things that won't work. That means I'm getting closer and closer."

Shortly thereafter, Edison discovered the filament that would work.

Being creative involves taking risks; but anything worthwhile involves some risk. You have two choices in life: You can dissolve into the mainstream of mediocrity, or you can be distinct and be a winner.

Another Lesson From Mary Kay

Mary Kay failed terribly at her first beauty show. Anxious to prove that her skin care products could be sold to small groups of women and looking for huge success, she sold a grand total of $1.50 that first evening. When she left, she drove around the corner, put her head on the steering wheel, and cried.

"What's wrong with those people?" she asked aloud. "Why didn't they buy this fantastic product?" She began to doubt her new business venture. She worried that her lifetime savings were tied up in a company that had just brought in $1.50 during her premiere presentation.

Then, she looked in the mirror and asked, "What did *you* do wrong, Mary Kay?" Immediately the answer hit her - "*I had never bothered to ask anyone for an order!*" Mary Kay had forgotten to pass out order cards and had just expected those women to buy automatically. She never made that same mistake again as she continued to try out her new idea.

Mary Kay Cosmetics did $34,000 in retail sales the first year. Fifteen years later, Mary Kay had 150,000 independent consultants and 3,000 directors with gross sales of $200 million.

I sincerely believe the key to starting new businesses is the ability to study customer needs and carve out a niche for you and your services. Offer service which far exceeds customer expectations. Become an expert in the field. Do common things in your field of interest uncommonly well. Always seek to improve. This type of lifestyle separates you from the person who just tries to get by, who works hard at doing as little as possible, who has very little expectations of life.

To be distinct, you must be creative. To be creative, you must be different. To be different, you must strive to be what no one else can be. And to be what no one else can be, you must take risks.

But people sometimes erect barriers to their creativity. People sometimes fear failure. They also feel the need to conform, to be like everyone else. And, they are afraid to try something new. They want to do things the way they have always been done.

Ask Yourself, "What If?"

I think it's always a good idea to ask yourself, "What if?"
"What if we changed this procedure?"
"What if we took this account?"
"What if I tried out for quarterback - or maybe split-end?"
"What if I took this job?"
"What if I really saw myself as a true professional?"
"What if I changed professions?"
"What if I retired early?"
"What if. . .?"

A Lesson From H. C. Booth

In 1901, H. C. Booth was sitting in his rocking chair on his front porch, watching the sun set. Living in the Midwest, he was also watching the dust blow. As he relaxed and rocked, he asked, "I wonder, what if we could reverse that wind and rather than blow dust, *pull* dust?" Well that was a crazy question to even him, but guess what? He went on to invent the vacuum cleaner.

Just think where we would be if those before us had not dared to ask "What if?" We would have no cars, planes, phones, fax machines, computers, electricity, radios, space exploration, traffic lights, microwaves, calculators, televisions and on and on.

I encourage you not to be afraid to ask questions everyday. That's the stuff dreams are made of and it's fun, too! It's a way to practice your creative skills. For example, take a look at anyone who might be in the room with you now and imagine how that person looked when he or she got up this morning; how he or she looked as a baby; how the person will look in 20 years. Picture how you might look as a doctor. . . as an astronaut. . . as a senator. . . as a game show host. . . as a clown. . . as the company president. . . as the company mail clerk. It helps you with creativity and helps you adjust to change.

A Lesson From Spud Webb

Spud Webb was well under six feet tall and, yet, he asked himself, "What if I was a professional basketball player?" He has starred with the Atlanta Hawks and has even won the NBA Dunking Contest!

A Lesson From Patty Calvert

Patty Calvert had some unhappy elementary school experiences. At a very early age, she asked herself, "What if I could become a teacher and help my students enjoy learning and the classroom?" She got her doctorate in education, founded her own schools and became president of a 5,000 member education association.

A Lesson From Steve And Andrea Williford

My friends Steve and Andrea Williford began this exercise for entertainment shortly after they got married. They took turns telling each other what they'd like to have if they could afford it or if they had the time. Over the years, they have discovered this type of fantasizing not only fun, but has helped them crystalize some goals. And over the years, many of those dreams have come true, but only because they have been able to use their creativity from the very beginning of the process.

Sometimes people need a push or nudge to try something new. Take for example, the sky diver who was asked by a friend, "What made you decide to jump out of an airplane thousands of feet up in the sky?"

The jumper replied, "A plane with three dead engines."

Being creative will help you make the right decisions at the right time. And you can train yourself to be more creative, similar to a child learning how to tie shoe laces. At first a child must force himself or herself to tie the shoelaces, step by step. Later, it occurs without thinking about it at all.

Do you want to be a better athlete, student, professional? Then, work to the point where you can do the right thing at the right time without thinking about it. If you want to win, if you plan to win, if you know how to win, and if you are creative about it, then you can win.

A Lesson From Carl

In the 70's, as my name began to appear on books, dramas and articles, people started calling upon me to speak to their groups. Living in the resort convention city of Gatlinburg opened many creative possibilities.

People would phone, indicating they were bringing a group to Gatlinburg, asking if I would speak to them. Later, they began asking me to suggest a place to stay and meet.

As I mentioned in chapter one, I invested $500 to start a convention hotel sales group "on the side." Ten years later, we had generated over 150,000 room nights for the hotels involved, resulting in a gross income of over nine million dollars in room revenue alone.

Last year, I leased my mailing list, contacts and expertise for $250,000 plus an on-going monthly retainer fee for consultation.

There are so many opportunities out there. For businesses, sports programs, schools, families or individuals, it's not a question of, "Can we do something?" Rather, it's a matter of, "What do we want to do?"

Creativity is doing a common thing uncommonly well.

Sometimes, however, creativity is doing an *uncommon* thing uncommonly well.

A Lesson From Scott Coleman

The *beginning of the adventure* is how my friend Scott Coleman describes the day he broke his neck in a water-skiing accident. That day, an outstanding football player and campus leader suddenly became a quadriplegic.

The accident left Scott paralyzed from the neck down except for the ability to use his biceps, which, in itself, took two years to develop. Some ingenuous devices have allowed him to use this one set of muscles to establish and grow successfully in a career.

This young Memphis man now earns a high income as an account executive for a major brokerage company. But it hasn't been easy.

The company gave him a chance to prove himself. Proof came when he made cold calls on the telephone. Dialing with his tongue, he made up to 100 calls per day. Then, in his wheelchair, he made door-to-door "cold" visits.

Approaching his career and his life with an appreciation of who he is and with a positive attitude, Scott mixes his creativity with a keen sense of humor. For example, many of Scott's clients only know him initially by his voice. Then when they meet him in person for the first time and see his physical condition, they often ask, "What happened, Scott?" His reply is, "I got a haircut."

He recently won a masquerade party costume contest when he and his wife painted him green, disguised his wheel chair as a space ship and Scott buzzed into the room.

Scott credits the people around him with supporting him and challenging him to use his creativity to turn what could have been a disaster into the adventure that he has made it.

Scott Coleman has set goals in his career and life. Now, he is working creatively to reach these goals. He has dreams of what is to be rather than nightmares of what was or regrets of what might have been.

What Is Your Challenge?

Daily, you and I are challenged to use our creativity. The challenge may come from a life-threatening experience. It may come from a business opportunity, a family situation, an athletic contest or a classroom project.

The enormity of the challenge shouldn't overshadow our creative abilities. At the same time, nothing is so small that it should not demand from us our very best.

A Review

To this point, we've discussed three principles in **A Strategy For Winning**:

Accept Yourself. If you don't appreciate yourself, if you don't realize your potential, don't expect others to.

Develop a Positive Attitude. I believe so strongly in what is written in the book of *Mark* in the *New Testament*, "Anything is possible if you have faith."

Be Creative. This gives legs to the first two principles. It requires effort to win.

There is an organization in North America named Optimist International. It was founded to help individuals and communities rise to levels of excellence. Their creed incorporates the three principles we've discussed so far:

The Optimist Creed

Be so strong that nothing can disturb your peace of mind. Talk health, happiness and prosperity to every person you meet. Make all your friends feel that there is something worthwhile in them. Look at the sunny side of everything and make your optimism come true.

Think only of the best, work only for the best and expect only the best. Be just as enthusiastic about the success of others as you are about your own. Forget about the mistakes of the past and press on to the greater achievements of the future. Wear a cheerful countenance at all times and give every living creature you meet a smile.

Give so much time to the improvement of yourself that you have no time to criticize others. Be too large for worry, too noble for anger, too strong for fear and too happy to permit the presence of trouble.

I like that! That's a goal worth shooting for. It sounds good, but it's not always that easy, is it? But should we want it to be easy?

The Oyster And The Eagle

When God made the oyster, he guaranteed him absolute social and economic security. He built the oyster a house, a shell, to protect him from his enemies. When hungry, the oyster simply opens his shell and food rushes in. He has no worries. He does not fight anyone. He doesn't go anywhere. He simply sits in his shell on the bottom, pushed by the currents, until something comes along and snatches away his treasure.

When God made the eagle, he gave him the sky as his domain. The eagle nests on the highest crag of the highest mountain where storms threaten everyday. For food, he flies through miles of snow, rain, sleet and wind.

He screams out in defiance against these elements, but goes his own way, building his own life. When attacked by an enemy, he is a vicious foe. The eagle, not the oyster is the symbol of America and the symbol of a winner.

If you want to be a winner, be a creator, be willing to take risks and to learn from your mistakes, as you reach out and grab success.

And, don't fear failure - a concept I will cover in chapter five.

Chapter 5

DON'T FEAR FAILURE

Have you ever been afraid to try something for fear you might fail? I think we all have somewhere along the line. Some people pass over certain courses in high school or college, afraid they might not do well. Some people don't try certain jobs or careers they would like. Others fear asking certain questions to certain people. Salespeople sometimes are afraid to ask for an order, fearing rejection.

Fear of failure may have loomed in your mind as you considered trying-out for a team or a school play, or asking someone for a date. Maybe you were afraid to apply to a particular college, train for a marathon or begin a new career for fear of failing.

When you think about it, *every* new project we undertake involves risk. Yet, consider what your life would be like if your fear of failure took complete control of your actions: You'd never get married or develop a relationship - it might fail. You'd never ask for a raise - it might get turned down. You'd never make an offer on a house or car - it might be rejected. You'd never offer a suggestion - it could be ridiculed.

But if life is to improve, we have to risk failure. Helen Keller said, "Security is mostly superstition. It does not exist in nature, nor do children experience it. Life is either a daring adventure or nothing."

Don't be afraid of life.

Challenge To Youth

A couple of years ago, I was the keynote speaker at the convention of the National Beta Club, an honorary society for high school scholastic achievers and leaders. Over 4,000 teenagers attended the meeting at the Sheraton-Washington Hotel in Washington, D.C. Even if I had not known a youth convention was in progress at the luxurious hotel, I would have learned quickly when I stepped onto the elevator with a delivery man who had a cart of over two dozen pizzas!

When I spoke to the youth, I said:

All of you are sharp or you wouldn't be here. All of you have something on the ball or you would not be representing your schools. But those among you who will taste the sweetness of success more than anyone else are the ones who are not afraid to fail - who are not afraid to take risks. I'm not talking about stupid, unintelligent, uninformed risks. But I'm talking about doing your homework, being prepared, then stepping out on the cutting-edge, realizing you may fall on your face, realizing people may laugh at you - but also realizing there is a big difference between temporary failure and total defeat. . .

Fear Distorts Things

In chapter four, I told of Mary Kay Ash's experiences in the cosmetics industry. When asked her opinion of what keeps most people from realizing their potential, she replied:

Fear is what holds people back. Fear of rejection, of not succeeding, of losing whatever money you have. All the fears that we have as human beings keep us from reaching our potential.

If there's one equal factor where many women are concerned, it's a lack of self-confidence. To see a woman so timid and shy she could hardly talk over the phone develop in a few months into a beautiful, personable woman is really wonderful.

David Viscott, M.D., author of *Risking*, wrote that it's amazing how little people know about risking failure. "At the very first sign of a reversal, they doubt themselves, hesitate, and fearing that the situation is about to fall apart, retreat untested, convinced that they were in over their heads, thankful just to escape. They do not understand that to risk is to exceed one's usual limits in reaching for any goal, and that uncertainty and danger are simply part of the process."

Temporary Failure

There's a *big* difference between temporary failure and total defeat. But some people believe that if at first they don't succeed, it wasn't meant to be!

Regardless of how many temporary failures you may experience, don't *get down* on yourself. That's when it's over. That's what turns temporary failure into total defeat.

Don't *get down* on your team, nor your job, nor your boss, nor your community, nor members of your family. When you start *getting down* on yourself, or on other people, you *get down*, period.

In the previous chapter, I told of Digital Equipment Corporation's Ken Olsen, recognized by *Fortune* magazine as "the most successful entrepreneur in the history of American business." In 1982, however, critics questioned whether DEC would ever recover from massive problems resulting from the dismantling of product line organizations that took five years to complete. The company's earnings were zapped by changes and delays. It appeared to many that DEC was in a tailspin from which it could not recover. As DEC's stock plunged, critics speculated that Olsen had succumbed to "founder's disease."

Olsen now recalls this period of temporary failure as a "sojourn in the desert." But the desert adventure brought Olsen and DEC greater strength and solidarity. During the trying period, Olsen worked in a frenzy, dictating memos at home into the night, keeping four secretaries swamped during the day. He suffered clashes with longtime co-workers and became paranoid, saying, "Everyone is out to prove the boss wrong."

He admitted he made some mistakes. He made some changes. He fought for what he believed in. The cream rose to the top.

It's hard to suffer a setback or failure. It's hard to get back up, dust yourself off and try again. But the difference between a loser and a winner is that when a loser gets knocked down, he stays there with his face in the mud and blames situations, circumstances or other people for his defeat.

But, when a winner gets knocked down, he gets back up. He gets knocked down again, he gets back up. He refuses to accept temporary failure as total defeat. As H. E. Jansen said, "The man who wins may have been counted out several times, but he didn't hear the referee." I like that!

Ron Guidry's Failure

Ron Guidry, a major league pitcher with the New York Yankees, almost quit baseball when he was sent back down to the minors early in his career. The manager told him that he just wasn't ready for the big leagues. Guidry felt his whole world begin to fall apart. He went home and told his wife, "That's it. I'm not going back to the minors! I've worked like the dickens to get here. I've made it and I can't go back."

They packed up and started driving to his home in the South. All the way, his wife kept encouraging him to go to the minors because baseball was his true love. Just as they were about to cross into their home state, they stopped at a restaurant. It was in that restaurant that Guidry picked himself up and dusted himself off. He said, "Okay, one more time. I'm going to give it one more chance."

So they turned the car around and he reported to his new minor league team. With renewed determination, he set new goals and worked on his control, his change-up, his curve and a far superior pitching technique. He finished the season in great form and returned to the majors the next year. Ron Guidry went on to win the Cy Young trophy, an award presented annually to the best pitcher in the major leagues.

You don't see "reacting to failure" statistics in the record books, but they determine the rest of the achievements.

People respond to failure in a variety of ways. Some turn to alcohol or drug abuse, overeating, a change of job or moving to a new location. Some sink into despair and depression. Others shut out their family and friends and pull into themselves. What these people really need to do is face up to the cause of the failure and take action to overcome it. Continued despair and despondency are certainly not fitting attitudes for people who would be winners.

17 Rejections = Success

When I was a sophomore in college, we were assigned to read Irving Stone's book, *Lust for Life*, the story of Vincent Van Gogh. I wasn't exactly thrilled about the assignment, but once I started reading the book, I was captivated. I thought (and still do) that it was one of the best books I'd ever read. I later learned Irving Stone's manuscript was rejected 17 times before a publisher decided to take a chance on it.

Now picture this: You have a thick stack of manuscript papers. You send them to a publisher. The publisher may keep them for a month to a year, only to send them back with an impersonal note that says, "Dear Writer: We're sorry but this does not meet our editorial needs." No encouragement whatsoever. Seventeen times over the years it went out and 17 times it came back. Each time, Stone would rework it and send it out, receive it back, rework it - 17 times. On the 18th try, a publisher said, "We're going to take a chance on this." *Lust for Life* became the year's number one best-seller, selling over a million copies, and an Oscar-winning motion picture. It was the first of 11 best-selling historical biographies by Stone.

I thought of Irving Stone and his experience with *Lust for Life* when my musical drama, *The Clown*, was rejected. In chapter four, I told of how this work has been presented in over 2,500 American communities and six foreign countries. Before it was presented anywhere, however, I took it through nine revisions. Before it sold over 350,000 copies of the book, cassette tapes, LP albums and instrumental accompaniment tapes, it had been rejected by those who did not think it would sell.

When *The Clown* began to sell well and was presented across the nation, a publisher for whom I'd previously written contacted me, asking why I had not sent the manuscript to them. I told the publisher that I *had* sent it to them first and that I had received a form letter from one of their editors telling me they could not use the material. I framed that form letter of rejection to remind me that there is a big difference between temporary failure and total defeat.

The Clown has been presented by schools, churches, YMCA's and other community groups that want to share a positive, upbeat message of hope. And, it just so happens that one of the songs in this musical drama focuses upon turning problems into opportunities - turning temporary failures into success:

Winter Rain

It's cold outside, rain coming down;
puddles are forming all around,
but I won't complain
'bout the Winter Rain.

Summer it seems was long ago;
the sunny days have turned to snow,
but I won't complain
'bout the Winter Rain.

Because I know spring is just ahead;
things come alive that once were dead,
and that's the way it is with you, my friend,
you can come alive. . . you can come alive!

Four seasons make life complete;
share this thought with those you meet,
and don't complain
'bout the Winter Rain.

Never, Never, Never, Never, Never Give Up!

Former Prime Minister of England, Winston Churchill, learned from his past failures and became the world's leading statesman in the 1940's. When asked to address students at the boys' school he had attended as a young man - and had flunked out of - he accepted the invitation. The headmaster was elated.

The headmaster called the boys into the auditorium and said, "Shortly, one of the greatest statesmen in the history of our country is going to speak to you from this very platform. I want you to be ready with pad and pencil. Bring an open and alert mind, because what he says may change your lives."

Churchill spoke soon afterwards. After a lengthy introduction by the headmaster, Churchill stood up, walked to the podium, looked at the young men and said, "Never, never, never, never, never give up!"

Then he sat down. That was his entire speech, but it was powerful.

I think Churchill was saying, "I wasn't born with anything that you don't have. I wasn't born with any special ability. The reason I have reached the place where I am today is because I refused to give up."

People sometimes make the mistake of looking at successful people where they are now, without taking into consideration what the successful people have gone through on the way to the top.

Nuggets From Helen Gurley Brown

Helen Gurley Brown is not necessarily my heroine, but this creator of *Cosmopolitan* and author of *Sex and the Single Girl* has some gold nuggets among her many words. I once heard this liberated New Yorker from Little Rock, Arkansas, say, "You can rarely grasp the sweetness of something, how precious it is, while you're in it." So true. Then she went on to say, "That's like being grateful for air. . . Being okay today and having survived, why did I worry so much about failing when I was young - that things wouldn't turn out okay? Why didn't I just do what I did and enjoy it?"

Helen Gurley Brown and I may not see eye-to-eye on what people should try to do, but we do see eye-to-eye on the fact that people should try.

". . . how precious life is," she said, "how fast you'll be 50, 60 and regretful that you were afraid to try, that you didn't drink it all in . . . guzzle, guzzle, guzzle."

Just as I know, Helen Gurley Brown knows that we often fail when we try, but we must never quit trying.

Elsewhere in this book, I write about the importance of "keeping on keeping on." However, right here as I write about "trying," I think I would be remiss if I didn't say that a better perspective is placed on trying and temporarily failing if we realize the significance of perseverance.

Calvin Coolidge: Persistence

Former President Calvin Coolidge said it so eloquently with the words:

Nothing in the world can take the place of persistence. Talent will not; unrewarded genius is almost a proverb. Education will not; the world is full of educated derelicts. Persistence and determination alone are omnipotent!

I've heard it said:

If you ride the merry-go-round,
and reach for the brass ring
and catch it, that's great.

If you ride the merry-go-round,
and reach for the brass ring
and miss it, the music doesn't stop.

Remember, the merry-go-round
will come round again
and you will have another chance.

Life is not a sprint, it's a marathon.

There's a big difference between temporary failure and total defeat.

Your Worst Critic

I think it's very important for you to remember, *you are your own worst critic!* You might be unusually critical of your golf game, or your tennis game, or your creative ability, or your business sense, or a weakness or shortcoming. What happens when you look in the mirror? What do you see? Well, it's probably not what others see when they look at you. When we look at ourselves, we tend to notice all the imperfections - hair out of place, blemishes, warts and all. We don't usually look in the mirror and say, "What pretty eyes!" or "What a great smile!" or "Great hair!" or "What an attractive person!" or "What a friendly face!" And yet, that's what others usually see when they look at us. Others recognize our strengths. We see our weaknesses.

In short, you're too hard on yourself. The people who feel "I'm Okay and You're Not" are in the minority. More people lean toward "You're Okay and I'm Not." Most of us tend to feel inferior because we know all of our weaknesses. We know where each wart is. We could make a list at the drop of a hat on what's wrong with us. Right?

You've heard the Golden Rule: "Treat others as you would have others treat you." Let me suggest that you turn this around:

Treat Yourself As You Would Others.

Be as patient with yourself as you are with others. Be as supportive of yourself as you are with others. Don't give up on yourself and your capabilities so quickly.

Don't be like the football coach who gave up on his team. He said they had a drug problem. Every time they went on the field, they got *drug* from one end to the other! My bet is, you're probably more patient with a total stranger than you are with yourself. That's very unfair. Don't give up on yourself. Eleanor Roosevelt said, "Remember, no one can make you feel inferior without your consent."

Low Self-Esteem

I am aware that low self-esteem is a tremendous problem in our country. That is why alcohol and drug abuse is so prevalent. However, I was shocked by a recent report that indicated the following:

Approximately 80% of all children begin kindergarten or the first grade with high self-esteem. Approximately five percent of these same children graduate from high school (or drop out) with high self-esteem.

There are three types of people in our society. First, there are people who make things happen. Then, there are people who watch things happen. Then, there are people who ask, "What happened?"

To make things happen, you need to keep in mind the wise words Yogi Berra shared when he talked of coming from behind in a ballgame. The great Hall of Fame catcher for the New York Yankees said, "It ain't over 'til it's over."

The Parable Of The Frogs

Two frogs accidentally jumped into a bucket of cream. The first frog said, "We may as well give up. It's no use. There's no way out. We're goners."

"Keep on paddling," said the other frog. "We'll get out of this mess somehow."

The first frog began listing all the reasons they were doomed: "It's too thick to swim, too thin to jump from and too slippery to crawl up. We're going to die sooner or later in this bucket, so it might as well be now." With that, he simply quit, and sank to the bottom.

But the second frog kept on paddling. By morning, all his paddling had turned the cream into butter. He hopped out and continued on his way.

It's easy to give up, but the only place that sends you, like the first frog, is to the bottom. Although you might not be able to see the solution immediately, that's no reason to give up on your ability to solve the problem.

So many feel like the man who went to the doctor to hear the results of his earlier physical. "According to the lab tests," the doctor said, "you have two days to live. That's the good news."

"Good news!" the man uttered. "How in the world could that possibly be perceived as good news?"

The doctor explained, "Well, according to this date, the report is two days old."

I think a lot of people feel like the first frog and similar to the news this man received. Life is just a series of disappointments and then you die. How pathetic!

Once a man was walking home after work. He decided to take a short cut through the cemetery. Since it was dark, he didn't see a recently dug hole and fell right in. Try as he might, the hole was too deep to climb out of. So, he sat down in the corner and went to sleep.

A couple of hours later, another man cut through the cemetery and also fell in the hole. Try as he might, he was unable to climb out. Just as he was about to sit down and await the morning light, he heard a sleepy voice in the corner say, "It's no use. You can't get out."

He got out.

All of a sudden he was able to jump a little higher and pull a little harder and dig a little deeper to get out of that hole. He just needed the proper motivation! Temporary failure doesn't always have to lead to total defeat.

Failure can be a blessing. Struggle is a blessing, because I believe it truly does bring the cream to the top. Anything that doesn't break us (and very few things do) will make us stronger. It just depends on your outlook. It depends on your perception of events. It depends on your attitude. Can you look at failure and see opportunity the way a sculptor can see a statue in a piece of stone? Or do you simply see a big rock?

Obstacle Or Opportunity?

Believe me, I've had my share of problems and setbacks. I've been disappointed and discouraged. I've run up against obstacles that in no way resembled opportunities.

For example, the cold, rainy January day on which I wrote *Winter Rain* had been preceded by:

(1) a publisher's rejection of a book for which we had already signed a contract. . . (I later sold the book to another publisher for more money.)

(2) the position I held in an organization being discontinued, leaving me with no regular income. . . (This

led to the forming of Creative Living, Inc., giving a shot in the arm to my speaking and writing career.)

(3) the company for which my wife worked being sold, leaving her with no regular income. . . (This eventually led to her coming to work with me, allowing me time for more creativity.)

(4) an uninsured driver running into my car and then leaving the state, never to be located. . . (As a result, I met a car dealer, began to work with him on some training programs and got a great deal on a new car.)

(5) a meeting in which Carl II's fifth grade teacher said he was creating an on-going disturbance with his incessant talking. . . (Later, his winning two national oratorical contests brought him several thousand dollars in scholarship money and propelled him to choose any university he wanted to attend.)

We all have obstacles/opportunities. I've shared a few of mine. Let me invite you to look at some current problems in your life and discover the possibilities. Don't be blinded by obstacles. Don't concentrate upon them so much that you cannot see the opportunities. Sadly, people have made this mistake for centuries.

Great Mistake - Or Land Of Opportunity?

On October 12, 1492, a lookout aboard the Pinta shouted, "Tierra! Tierra!" ("Land! Land!"). In his effort to find a new sea passage to India, Christopher Columbus accidentally stumbled onto two continents previously unknown to the Europeans. For the rest of his life, Columbus tried to prove he had actually discovered China.

Amerigo Vespucci recognized within a decade that Columbus had discovered a hitherto unknown land mass. Yet, Vespuuci, too, saw (what came to be called) North and South America only as an obstacle to reaching India by sea. Europeans did not realize that this obstacle on the way to India represented tremendous possibilities. These continents contained a wealth of gold, silver, unsettled territory, farmable land and undreamed of opportunities. All that was required was for someone to see the potential and the opportunity instead of merely the obstacle or failure.

Many of us have faced obstacles to accomplishing a task. Too often, we do not see the opportunity in the obstacle or temporary failure.

Think about where we would be if people had not dared to fail. We would have no electricity. After 10 or 15 attempts, Edison could have looked at his percentages and quit. We would have no air travel. The Wright brothers would have quit after their first or second failure. We would have no computers, no televisions, no telephones and no bathrooms (the indoor kind, that is).

As a matter of fact, Thomas J. Watson, the founder of IBM, said, "The way to succeed is to double your failure rate." Dr. Roger von Oech, author of A *Whack on the Side of the Head*, put it this way, "We learn by our failures. A person's errors are the whacks that lead him to think something different. . . The creative director of an advertising agency told me that he isn't happy unless he's failing at least half the time. As he put it, 'If you are going to be original, you are going to be wrong a lot.' " Or, as Woody Allen said, "If you're not failing every now and then, you're probably playing it too safe."

But how should you handle failure?

Handling Failure

After the rare loss of a game by a football team I was working with, I asked the players and coaches to complete several sheets of paper.

On the first sheet, they listed things they'd done to contribute to the loss. On the second sheet, they listed any project or activity in school on which they'd performed less than perfect. On the third sheet, they listed failures at home and other problems in their lives.

I took all the papers and placed them in a container, lit a match, dropped it into the papers and watched all those mistakes burn up.

Then I asked the players to concentrate as I said the following words:

I will have the character, the desire and the enthusiasm that it takes to rise above temporary failure to win again. I will admit my mistakes; I will learn from them. I will do what needs to be done to correct them. I will reflect upon my mistakes only to learn from them and to gain experience. Then I will burn these mistakes and watch them go up in smoke.

I will forget the past and look forward to what lies ahead. The pursuit of excellence is my challenge, and my challenge begins today as I prepare to set higher goals and to climb higher mountains. I am thankful for life, for opportunities, for the ability to learn from mistakes and for the privilege to pursue excellence.

One of the keys to success is the ability to adapt to circumstances and turn them into positive opportunities. Losers blame others, or the weather, or anything else they can think of for their failures. Losers want to change the environment or people or institutions, but winners change their attitudes toward the environment, people, institutions and other circumstances.

We Can Always Change

I think one of the greatest things about life is that we can always change. From negative thinkers, we can become positive thinkers. From failure, we can rise to victory. From the bottom, we can rise to the top. From losers, we can become winners. It begins with the mind. It concludes with desire, determination, dedication and plain hard work. We can always change.

It's like the young man who told the girl, "Just call me Tex."

"Why?" she asked. "Are you from Texas?"

"No," he answered, "I'm from Maryland, but I'm tired of being called Mary!"

We can always change, if we have enough motivation. We can always adapt in some way. And the changes we make should be designed to bring us out on top. And to come out on top where we want to be, we need to follow another precept - *We've Got To Play To Win Rather Than To Play Not To Lose.*

Play To Win

In a big game between two college football teams, the visiting team had not defeated the home team in nine years. At halftime, the team that had not won in nine years was ahead 21 to 7. When the game ended, however, the score was 35 to 28 in favor of the team that had always won.

The local sports editor asked one of the players on the winning team, "When you were behind at halftime, what were you thinking?" The player replied, "I knew we were going to win. It was just a matter of time."

Meanwhile, a reporter asked a player on the losing team, "When you were ahead at halftime, what were you thinking?" He said, "I was just hoping we could hang on."

His team was treading water, hoping the clock would run out. They were playing "not to lose" instead of playing "to win."

And guess what? There are people like that in all aspects of life. They never get ahead because they're too busy treading water. Trying to keep their heads above water, just hoping they can hold on. Hoping they won't drown, rather than setting goals and accomplishing the things they have the potential to do. Just as there's a big difference between temporary failure and total defeat, there's a big difference between playing to win and playing not to lose. People who play not to lose are easily defeated by temporary failure. People who play to win attack a problem or obstacle and push forward even harder.

The Common Thread Of Winners

A group of researchers tried to determine the major difference between winners and losers in the business world. What separates those who make it from those who linger somewhere at the bottom?

As the researchers inspected the lives of successful people, they looked for a common thread. Was it something physical? Some were tall, some were short, some were average. Some were good looking, some plain, some downright ugly.

Was it intelligence? Most of their IQ's were average at best.

Was it inherited wealth or power? Not only were most not born with silver spoons in their mouths, many were poor and many had to overcompensate for being below average before they could become above average.

But the researchers did discover one variable that separated the two groups. They found that very successful people are not defeated by setbacks, or disappointments, or temporary failures. A winner has a belief in herself or himself that is more powerful than the problems, troubles and roadblocks they encounter. A winner chases after his dreams. Everytime he or she gets knocked down, it's an opportunity to get back up, dust off and resume the chase.

The research also pointed out that most successful people have many more failures than unsuccessful people. But, ultimately, successful people keep on trying long enough to make it. Unsuccessful people give up early and settle for less. They stop daring to pursue their dreams. And thus, the temporary failures become total defeats.

Remember, if you stop daring to pursue your dream, if you become afraid of failure, your life becomes a reaction to what you encounter, instead of a life with direction.

Dealing With Pressure

Fearing failure can cause you to perform very badly when pressure arises. When you feel the pressure of passing a test, shooting a free throw in basketball, not striking out when the count is 0-2 in baseball, competing for a job, making a sale or obtaining a contract, you need to quit thinking about failing.

Also, you need to shift the focus from yourself and put things on automatic. Rather than growing tight, let your mind and body take advantage of the preparation you have made to bring you to this point.

Some people under pressure become so involved with making sure they do everything just right that they increase the pressure. They begin to pay too much attention to what they are doing and performance is hindered.

For example, a few years ago when I was interviewing potential secretaries for a position, one lady became so flustered during a typing test that she actually forgot how to type!

If you are a good typist, you don't consciously pay attention to where the keys are. However, under pressure, you might begin to pay attention, making sure you do everything just right, resulting not only in a slower typing speed, but, also, more mistakes.

In the '88 Olympics, no one expected ice skater Elizabeth Manley to do well because of her poor record in competition. She let it be known that she was going to have a good time and enjoy the experience. She didn't worry about failing; she tried things she wouldn't ordinarily try, and was relaxed in doing so. She ended up winning the silver medal.

At the same time, Debi Thomas was favored to win the gold. However, she drew the last slot and waited anxiously as the other skaters, including Elizabeth Manley, performed well. When Debi's time came, she did as most all of us have done at times; she suffered under the pressure and her performance was not up to her usual standard.

Recently, my son Carl II was scheduled to test for a higher level in the martial art of Kung Fu. As I spoke with him on the phone about his test, I said, "You need to watch one of my video tapes to get psyched-up." There was a brief silence. Then he said, "What I need is something to get me psyched-down!"

Do your homework. Prepare. Practice. Plan. Then when the time comes to perform, try not to overthink. Put things on automatic as much as possible. And, most of all, don't fear failing.

Have Loose Enthusiasm

When working with athletes, I often talk about the importance of having "loose enthusiasm." Athletes can relate to this. A common problem among athletes is having "tight enthusiasm."

For example, if you have played football, can you remember your first game? Can you recall the number of times you visited the restroom prior to the contest? What about when you went onto the field for warm-ups? Following calisthenics and group drills, was your uniform wringing wet? Were you ready to go somewhere and lie down because you were so mentally and physically drained?

This doesn't just happen to athletes, though. It happens to students taking exams; to salespeople preparing to call on prospects; to speakers preparing to address audiences; and to various people in various situations - even to brides and grooms as the wedding time nears!

"Tight enthusiasm" causes your muscles to become tense and causes you to burn excess energy. Being afraid of failure can do strange things to you.

But it's okay to have some stress. As a matter of fact, I've often told athletes, "If you go into a game and don't have some butterflies, you are in trouble. You are going to be 'flat.' And if you are flat, it's going to be a long day or a long night!" Any athlete, salesperson, manager, student or anyone else going into an important situation should have some stress. But a winner learns to use stress wisely, to make it work for him or her in order that he or she can grow stronger rather than weaker.

Stress is triggered by fear of failure and failure itself, just as it is triggered by the pressures of success and success itself. So, how can we make stress work for us rather than against us? How can we grow stronger rather than weaker? How can we experience "loose" rather than "tight" enthusiasm? Well, if you'll think about it, that is what this entire book deals with. The more you get involved with the nine principles of **A Strategy For Winning,** the more you will experience loose enthusiasm in all your endeavors.

The "fight or flight" syndrome has been with us since early man stepped from his cave and encountered a wild animal. His mind and body worked together to provide him with additional strength to either fight the animal or run away. If we can properly channel and use the extra power instead of letting it take a toll on us, we can perform beyond our potentials.

The Fear-Stress Expert

So how did I become such an expert on the fear-stress syndrome? Beyond research and study, I have been there. Oh, have I been there!

144

As a freshman, I was the starting guard on a basketball team comprised of all upperclassmen. That in itself presented fear and pressure. But one game early in the season brought an additional dose as a result of the opponent's tenacious defense. Their main weapon was to attack, trap and annihilate the point guard. In this case, me!

The opponent's plan was studied and our plan of attack and counter-attack was practiced and discussed all week. The big night arrived. And even though I was jittery, I thought I was well prepared. The teams took the court in front of a packed house. We went through our drills and took our shots. Then our coach told the starting five to take off our warm-up pants. With the other four, I went to the bench and sat down to unzip the legs and kick off the pants. I didn't get very far, though.

Can you imagine the feeling I had when I discovered I had forgot to put on my game pants? I mean, this was not the place for a *jock strap commercial!*

Red-faced, I explained the situation to my coach. He enjoyed it. Too much, I thought. The other guys enjoyed it, also. Again, too much, I thought. But it did something for us. It cut through some tension and helped transform our "tight" enthusiasm into "loose" enthusiasm. I went to my locker, located my pants and returned to the floor. We won the game by 12 points. I scored 18, had 10 assists and only two turn-overs. It was a game I will remember forever - for more reasons than one!

I've been under more pressure and endured more stress since that time, but that evening taught me something else that should be mixed and stirred with the principles of **A Strategy For Winning:** A good sense of humor. You need to learn to laugh at yourself and not take yourself too seriously.

A sense of humor helped my favorite football team this past year. With a lot of new, untried-under-pressure players and our team coming off of a 10-0 championship season the year before, they were tight, tight, tight prior to their first game. I talked to them the afternoon of the game and closed my presentation by giving each player and each coach a nail. (Have you heard the saying, "He's so tight, he could break a nail. . ."?) I told them I didn't want to see one broken nail when they all showed them to me after the game. To the head coach, I gave an extra large nail. This was so off-the-wall and unexpected that it served to loosen-up the entire squad.

Usually conservative with his offense, our head coach called for a pass on the first play of the game and it went 75 yards for a touchdown. We were well on our way to another championship season!

Humor Plus Courage Removes Fear

Homer Rice, Athletic Director at Georgia Tech and former head coach of the Cincinnati Bengals, said, "Fear is man's greatest enemy. Fear often causes failure, sickness and poor human relations. Fear is indeed crafty. It doesn't come alone. It runs in a pack with worry, its partner in crime. It spoils our present and clouds our future."

To get rid of fear, laugh at it and challenge it. Let it know that you are not going to continue to let it grow. You are going to look at it full in the face and use it to your advantage.

The 99 Yard Opportunity!

It was a close championship football game, a defensive struggle with neither team being able to score. Both teams had come in undefeated and our opponents' home stadium was packed. When the opponents punted the ball to our one yard line, their fans erupted in the stands, cheerleaders turned cartwheels and the players slapped high-fives. Their coaches were elated. Our team wasn't too thrilled!

I caught the look in our offensive team's eyes. It was a worried, distressed look, so I called them aside. "What a break!" I told them, with excitement in my voice and on my face. "You have a great opportunity!

"You have the greatest opportunity of any team that has ever represented this institution. Look at them; look at their fans, cheerleaders and coaches. Listen to their band. Can you imagine what is going to happen when you take that ball and march 99 yards for a touchdown?" I paused, surveyed the group, looked into each player's eyes. "Can you imagine? What an opportunity!"

The players looked at me, at each other and then back at me. Their eyes lit up with a new understanding of the situation. "Guys, this game will be over when you do it. When you go 99 yards, this game will be history!"

The game became history. It took a while. About seven minutes. It wasn't easy, but it became easier as we drew nearer to their goal line. You could see the momentum shifting - fading from them and growing in us. We scored - and won the game by three touchdowns.

It is important how you view a situation. You can usually find opportunity in the middle of what appears to be adversity. Were we pinned in on our one yard line - or did we have a great opportunity to march 99 yards for a touchdown? The major difference between an obstacle and an opportunity is the way it is perceived, the way it is viewed.

Winners see risks as opportunities. Winners see rewards of success in advance - the reward of a victory for taking the ball 99 yards rather than the adversity of having our backs to the wall.

The Three "R's"

This style of thinking makes all the difference in the world. I often talk about the three "R's". Not reading, 'riting and 'rithmetic, but Receptive, Resourceful and Resurgent.

Being receptive means accepting things as they are, facing up to the situation.

Being resourceful means reaching down and utilizing your creativity.

Being resurgent means rising again and again after you've been knocked down or after you've stumbled and fallen on your own.

Being "Down But Not Out"

Being "down but not out" is one of the greatest attributes one can possess. Overcoming seemingly insurmountable odds to taste the sweetness of victory leaves us with memories we can build upon and grow from. Most of us have experienced such moments. We savor them and are encouraged to call upon them again when it seems like something or someone might have us *down but not out.*

I shared with you the account of that memorable "missing pants" basketball game which will forever be branded in my mind for obvious reasons. And, the most memorable football game in which I was involved as a player was one in which our team was behind 25-6 going into the final five minutes of play. We had to win the game in order to remain in the race for the conference championship. Needless to say, things didn't look too great for us at this point, especially since the opponents had possession of the ball. But a hard tackle caused a fumble. We recovered and were on our way.

A couple of plays later, I took a hand-off from the quarterback, found an opening in the line, picked-up a couple of good downfield blocks and went into the end zone with about five minutes left in the game. The extra point was good and the score was now 25-13. Then. . . well, let me dust off an old scrapbook and open it up for you. The following account was recorded in the *Jackson* (Tennessee) *Sun* newspaper, telling what happened after we kicked-off to the opponents and held them on downs, causing them to have to punt to us:

> *An inspired bunch of Humboldt Rams rose to superb heights to pull an almost certain loss out of the fire and edge a strong, highly-favored Jackson Golden Bear eleven by a 26 to 25 one point margin, with barely seconds remaining on the clock. . .*
>
> *In as dramatic a finish as you will see in many a moon, the Rams were still behind two touchdowns with less than four minutes to play. . . and here is how it happened in those last three minutes. . .*
>
> *Quarterback Jerry Williams sent Carl Mays straight down the field where Williams threw the speedy Mays a strike at the 25-yard line. One Jackson man hit him solidly on the 20 but slid off as Mays refused to be denied. He hit paydirt with two minutes and 27 seconds remaining in the game. Still, after the extra point was made, Humboldt trailed 25-20.*

Playing the game to the hilt, the Rams successfully tried an onside kick. . . Humboldt covered the loose pigskin. . .

With 48 seconds remaining, Humboldt picked-up a first down at the Jackson nine.

A play into the line netted one yard. A pass fell incomplete. Nothing daunted, Williams tried again, a sharp rifle shot down the line to Mays in the flat. Once again Mays was hit immediately, but shook off his would-be tackler and zipped into the end zone with the winning points and pandemonium reigned.

Yes, we all have moments we like to relive in our minds - moments when it seemed like we were down for the count but rose to fight again. Scoring three touchdowns in the last five minutes of that game has not only provided me with some good memories, but has provided me with ammunition in all of life to agree with Yogi Berra's, "It ain't over 'til it's over."

We Can Learn From Them

Beethoven rose above deafness to compose majestic music.

Milton defeated blindness to write words of depth and beauty.

Helen Keller, who could neither see, hear, nor speak for a long time, achieved a victory that few people can imagine.

Louisa Mae Alcott was told by an editor that she had no writing ability and should forget about attempting such endeavors. *Little Women* came shortly thereafter.

When Walt Disney submitted his first drawings for publication, the editor told him he had no talent.

F.W. Woolworth was not permitted to wait on customers in the store where he worked because his employer said he did not have enough sense to meet the public.

The Human Spirit

When I was a child, my dad took me to to Nashville to see a minor league baseball game. I was amazed to see an outfielder, Pete Gray, who had only one arm. He batted with power. He could catch a ball, toss his glove and ball in the air, catch the ball and fire the ball back to the infield with amazing agility and speed. He later played in the major leagues.

Jim Abbot was born with only one hand. He played baseball (pitcher) and football (quarterback) in high school, then went to the University of Michigan on a baseball scholarship. He pitched in the 1988 Olympics and went straight to the majors with the California Angels.

When asked about his record of achievement, Abbot responded, "I think the main reason I have done what I have done is because no one ever discouraged me."

Isn't it amazing what human beings can do, what we can accomplish, what we can overcome when we have the proper motivation? As we've discussed in this chapter, that type of motivation consists of desire, dedication and daily discipline.

That type of motivation gives meaning to the saying: *It Isn't The Size Of The Dog In The Fight But The Size Of The Fight In The Dog That Determines The Winner.*

But, Winning Isn't Everything . . .

Jeff Blatnick won a gold medal in Grecco-Roman wrestling for the United States in 1984. I think he won even greater respect of the entire world by the way he adapted to and bounced back from his bout with cancer prior to the Olympics. I watched on television that day as he did the impossible. As he accepted the gold, tears were in the eyes of this giant of a man. Not only a physical giant, but a mental giant, because he fought and won with both his mind and his body.

Then it was discovered that the cancer had returned. At first, Jeff was devastated. But then he adapted. He continued his training, despite his weakened state, and placed third in the 1987 National Championships even though he was barely able to walk just months earlier.

Jeff Blatnick is a winner because he desired to be. He certainly had plenty of reasons to quit. Plenty of things on which to blame his misfortunes. As I have said on numerous occasions: Winning isn't everything - but wanting to win, planning to win and knowing how to win is. Jeff wanted to win, he planned to win and he knew how to win.

Winners continually look for ways to win while losers look for excuses.

The Quitter

It's easy to cry that you're beaten and die.
It's easy to wallow and crawl.
But to fight and to fight when hope's out of sight,
that's the best game of all.
And though you come out of each grueling bout
all broken, beaten and scarred,
just have one more try.
It's easy to die,
it's the keeping on living that's hard.

Robert W. Service

Yaz

You might remember when Carl Yastrzemski, the Boston Red Sox first baseman, was about to get his 3,000th career hit. As you might imagine, it was quite a media event with reporters following games by the herds. As the magic number got closer, Yaz's following grew even larger. A reporter, trying to ask a different question, said, "Hey Yaz, are you afraid all of this attention will go to your head?"

Yastrzemski smiled a tired smile and said, "I look at it this way. I've been up to bat probably over 10,000 times. That means I've been unsuccessful at the plate over 7,000 times. That fact alone keeps me from getting a swollen head."

I think what we have to realize is that every swing is not going to be a home run. We're going to ground out, pop up and strike out. But if we keep practicing, keep our attitudes up and keep swinging, we're going to get to first base with regularity. As Roger von Oech suggests, "Most people think of success and failure as opposites, but they are actually both products of the same process."

Of course, you can't get on base if you quit when you're making more outs than hits. You have to be able to see past the failures. You have to develop the type of attitude that sees opportunities in failure. You have to develop the type of attitude that says, "I learned from that mistake. Next time, I'll try it differently."

My friend, humorist Grady Jim Robinson, tells the story about his young son Ryan playing a Pee Wee baseball game. After the first half of the first inning, Ryan's team was down by 18 runs. Ryan ran into the dugout and said, "Alright men, 18 more runs and we're back in this thing!" Well, that's the spirit it takes. It might be the next game or the next season or maybe 10 years later, but opportunity comes from failure.

Clifton Burke said, "The most you can expect out of life is what you can expect out of life." I like that. I also like the words that have been around for thousands of years and translated into hundreds of languages:

Look Well To This Day

Look well to this day, for it is life,
the very life of life.
In its brief course lie all the truths and
realities of your existence -
the joy of growth, the glory of action, the splendor of beauty.
For yesterday is but a memory and tomorrow is
only a vision.
But today, well lived, makes every yesterday
a memory of happiness and every tomorrow a
vision of hope.
Look well, therefore, to this very day.

Don't Fear Failure.

Don't miss smelling the flowers for fear you may get stung by a bee!

And, in order not to miss out, you need to "act rather than react," a concept covered in chapter six. . .

Chapter 6

CLARIFY YOUR VALUES - ACT RATHER THAN REACT

Years ago, a boy living in the mountains of East Tennessee was always getting into trouble. You know the type. It was as if he was drawn to mischief like a magnet. Living out in the country, he was waiting for the school bus one morning and, sure enough, he found something else to get into.

He pushed the family's outdoor toilet off the side of the hill and watched it tumble into the hollow below. Then he got on the school bus and went off to school as if nothing had happened.

When he returned home that afternoon, however, his father was waiting for him. "Son, did you push the toilet over?"

"Yes, Dad," replied the son. "Like George Washington, I cannot tell a lie. I did it." The boy's father took off his belt and began to whip the boy.

"But Dad," the boy protested, "Mr. Washington didn't spank George when he admitted chopping down the cherry tree!"

"Yes," the angry father replied, "But Mr. Washington was not sitting in that tree!"

The question here is not whether you get caught. The question is, do you lie? Do you cheat? Do you steal? Do you do anything to keep you from becoming the person you have the potential to become? It's a question of character.

The Truth? The Whole Truth? And Nothing But the Truth?

It has been my privilege to speak to numerous insurance organizations over the past dozen or so years. Along with sales and marketing personnel, I have spoken to several insurance claims groups. The professional claims adjusters who comprise these groups encounter a lot of stress and are constantly involved in "problems." It is the nature of their work. And even though they feel they have "heard it all" as far as accounts of accidents are concerned, people involved in mishaps always seem able to come up with new descriptions of their latest run-ins.

There have been many lists of accident descriptions supplied to claims adjusters. Magazines, newspapers and even Johnny Carson on the *Tonight Show* have had a field day with such excuses as:

- *An invisible car came out of nowhere, struck my vehicle, and vanished.*
- *The pedestrian had no idea which direction to go, so I ran over him.*
- *My car was legally parked as it backed into the other vehicle.*
- *I was on the way to the doctor with rear-end trouble when my universal joint gave way, causing me to have an accident.*
- *I pulled away from the side of the road, glanced at my mother-in-law, and headed over the embankment.*

People have come up with some wild tales as they have tried to describe the event in as few words as possible, all the while being careful to try to shift the blame from them to someone or something else. The descriptions often end up being humorous, yet they illustrate a point we should be concerned with. We're talking about values. About honesty. About character.

It's sometimes difficult to be truthful, knowing the consequences are not always desirable. It's tempting to deny guilt when reporting an accident to an insurance company. Likewise, it's tempting to lie about why you're late for work (and employers have heard some good ones here!). It's tempting for a student to make up an excuse for not turning in homework on time (the dog ate it?). Income taxes are another good example. It's very tempting to "fudge" on how much you make when reporting to the IRS.

Thinking along these lines reminds me of the 10 year-old boy who protested loudly when his mother asked him to take his younger sister with him when he went fishing.

When they returned shortly with no fish, the mother said, "Well, that didn't take long. I hope Cindy didn't make too much noise."

"It wasn't the noise, Mom," the boy said. "Cindy ate all the bait!"

We're talking about a question of priorities. Sister Cindy wanted the bread (did you think it was worms?) more than the fish. Which is more important to you? Avoiding consequences through dishonesty or deception - or developing character?

Professional Creed

As a professional writer and speaker, I recently led in a seminar for other such professionals and would-be professionals from across the nation. Focusing upon how to succeed in the world of paid speaking, here are some of the suggestions presented:

(1) Be professional from the first contact.

(2) Be warm and cordial with all contacts on all levels.

(3) Be prompt and concise with needs, schedules, contracts, travel arrangements, etc.

(4) Be the same person before, during and after your presentation.

(5) Be thankful for the opportunity to speak; let them know you are thankful.

(6) Present what is expected in (a) content, (b) style, (c) length.

(7) Promise much and deliver more.

(8) Never even consider padding expenses; pull no surprises.

(9) Go out of your way to help the client get the best deal for his money.

(10) Consider flying first class on frequent flyer points or small payment while still billing client for coach fare, and let client know.

These 10 hints form the basis of a value system for a professional speaker which in the long run will result in success. In and out, "zap 'em when you can" prima donnas won't get the job done in professional speaking or in anything else.

A Matter Of Ethics

Our society is running over with stories of unethical behavior in all areas of life. Accounts range from the Watergate scandal of the 70's to the bank frauds, political deals, athletes' wrong doings and religious leaders' sexual adventures of today. From immorality and drugs in our schools to insider trading schemes on Wall Street, improprieties abound.

The need has never been greater for the wisdom and the knowledge of what is right and wrong and the everyday practice of doing what is right in our business and professional lives, home lives and personal lives. When a person adheres to a set system of values, this person, more often than not, will discover more productivity, harmony, fulfillment and profitability in all areas of life.

Having the right values requires having discipline; having discipline requires having character.

One of the sports teams with which I work has a large sign in the locker room: *We're Not Looking For Players Who Are Characters; We're Looking For Players Who Have Character.*

That says it all.

An Example Of Character

Let me share an example with you about character and courage. In the early 40's, a mother of several children was determined to keep her family together when her husband died. She worked at four different jobs: waiting tables, cleaning offices, working in a bakery and delivering coal in Pittsburgh where she

156

lived. Later she took the civil service exam and eventually became the chief bookkeeper for the city treasurer.

She held her family together with love and courage. She couldn't give her children money but she did teach them courage and the meaning of character.

One of her children wanted to play football in college but none of the large colleges to which he applied wanted him. They said he was too little and too slow. So he played for a small college and excelled. Then he wanted to play professional football and tried out for his hometown Pittsburgh Steelers but was cut from the team in short order.

He found a job in construction, helping to build some of the skyscrapers you can see today in Pittsburgh. But he didn't give up on his dream. He chose how to respond to rejection. He didn't see himself as a victim of circumstances, helpless to do anything about it. He didn't curse his size and develop a bias against larger men. Here's what he did: (1) He took a look at his options. (2) He played in a league that paid him $6.00 a game and was able to maintain and improve his skills. (3) He continued to write and telephone NFL teams in hopes of an opportunity to try out. After seven months of asking, he received an invitation to try out for the Baltimore Colts.

The rest is now sports history. Johnny Unitas, honored in the NFL Hall of Fame, was one of the greatest quarterbacks to ever play the game.

It takes character to get up and go again when you've been knocked flat. It takes character not to give in to the easy way out, to the easy money, to the unethical deals, to the immoral behavior, to the "what's in it for me?" and the "you go to hell!" attitudes.

Character leads to values, and values are standards by which choices and decisions are made. Values are revealed in our day-in, day-out activities and relationships.

What do you do at a crucial point in your life? Do you just give up? Do you make excuses? Or, do you have character? It's pretty easy to have what it takes when everything is going your way. But what happens when things stop going your way?

What do you do in business when obstacles start appearing in several directions?

What do you do as a coach when your team loses a key player?

What do you do as a family when Dad loses his job?

How do you handle rejection? How do you handle failure?

Do you just give up? Do you do something a little shady? Do you make excuses or rationalize? Or, do you have character?

The Lean Dog

My friend and associate, Steve Williford, was getting some coffee one morning before Sunday School class. When he by-passed the doughnuts, saying he was trying to watch his weight, one of the older ladies in the group observed, "It takes the lean dog to make the long run!"

Well, that's true, isn't it? Any old dog can lie around on the porch or in the yard, regardless of its condition. But it takes a certain type dog to run for hours at a time through the woods, thickets, meadows, swamps, hills and hollows. It not only requires a degree of fitness, but also the desire and the character to stick it out.

A young man was filling out his first job application. When he came to the space, "person to notify in case of accident," he wrote, "anybody in sight!"

The fact is, employers don't look for just anyone in sight. When a coach comes down to a crucial part of the game, he doesn't choose just anybody. He chooses someone he knows has character. Someone he knows has courage. Someone he knows has a strong possibility of coming through when it's needed. And what's true in sports is true in all other areas of life.

Over The Long Haul

Back when I was in radio and TV work, I sold commercial time for my own show as well as spots throughout the day. I had just come on board with a station when the manager devised an advertising promotion. It was a good promotion, but I didn't think it was well-suited for all my clients and told the manager so.

At first, the manager was upset that I did not want to sell the promotion to everyone I could. He was focusing on all the money the campaign would bring in to the station. I shared with him my focus: "I want to do what is best for my client over the long haul, rather than see how much money I can bring in during a short period of time."

The manager finally gave in to my form of reasoning, letting me determine who and who not to approach with the promotion. That year, I sold more commercial time than anyone else at the station. Later, when I moved on, the manager told me he hated to see me go, that he was grooming me to become the assistant station manager and to eventually take over his job.

Over the long haul, maintaining high principles in sales or in life increases your effectiveness - a concept I will continue to develop in this chapter.

This occurred back in the 60's. I visited with my former manager a couple of years ago, and one of the first things he brought up was, "Remember that ad promotion we disagreed upon - initially?"

Spiritual Values

Several years ago, I sponsored a conference for about 2,500 young people. One of my guests was Olympic Gold Medalist, Paul Anderson, known at the time as the World's Strongest Man. I introduced him and he walked out on stage, standing 5'9" and weighing about 300 pounds. He looked powerful.

At one point in his presentation, he asked, "Are there any football players in the audience?" Quite a few hands went up. Then he asked players weighing over 200 pounds to stand up. Quite a few stood. Then he said, "If you weigh under 225, please sit down." He finally reduced the group to 11 of the heaviest players and invited them on stage. He asked them to sit on a specially made table. He crawled under the table and stuck his head through a hole in the center. With the table resting on his shoulders, he stood up, lifting the 11 football players.

Now that got my attention and the attention of each of the 2,500 young people present. Then he said, "I'm Paul Anderson.

I'm known as the world's strongest man. But without the spiritual power that is available to me, I am nothing. Without the power I receive through my Maker, I am weak."

With that, he encouraged each person to get his or her spiritual priorities straight; to realize there's a power far stronger than any person; to find this power and to become one with it.

That's the first area in which you need to clarify your values. What are your spiritual beliefs? Do these beliefs affect your life in a positive way and help you reach your potential?

Moral Values

Are your moral values solid and dependable? Or, are you like the chameleon that changes colors with its surroundings? That's appropriate for lizards, but not for people! True winners need to be stable and not be swayed by circumstances. And, of course, this is not always easy. Intimidation and peer pressure are always present.

We want others to like us. Although peer pressure may be more obvious during adolescence, it's always with us. It just changes form slightly. If we think we'll be more accepted or respected for wearing a particular style shirt, pants, suit or driving a certain car, we'll try to obtain it. But what if it appears that you'll be more accepted if you participate in something which violates your moral values?

A recent survey of men across the nation asked, "From what do you derive your self-esteem?" The majority of men chose the response, "peer perception." The men said the way they felt about themselves was determined by the way others felt about them. Don't tell me peer pressure ends with the teenage years!

This is a very dangerous position. If you take this stand, which many take, you are dependent on the attitude of others to determine your own attitude and esteem. You are dependent on others to determine your value system.

Wishy-Washy?

This intimidation could be physical, emotional, financial or mental. It reminds me of a commercial that was popular a few years ago. In the commercial, there are three people. On one side is a former pro football player, standing 6'5", weighing about 300 pounds. On the other side is another former pro football player, about the same size, and in the center between the two is the late Billy Martin, standing about 5'8", weighing about 140 pounds.

The big fellow on his right says, "I like this beverage because it tastes great." The guy on his left says, "I like it because it's less filling."

The guy on the right says, "Tastes great."
The guy on the left says, "Less filling."
"Tastes great." - "Less filling."
"Tastes great." - "Less filling."

They had been carrying-on this conversation above Billy Martin's head. Now they look down at him and one says, "What do you think, Billy?"

The other says, "Yeah, Billy, what do you think?"

He takes a moment to look at the twin towers, turns toward the camera and says, "Well, I feel rather strongly both ways."

In short (no pun intended), he's afraid to let his feelings be known. He's afraid to make a decision. He wants to straddle the fence. That's what peer pressure can do to you.

We Have To Decide

Jack Donohue, Olympic coach of the Canadian basketball team, wrote to me and ordered copies of my book, *You Can Do It!*, for his players and himself. Naturally, I was pleased that he wanted the books. And naturally, I wanted Coach Donohue and his team to do well in the Olympics.

They did well. In fact, they earned the right to play the U.S.A. in the semi-final round. This placed me in an awkward position. I couldn't be against America - but it would have been great to see Canada continue to win, thinking that through my book I had a little to do with their better-than-usual showing.

In the end, though, as I sat down to watch the game on TV, I had to make a decision. Of course, I decided to *stand up for America*.

We all have *stands* to take. Some are relatively minor, like my Olympic predicament. Some are major. Others are somewhere in-between. But, daily, we have to get off the fence. We must make decisions about the things we think, say and do. And, we must make decisions about the people with whom we associate.

Choose Associates Wisely

Winners must surround themselves with positive, uplifting people who share the same values. One of the most important things a person can do is choose associates wisely. We seem to take on the characteristics of those around us and become much like them. So, the friends we choose are important in helping us develop positive values. I'm not just talking about teenagers' friends. This also applies to adults' friends and to co-workers and the company you work for.

If you want to look at where you're heading, take a look at your friends, your co-workers and your company. Are they building you up or tearing you down? Are they helping you reach those goals and objectives you've set for yourself? Do they have their own goals? Are you able to support each other? Do you have similar value systems? Do they respect and support your code of ethics?

Remember, enthusiasm is contagious. You can build up your friends, co-workers and organization as they build up you. Choosing to look at the world with enthusiasm, confidence and a sense of humor is a choice you make. I think it's also something to look for in your associates. Avoid pessimists. They can poison life. But a positive associate can radiate energy, enthusiasm, motivation and can make good times even better and bad times easier to endure.

A winner is able to let his or her feelings be known, realizing that true friends, positive co-workers and a valuable organization will respect your opinions and beliefs.

Eagle Or Turkey?

Of course, it goes without saying, you should choose the people you date and, especially, the person you marry with extreme care. You've heard it said, "It's difficult to soar with the eagles when you're surrounded by turkeys." But, consider the consequences when you date or - heaven forbid - marry a turkey!

In chapter two, I stated that some people become winners with a lot of help from good, positive uplifting "contacts." Other people become winners in spite of bad, negative, debasing "contacts." The former is much easier than the latter.

However, should you discover that your mate is of the turkey family, remember: Anyone can change. And, you can be a very positive influence in bringing about such a change.

The bottom line is, date with care and marry with care - something that, apparently, many people do not do. According to *American Demographics*, 51.6% of new marriages will end in divorce.

High Values Equal Greater Achievements

In 1987, the respected Gallup poll made a sweeping statement to the effect that America is facing a moral and ethical crisis of huge proportions. The report went on to pose the question as to what happened to the value system that once characterized our society and allowed business to be done on a handshake.

This is a good question, considering that the individuals and companies with higher ethical values appear to have greater productivity and profitability. That is why I consider this chapter a vital one in **A Strategy For Winning.**

The best-seller, *In Search of Excellence*, pointed to the success of corporations that emphasize moral responsibilities. The authors told how the excellent companies seemed to develop traits that incorporate the values and practices of their leaders. And, these values and practices can be seen to survive decades after leaders have passed from the scene.

It is refreshing to know that J. C. Penney personally built his business on "The Golden Rule" of treating employees and customers as he would want to be treated. The early Penney stores were often referred to as "Golden Rule" stores.

Likewise, Milton S. Hershey built the Hershey Corporation on a values base that paralleled his own lifestyle. Integrity, industry, benefit to others, and family and community involvement were reflected in the company he founded. Those values, still identified and visible, have given the company profitable staying power for over 80 years.

Ethics During Crisis

During Johnson and Johnson's Tylenol crisis of 1982, when seven people died after taking cyanide-laced Tylenol, Chairman James Burke said, "Our code of ethics, instituted in 1947, played the single most important role in handling the situation correctly." It is commonly believed that if Johnson and Johnson had not responded based on its established code of ethics, the company would have run head-long into financial disaster.

And the examples of what high ethical values can do for corporations are numerous. One such good example is the Boeing Aerospace Corporation.

The Boeing Example

The Boeing Company today has a reputation as one of America's best managed, most successful - and most ethical large corporations. In its most recent annual survey of corporate ratings, *Fortune* magazine reported that Boeing was considered by other executives to be one of America's three best managed companies.

Every discussion with company executives and managers about the origin of Boeing's strong values starts with an emphasis on the leadership of former chief executive William Allen. Allen is remembered as a man of great sincerity and honesty who "exuded integrity." On the eve of his acceptance of the company presidency in 1945, Allen jotted down a list of resolutions that reflected his personal values:

- *Be considerate of my associates' views.*
- *Don't talk too much . . . let others talk.*
- *Don't be afraid to admit that you don't know.*
- *Don't get immersed in detail . . .*
- *Make contacts with other people in the industry . . .*
- *Try to improve feelings toward the company.*
- *Make a sincere effort to understand labor's point of view.*

- *Be definite; don't vacillate.*
- *Act - get things done - move forward.*
- *Develop a post-war future for Boeing.*
- *Try hard, but don't let obstacles get you down. Take things in stride.*
- *Above all else be human - keep your sense of humor - learn to relax.*
- *Be just, straightforward; invite criticism and learn to take it.*
- *Bring to the task great enthusiasm, unlimited energy.*
- *Make Boeing even greater than it is.*

Do You Have A Price?

We also need to assess what we base our values on. Too often, people determine value by price. For example, a man asked a certain woman, "Would you go to bed with me for a million dollars?"

Without hesitation she replied, "Yes."

Then he asked, "Would you go to bed with me for 10 dollars?"

She became indignant and replied sharply, "No! What do you think I am?"

"I know what you are," he said. "Now I'm just trying to find your price."

This has become an epidemic in our society. People with the potential to be real winners are becoming losers because they allow price to determine their values.

Some determine value by position; some by education; some by athletic ability; some by salary; some by physical appearance.

Criteria For Value

But just because a person is wealthy, well-educated, athletic and/or attractive doesn't make him or her a winner. Let me suggest some criteria for value other than the traditional measures of money, fame and power: time, family, knowledge, friends.

As we've discussed and will continue to emphasize, *time* is a precious commodity. The *family* is also a tremendously valuable institution designed to help us enjoy life to the fullest. *Knowledge* unlocks the mysteries of the universe to us and is available to anyone. And as we've discussed, *friends* can make all the difference in the world. It's hard to put a price on a good friend.

In his book, *A Father, A Son and a Three Mile Run*, Keith Leenhouts shares how he resigned his judgeship to be able to spend more time in the afternoons with his son. As he explained it, his career and salary were secondary to being able to show his love to his son.

I believe that families send and receive conflicting messages. On the one hand, parents seem to think that if they don't provide the finest cars, houses and clothes possible, somehow they've let their children down. This also requires more work and pressure, and less time with their children.

The Price Of Success

American families have felt the impact of misplaced priorities. Historically, the home has been the center for teaching values, morals and ethics. If, as the Gallup poll reports, America is facing a moral and ethical crisis of huge proportions, the home or family is at fault.

When parents spend more and more time making money to satisfy the economic demands of their children, time invested in the development of the children is reduced. Meanwhile, the young people are elsewhere, learning other values and involved in a different culture from their parents.

Calendar Commitment

Having worked with young people in various ways, I saw the effect of absentee parents. Therefore, when our son Carl II was young, I made the commitment to be present for his important times. For example, I'd take his sports schedule and mark out those dates on my calendar as well as other dates important to him. When someone asked me to speak on one of those dates, I'd say, "I'm sorry, but I already have a commitment for that time."

Did I need the money? Absolutely. Were we independently wealthy? No. But we managed to make it, even though it cost us

166

financially. Now that Carl II is grown and living a thousand miles away, I'm thankful that I realized and acted upon what was most important in my life at the time.

Just recently, my friend and fellow speaker, Kyle Rote, Jr., wrote me a letter asking about juggling career demands and family time. Kyle is the only American-born professional soccer player to be voted MVP in the World Soccer League. And, he won the popular televised *Superstars Competition* more times than any other professional athlete. Now, he is growing in demand as a speaker and TV sports commentator. He also has children now - and some decisions to make.

Knowing that I have gone through what he is currently experiencing, he wanted to know how I handled it. I shared with Kyle what I have shared with you. I placed my family on my calendar. For example, Carl II began playing organized football in the second grade. Through those early years, then through junior high school and on through high school, I only missed one game in which he played. That was during the Air Controllers' strike in 1981. I was stuck on an airplane on the runway in Dallas, Texas, for two hours and 45 minutes, causing me to miss a connecting flight home.

The bottom line: Think carefully before you sacrifice something in the present that you cannot experience in the future. Think carefully before you choose what you are going to postpone.

Harry Chapin wrote a very perceptive song entitled, *The Cat's In the Cradle*. Remember that song? A child was born, but his father was so busy taking care of business and assuring his son of a secure future that he didn't have much time for the child as he was growing up. Still, the boy admired his father and claimed, *"I'm going to be like you, Dad. You know I'm going to be like you."*

The son continued to grow and the father continued to take care of business. The same relationship remained as the boy advanced through grade school, high school, college and into the business world. No time to play ball. No time to talk. No time to share.

Then, the father retired. He and his son lived in distant cities. He was anxious to visit with his son, to talk with him. But the son was so busy that it seemed as if they just couldn't get together. Contemplating the situation, the father discovered that ". . . he'd grown up just like me. Yeah, my boy was just like me."

The bottom line here: You must clarify your values and set your priorities if you want to be a winner. You must decide to *act rather than react*.

Act Rather Than React

A friend of mine and founder of the National Speakers Association, Cavett Robert, told about something that happened to him years ago that's had a tremendous positive influence on his life. As a small boy, he and his grandfather were walking down the sidewalk in a little Mississippi town when a woman came from the other direction. The grandfather stepped aside, took off his hat and said, "Good day, ma'am."

The boy was puzzled. Even *he* knew this was the woman that mothers warned their daughters not to be like. So, he asked, "Grandpa, why did you do that?"

"Boy," he answered, "I was polite to her not because of who she is, but because of who I am."

How many people go through life reacting rather than acting? "If you're nice to me, I'll be nice to you. If you're nasty to me, I'll be nasty to you."

As we've discussed, there are a lot of things we have no control over: the weather, our height, the color of our skin, our parents and how others treat us. But we do have control over how we act toward others. We do have control over what we choose to initiate.

Important To Be In Control

It's important to be in control of yourself and of situations in all areas of life: athletics, business, family or whatever.

I was involved in a conference for chief executives of the fastest growing private firms in America. On the program was Robert Donnelly, author of *The Guidebook Of Planning*. He claimed that when a company is growing like gang-busters, the CEO spends most of the time reacting. He said that a measley five percent of the CEO's time goes into planning how to cope with growth, and the result is: "Things go a little wacky."

According to Donnelly, customers begin complaining about delivery and quality, employees complain about "burning-out," and suppliers complain about not getting paid. And, there is usually a lack of office and production space. All these things are signs that a company is growing too fast and the CEO is having to spend time reacting rather than acting.

Companies sometimes grow so fast that they self-destruct. Too much reaction and not enough action or planning takes them under. Donnelly advised the CEO's not to think of their business plans merely as financial documents needed to get bank loans. Business plans should help you plan for changes in customers, products and competitors. The plans should lead to action, not simply reaction.

Too much reaction and too little action can kill you in all endeavors. When you are not in control, then people, circumstances and situations control you. Rather than making decisions, decisions are made for you. Rather than clarifying your values, your values might become vague.

Thermostat Or Thermometer?

When you clarify your values, you act rather than react. You become a thermostat rather than a thermometer. A thermostat sets the temperature. A thermometer only measures the temperature that's present. A thermostat is someone who makes things happen. It is someone who shoulders responsibility. But a thermometer just watches and records what happens.

Remember in an earlier chapter, I said there are three types of people? First of all, there's the person who makes things happen. I put a sign above the light switch in my son's room with the words, *Shoulder Responsibility*. That's like a thermostat. If you go in the right direction, you get the credit. If you go in the wrong direction, you get the blame.

Then there's the person who watches things happen. That's like being a human thermometer. The third type just asks, "What happened?" He is neither a thermostat nor a thermometer . He neither acts nor reacts. He just exists, content to breathe, eat and sleep. As the old saying goes, "Good things may come to those who wait, but only the things left by those who hustle."

Which kind of person are you? It's not an easy task to accept responsibility.

If It Is To Be, It Is Up To Me!

A football team I work with has this sign in their locker room: *If It Is To Be, It Is Up To Me.*

This means that when crunch time comes, I'm not going to hope that someone else takes up the slack. When we need a big play or need to make a major decision, I'm not going to look to someone else to make it. The responsibility is on my shoulders. Winston Churchill's motto was "The price of greatness is responsibility."

The business world is hungry for people who can excel under pressure. It is not just military personnel who are held in high esteem in keeping their heads and performing beyond themselves when bullets are in the air. Cool-under-fire managers are worth their weight in gold. If you build a reputation as a "take charge" person, you have a much better than average chance to go far in any endeavor. Workers are motivated when they feel they have a fair but decisive manager who is in command of the situation at hand.

In working with people in customer relations seminars, I emphasize to high-contact employees the importance of being responsible. For example, if a representative from the electric system goes to a home to read a meter, someone may come out of the house to tell the reader about a problem. The reader could say, "That's not my responsibility, you'll have to call the company." Or, he could say, "I'm sorry you're having this problem. Let me pass along this information to the proper department. Someone will be back in touch with you tomorrow morning before 10:00."

Then, the meter reader shares the problem with the department and tells of his commitment to the customer. The next time he goes to the house to read the meter, he makes it a point to follow-up, asking the customer if the problem has been taken care of.

If you work for an organization and a customer comes to you with a problem, don't say, "That's not my responsibility, see someone else." You make it your responsibility. If you can't handle it directly, get in contact with the person who can. If a customer asks you a question you can't answer, don't say, "I don't know." Instead, reply, "I will put you in contact with someone who can answer that." Then do it.

Last month, I was in a hotel ballroom preparing for a speaking engagement. Checking out the sound system, I discovered the volume to be too low and I could find no way to adjust it. The only person around was a lady cleaning the room. I told her of my problem. She replied, "I'll go get someone from the audio-visual department."

A few minutes later she returned and said, "No one was in the office. I'll go to the front desk and have one of the men paged." Shortly, she returned again and said, "Someone will be here within five minutes." Four minutes later someone did arrive to address the problem. I thanked the lady, then joined the audio-visual representative. We resolved the volume deficiency.

I turned to thank the lady again, but she was gone. I noticed that she had not finished her work as I continued to prepare for my presentation. Then, she returned. Talking with her, I discovered she had left the room to punch-out on the time clock, but had come back to finish her work in the room before going home. You can find excellence on all levels!

Vince Lombardi said, "The quality of a person's life is in direct proportion to his commitment to excellence, regardless of his chosen field of endeavor." And when all the people in a business, organization or all the members of a sports team say, "If it is to be, it is up to me," you will have a winning group.

We all make a choice as to the role we'll play in the group. We either join it as an actively participating and caring member, or, we go through the motions from the sidelines.

I Make A Difference

The Dartnell Corporation printed this philosophy for employees to internalize:

I make a difference. I know that what I do makes it possible for my office to run smoothly. The effort I put into my job shows up in the quality of my office's services and in my company's earnings.

I'm part of what outsiders see when they judge my organization. With every letter, every phone conversation, every personal contact, I make a statement about the caliber of service we offer. In the course of a year, I make hundreds of valuable business contacts for us.

How I feel on a given day affects the people I work with. I help to set the tone here. I know that when I bring real enthusiasm to the job, I make a contribution few others can equal.

I also take responsibility for what bothers me...Whether it's a procedure that isn't working, a practice I feel is unfair, or a person I'm having difficulty with, I do what I can to change the situation. When I can't get a situation changed, I look for ways to minimize its effect on me. Most important, I remember that I've chosen to work here, and as long as I'm here, I'll give my best.

I'm proud to be a strong, reliable member of my company's team. I know that my success, as well as the company's success, depends on it.

We Represent Each Other

Here is what may be a somewhat unusual philosophy: As I have enlisted people to work with me in my organization, I have always emphasized that we are responsible to one another. People who work with me are more than "just employees." They represent me and I represent them. In their business contacts and in their personal lives, my people are an extension of me. Likewise, I am an extension of them. We have a mutual responsibility to represent each other well.

172

For example, my business manager is in charge of all of my speaking engagements. How she manages details reflects upon me. In all her contacts, she must represent me, my message and my philosophy. Should she not reflect in her professional or personal life the principles I have emphasized in this book, she would be letting me down.

At the same time, I have the responsibility not to let her down. I must represent her well. I must live up to the obligations to our clients, to her and to myself. I must always be prepared and do the best I can. My professional and personal endeavors must reflect the contents of this book.

The people of our organization know we are not perfect. We know we are going to make some mistakes - to experience some temporary failures. However, we also know that we are going to do what we can to continue to grow positively and perform accordingly. Just as I have challenged you throughout this book, we challenge ourselves to take the initiative to make good things happen.

Winners Take The Initiative

Winners don't wait for someone else to step forward. Winners don't sit on the sidelines and hope someone else will say something that's significant or make the right decision. Winners take the initiative. Winners take the responsibility. Even in meeting people, winners step forward and introduce themselves.

I've instructed game captains in football, "When you go out onto the center of the field for the coin toss, take the initiative. Step forward and give a confident smile. Introduce yourself to the officials and the other team captains before anyone else has a chance to do anything. With confidence and a sparkle in your eyes, say, 'I'm looking forward to a great game.' "

This disarms people. It lets them know up front that they're dealing with a winner.

I've had game captains come off the field and tell me, "They wouldn't even look us in the eyes. The game is ours!"

This is not to say that I encourage you to manipulate and intimidate people in life. It is to say that I encourage you to step forward and not hang back, waiting to do what someone else "allows" you to do. Be the captain of your ship. Sail to the horizons that, before, you have only dreamed of.

Have you ever had an idea you wanted to share with a group, but hesitated because it was *your* idea? Then later, someone else introduced an almost identical idea to the group? Have you ever wanted to apply for a position, but hesitated because you questioned your worthiness? Then someone else successfully applied, and you knew you could have done a better job in the position than this person?

The more you take the initiative, the more you are going to be in control of your life. And, the more you are in control of your life, the more input you will have about the values by which you live.

Three Valuable Lessons

When Carl Erskine, a former pitcher with the Dodgers, first came to the big leagues, he learned three valuable lessons. In his first interview with Branch Rickey, owner of the Dodgers, Mr. Rickey asked Carl if he went to church. Carl said he did. Mr. Rickey then responded, "I ask that question of every young man that I sign. The reason that I ask it is that I've found if a person will discipline his life to sit in a place of worship and get his spiritual values in place, that person will develop a quiet confidence that he cannot get anywhere else. His faith will stand him in good stead under all the pressures of life."

Carl's first major league game was in Pittsburgh. Carl didn't know anyone on the team, but an older pitcher named Hugh Casey came up to him and gave him some advice. He said, "I've never seen you pitch. I don't know if you throw underhand, overhand or sidearm, but there are guys in this league who are going to hit you. You're going to get your lumps in this league. I want to tell you something else. There are certain things in this league you can't change. You can't change the weather. You can't change the ballpark you're pitching in. And you can't change the guy calling the balls and strikes behind the plate. So concentrate on the things you can do. Keep your fastball where you want it.

Keep your curveball where you want it. And take the initiative. Be in charge."

Carl Erskine became a big winner in the major leagues. And branded in his mind were these three lessons:

(1) Spiritual discipline makes you stronger in all aspects of life.
(2) A person should concentrate on what he or she can control.
(3) A winner takes the initiative.

Courage . . . Character . . . Faith . . . Persistence

Whenever I talk about initiative, character and courage, I always think of the girl born to very poor parents in Tennessee. She was a premature baby and weighed only four and a half pounds. At four years of age, she had double pneumonia and scarlet fever. That left her with a paralyzed and useless left leg.

But she had courage, character and faith. And at nine years of age, she did away with the brace and took her first step. At 13, she entered a race in high school and finished last. But she didn't quit. Finally she began winning races and went on to run in college and later in the Olympics.

In the Olympics, she had to race against the greatest female runner in the world, Yetta Hynie. But when the Olympics were over, Wilma Rudolf had won three gold medals.

How did this girl from a poor family in Tennessee, not expected to live, then not expected to walk, and never expected to run, win three Olympic gold medals? Courage. . . Character. . . Faith. . . Persistence. She demonstrated the concept: *If It Is To Be, It Is Up To Me.*

President Harry Truman liked to use the Horace Greeley quote:

> *Fame is a vapor, popularity an accident, riches take wings, those who cheer today may curse tomorrow, only one thing endures - character.*

To be a winner, concentrate on character and courage.

175

Be like the little boy who was outside playing baseball. When he came into the house to get a drink of water, he yelled to his mother, "The score is 20 to nothing in their favor. But don't worry, Mom. We haven't come up to bat yet!"

Remember, success in life is not reserved for the most talented, for people with the highest I.Q.'s or for people with the most ability. Success is almost totally dependent on character, courage, desire, drive and persistence.

Those who make another effort, those who try another approach, those who keep on trying when others give up - these are the winners.

And when you might experience temporary failure, and when others might criticize you and get down on you and cause you to get down on yourself, think about these words of our past president, Teddy Roosevelt:

> *The credit in life does not go to the critic who stands on the sideline and points out where the strong stumble. But rather, the real credit in life goes to the man who is actually in the arena, whose face may get marred by sweat and dust, who knows great enthusiasm and great devotion, and learns to spend himself in a worthy cause; who at best if he wins, knows the thrill of high achievement, and, if he fails, at least fails while daring greatly, so that in life his place will never be with those very cold and timid souls who know neither victory nor defeat.*

Are You Ready?

Do you have the courage to be in the arena?

Are you ready to be marred by sweat and dust?

Are you ready to do what it takes to experience the great enthusiasm and the high achievements of life?

Before you answer these questions, think logically as well as emotionally. Consider what you currently have to give up, what you have to get rid of. Consider what you have to dedicate yourself to do. It's not easy. If it were, then everyone would be a winner. And, you and I both know there are losers in the world.

However, if your answer to these three questions is, "Yes," then let me challenge you to clarify your values if you have not already done so. The more you clarify your values, the more you will act rather than react. And, the more you act rather than react, the more you will find purpose and meaning in life.

Purpose and meaning in life will lead to greater self-esteem. Greater self-esteem will help you to respect other people more. This respect for others will lead to a more positive perspective of people and situations, which will give you an almost unbeatable desire, dedication, determination, discipline and powerful persistence to become a winner.

But, it's not easy. . .

Don't Give Up!

Paganini, the great violinist, was once performing before a distinguished audience when, suddenly, one of the strings on his violin snapped. The audience gasped. The master musician, however, continued to play on the three remaining strings as if nothing had happened.

Snap! A second string broke! Paganini played on without hesitation. Then, unbelievably, a third string gave way with a sharp crack!

For a brief moment, the violinist stopped. The audience knew he couldn't continue. But he calmly raised his famous Stradivarius violin high with one hand as he announced, "One string. . . and Paganini."

With a tremendous, furious skill and the matchless discipline of a gifted artist, he finished the selection on a single string. The performance was done with such matchless perfection, the audience rose together to give him a standing ovation.

There are times in all our lives when one string after another seems to snap. It would be easy to quit, easy to lower our standards and easy to forsake our values. But it is much more rewarding to continue. When we struggle through circumstances that would make quitters out of lesser men or women, we come to understand the real meaning of the word, "Winner."

I challenge you to set your goals to be a winner in all of life. And, goal-setting is the important principle coming up in chapter seven. . .

Chapter 7

SET GOALS

"What Exactly Do You Do?"

"What exactly do you do?" is a question I hear frequently. I hear it because people like to have a good handle on what other people do in life. People like to pigeon-hole people. We like to label someone as a teacher, a salesperson, a doctor, a lawyer, a hotel desk clerk, a company president, etc.

So, then, how should I answer the question, "What exactly do you do?"

I could say that I help people to win. My answer could be that I assist in human relations, customer relations and performance improvement. Or, I could describe myself as a professional motivator. To some, I'm a leadership or management consultant. I'm a professional writer and a professional speaker.

Whatever it is that *I* "exactly do," though, unless I do it, I don't get paid. And that, my friend, has led me to realize the importance of . . .

Setting . . .

Planning . . .

Working . . .

and Reaching goals!

Professional Entrepreneur

Maybe more than anything else, I'm a professional entrepreneur who signs his own checks.

I have had an opportunity to work "with" a large number of people and organizations in the past dozen or so years, but it has been a long time since I have worked "for" anyone.

My annual income has depended upon fees, royalties and commissions. I have been in the type of situation in which I don't receive if I don't produce. And, I have loved it. However, it has caused me to be extremely goal-oriented.

Years ago, I sat down one December and wrote out in detail my various goals for the coming year. Family goals, social goals, spiritual goals and professional goals were all considered.

In dealing with writing, speaking and consulting, I listed my desired financial goal for the next 12 months. When the following December rolled around, I discovered I had come within $1.19 of my proposed earnings. That made a believer out of me as to how we program ourselves with goals.

You should never set a goal just for the sake of setting a goal. The one purpose of goal-setting is to help you accomplish what you want to accomplish. Setting, planning and working toward goals has helped me tremendously in my accomplishments. And I am no more special than anyone who reads this book. Therefore, if goals have helped to make me successful, they can do the same for you. And that is why I want to share with you some goal-setting guidelines that have been important to me.

Not Many Goal-Setters

It's difficult for me to understand why more people are not goal-oriented.

Because of a lack of goal-setters in America, only three percent of Americans reach 65 with any degree of financial security. According to the U.S. Department of Labor, 97% of Americans must depend on Social Security checks to survive!

How sad. In America, the "Land of Opportunity."

What's more, only five percent of Americans who we consider to be "high income" professionals such as lawyers and doctors reach age 65 without having to depend on Social Security!

The lack of goal-setting is apparent in the area of finances, but it is likewise as bad in people's family, social, spiritual and professional lives.

The Zoo Parable

When Carl II was a small child, my wife Jean and I were excited over taking him to the zoo for the first time. We discussed how he might react to the lions, elephants, giraffes and other animals.

He looked at the sparrows.

As we pushed his stroller and pointed out all the exotic wildlife, he would glance briefly at our findings and then quickly turn back toward the little birds that flocked to pick up stray peanuts and popcorn.

Carl II was so engrossed by the little things around him, he could not concentrate upon the larger, more distinct, more unique things he had an opportunity to view.

Most people are like that. They become so involved in taking things as they come that they can't concentrate upon the larger, more distinct, more unique things that can add value and purpose to life.

Not That Easy

A golf pro was approached by two women, "Do you wish to learn to play golf, Ma'am?" he asked one of them.

"Oh, no," she said. "It's my friend who wants to learn. I learned how yesterday."

Well, learning how to play golf is just not that easy. You can't learn in one day. As a matter of fact, doing anything well is not all that easy. But there are certain things we can concentrate on that will make doing them well a lot smoother and a lot more satisfying. Setting goals makes life go smoother and allows you to achieve a great deal more in life.

"Never-Miss" Nelson

Champion bowler Nelson Burton said he reached the top because he never knew what it was like not to be able to bowl well. He said that when he first began bowling, his father made sure that he had a small bowling ball that he could handle easily. His father set up the pins in the gutter rather than in the alley because he knew that's where Nelson's ball would go. Then when Nelson was able to control the ball and keep it from going in the gutter, the pins were moved back onto the alley.

Nelson said his father made sure the pins were always in the front of where the ball was going. According to Nelson, "I don't ever remember missing." Winning programmed him to become a winner.

"Pistol Pete"

Basketball great Pete Maravich began the road to his scoring fame at the age of two when his father, Coach Press Maravich, handed Pete a tennis ball and helped him toss it into a large basket at a low height. Pete hit the first one he ever tried and continued to hit. As he grew, the ball became larger, the basket's rim became smaller and the goal became higher, but it was all relative to Pete as his body and his subconscious mind worked together to make him the proficient scorer he became. Winning programmed him to become a winner.

In your mind's eye, compare these two true examples with the picture of a child lifting a huge bowling ball with both hands, giving it a throw toward the pins set up seemingly miles away at the end of the alley and then watching it fall into the gutter after it has gone only a few feet. Or, see the picture of a small child, standing under a 10 foot basketball goal, lifting a huge basketball and shoving the basketball upward with a great heave, only to watch it come back down, getting nowhere close to the distant goal.

Winning Tradition: 83-7

When I began working with the football team that turned its 43-47 record into a record of 83-7, I told the team that the coaches, the players and I were going to work to establish a winning tradition. And the only way to establish a winning tradition is to win, and the only way to win is to set goals, make plans to reach these goals, work the plans, expect the positive results and be grateful for the winning tradition that is going to come.

We program ourselves to be winners or losers. And winners, through programming, set goals. The two fathers mentioned previously knew something about goal-setting, and they realized that one of the most frustrating things in the world is for a person to set a very high goal and to try to reach it in one step.

Have you ever taken a cross-country car trip? If so, what did you do to make the trip a little more enjoyable? Did you say, "Only 2,000 miles farther to the Grand Canyon," or did you say, "Only 50 miles to lunch!" You broke the trip into segments or stages or steps. We read a book by chapters, we paint a house by rooms and we save for our children's college education a month at a time.

Chart Your Way To The Top

Here's a chart I've used with with sports groups, business groups and other organizations. It's been modified in various ways, but basically it's the basis of goal-setting.

There are a series of steps representing short term and intermediate goals leading to the far-away ultimate goal. It is important to reach smaller, quicker goals as we strive to reach our ultimate goals. We need the successes that we experience along the way. We need the feeling of winning. We need the reinforcement that comes as we reach smaller steps striving for the top.

It is great to see parents, teachers, coaches, business leaders and other people in authority who understand this principle and who encourage those under them to achieve. It is heartening to see leaders who believe in people and help them to believe in themselves through the process of goal-setting. Reaching small, day-by-day goals and month-by-month goals lead to larger ultimate goals.

It is unfortunate, however, that many people in their early years are influenced by authority figures who discourage rather than encourage. They're programmed to be losers rather than winners.

182

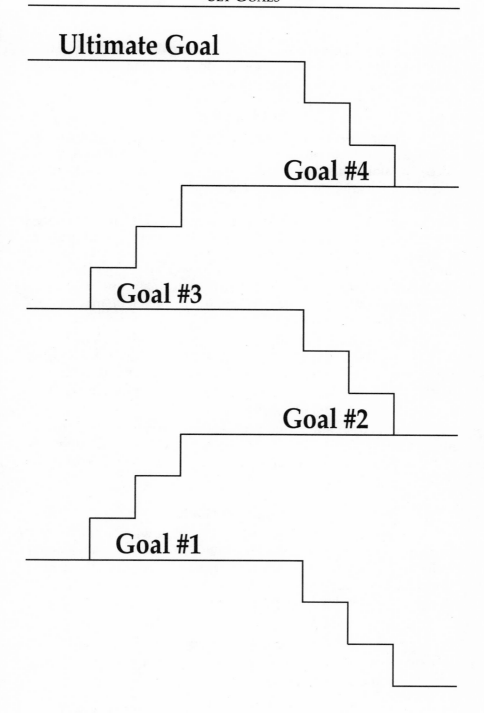

Ultimate Goal

Goal #4

Goal #3

Goal #2

Goal #1

They are told all the ways they can't do something rather than being told all the ways they can do something. They learn to picture ultimate goals as frustrating and overpowering.

The Elephant Parable

Many people never learn the method of reaching far away ultimate goals by using small steps and by experiencing small successes along the way. Thus, they become like the elephants in a circus. The full-grown elephants are kept in line by tying a small rope around one leg and securing it to a small wooden peg. The reason? As young elephants, a heavy chain secured to a large steel stake was placed around a leg. After pulling and pulling, the elephants eventually decide there's no way to get loose, and take their captivity for granted, ceasing to pull on the chain. At that point, the chain can be replaced with a small rope. The mere presence of the wooden peg and rope tells the elephants that escape is impossible and they accept it.

This is a perfect example of being programmed negatively. It's amazing how many barriers are mental rather than physical. But setting goals wisely, making plans to reach those goals and working the plans to make it happen will destroy the barriers that keep us from reaching our potential.

Some people have been programmed that they are not supposed to win. Others have programmed into them a winning tradition, so they simply go out and do the things they need to do in order to win.

Setting Your Goals

As you set your goals, first of all, think wisely, "What do I have and what can I do with what I have in order to reach where I want to go?" Don't just haphazardly set goals, like the young man who went up to the coach and, trying to impress him, said, "Coach, you're going to be proud of me."

The coach replied, "Is that right?"

"Yes," the young man said. "You know, someone has already gone to the moon."

"Yes," the coach said.

"Coach, I'm going to build a rocket that will take me to the sun!"

The coach looked at him and said, "Boy, don't you know you'll burn up?"

The boy thought about it for a few seconds and said, "Coach, I'm going at night time!"

Some people set goals with about that much thought. But in order to win - good, well thought out goals are necessary. It's sort of like Alice in Wonderland. As she walks along, she comes to a fork in the road and tries to determine which direction to take. She sees the Cheshire Cat sitting nearby, walks over to him and asks, "Which road should I take?"

The cat looks at her and asks, "Where are you going?"

"I don't know," Alice replies.

"Well," the cat says, "then I guess it doesn't matter which road you take, does it?"

If we don't know where we're going, we're probably going to wind up somewhere else. But as we plan our days, our weeks, our months, our years and our lives, things begin to fall into place and more and more, rather than just taking things as they come, we begin to cause things to happen.

Barbara Sher, an encourager, speaker and author of *Wishcraft: How to Get What You Really Want*, wrote:

> *Because so many of us never were told how to make our dreams happen, after a few times of trying, we assumed it was impossible or horribly difficult. So, we adjusted our sights downward and settled for what we thought we could get. . . Winning to me means getting what you really want.*

In a previous chapter, I said we should be realistic in setting our goals and dreaming our dreams. But when we know our strengths and weaknesses, our likes and dislikes - when we know where we are and where we want to go and what it will take to get there - we should then bring all our energies together and go for it!

Going For It

Step Number One: Set Specific Goals

I refer back to that December a number of years ago when I wrote down exactly what income I wanted to realize in fees, royalties and commissions during the next year. It was important that I didn't use vague terms like "a lot of money" or "enough to live on."

Rather than someone saying his goal is to be a better husband, he should state specifically what it is he must do in order to become a better husband - or father - or businessman.

An athlete may say to me, "My goal is to run faster."

I might reply, "That's not a good goal. It's not specific enough." I would then ask him how fast he is currently running the 40 yard dash. If he tells me his time is 4.8 seconds, then I would ask, "How fast do you want to run the 40? Do you think you can eventually do it in 4.7? 4.6? 4.5?"

In other words, I want the athlete to state specifically what he is shooting for. The goal he sets should be one he would really have to work for in order to reach it. Realistically, though, it should not be out of sight.

What are some of the specific things you want to achieve? Project as far as you can, naming some of your ultimate desires. As I have suggested previously, consider financial, family, social, spiritual and professional goals.

Setting your specific goals will help you to feel that you are in charge of your life. The goals will give you more purpose and meaning. They will lead you to believe that your future is up to you and is not just one big unknown.

As you set your specific goals, please keep in mind that people who set goals just beyond what they can reasonably expect of themselves are the ones who accomplish more and find more happiness.

Stretch As You Reach

Weight lifters know that strength cannot be increased by lifting weights that do not challenge the muscles. Strength is increased by lifting weights that are difficult, that stretch the muscles, but can realistically be accomplished.

Step Number Two: Put Your Goals In Writing

A professional speaker made a presentation on goal-setting at a major American university in the East. He especially emphasized the importance of putting goals in writing. Following the address, a group of the school's intellectual elite discussed the speaker and his comments. They felt he was wrong and decided to prove it.

The group surveyed the senior class and discovered that only three percent of the students had any written goals. Ninety percent had no specific goals at all, written or unwritten. The group kept track of the graduating class. Ten years later they conducted another survey.

The group found there must be something to written goals after all. And, to their credit, they let the results of their survey be known: The three percent with written goals had achieved more than the other 97 percent combined!

Crystalize

When a goal is written down, it is crystalized. You know exactly what you want to do and, as we shall inspect in the next step, you can better make plans to reach your goal.

Also, putting the goal in black and white will help you to remember it better. Consciously, you will be more aware of it. And, the writing of the goal will impress it upon the subconscious mind more. This will lead the subconscious mind to work 24 hours a day to help you obtain the goal.

After you have written down your goal, be sure to look at it as often as possible. I have my goals written on little cards which I have covered with plastic and carry with me. While waiting in airports, offices and riding in cabs, I have taken these cards out and read them.

The World Within Makes The World Without

In working with sales groups, I have asked them to commit to paper exactly what they want to sell this year, this month, this week, today.

To help athletes improve or prepare for certain contests, I have asked them to put on paper exactly what they must do.

As you write down your goals, remember it is the world within that makes the world without. What you write, what you truly believe and what your subconscious mind accepts will lead to what you achieve.

Be specific and concise when you write your goals so there will be no doubt in your mind of exactly what you are going to accomplish.

Step Three: Develop A Plan And Determine A Deadline

To Make $100,000

Let's suppose a few years ago I was receiving $1,000 per speech presented, $500 per magazine article written and five dollars for every room booked into a convention hotel.

Then, let's suppose I set a goal to make $100,000 in a certain year. To break it down into a plan and deadline situation, I set my sights for the year on making 50 presentations ($50,000), writing 30 magazine articles ($15,000) and booking 7,000 rooms for the convention hotel ($35,000).

To realistically accomplish this, I determine I must make about four presentations per month, write about two articles per month and average booking about 585 rooms per month.

This would amount to about one presentation per week, one-half article per week and 135 rooms per week.

To Press 250 Pounds

Suppose a young man who is a freshman in high school has a goal to bench press 250 pounds by the beginning of his senior year. If he now presses 160 pounds, he will have to press 175 by the end of his first semester, 190 by the beginning of his sophomore year, 205 by the end of the first semester, 220 by the beginning of his junior year and 235 by the end of the first semester of his junior year. He can then realistically reach his goal of bench pressing 250 pounds by the beginning of his senior year.

As he continues to climb, step by step, session by session, week by week, success by success, all the way to his ultimate goal, he enjoys smaller successes along the way.

But suppose this freshman who could press 160 pounds told me that he wanted to bench press 250 pounds, and the next day goes into the weight room and places 250 pounds on the bar? He gets on the bench and tries to raise the bar and nothing happens. He says, "Well, I'll do it tomorrow." The next day he puts 250 pounds back on the bar and still can't budge it. He could continue to do this for a long time, but he'll never reach his goal. Eventually he'll get discouraged, overwhelmed, snowed under and quit.

Goal-setting helps prevent this situation. If you plan wisely, if you do it step by step, if you experience smaller successes as you reach toward your ultimate success, good things will happen, because you will make them happen.

Distorted Notion

Many people have a very distorted notion of how things actually get done in this world. They think that accomplishments come from great, all of a sudden, overnight deeds. In sports, they see champions winning suddenly. They see Olympic divers simply striding out onto the board, pushing off and entering the water. They see swimmers simply diving in and naturally pulling themselves along in a smooth fashion. They see basketball greats all of a sudden picking up a basketball and doing magic with it. They see golfers strolling onto the golf course and shooting under par.

People who think like this need to talk with Mary Lou Retton about the six to eight hours daily she worked to reach smaller goals on the way to her ultimate goal. They need to talk with Greg Luganis, who set so many goals and worked so many hours to reach these goals in diving, that his hands became calloused from entering the water. They should talk to Mark Spitz who was disappointed when he won only two gold medals in the '68 Olympics and then reached his ultimate goal of seven medals in the '72 Olympics. They should talk to Larry Bird who literally locked himself in the gym to practice to reach the personal goals he set for himself. They should talk with Arnold Palmer who spent up to 10 hours a day on the golf course working to reach the personal goals he set until he said the club felt like an extension of his body.

In the business world, many people see successful operations and decide they, too, "can do that." Then, when they fail because of a lack of planning and proper preparation, they can't understand what happened.

At least a dozen people have seen my hotel sales organization book over 15,000 room nights annually and have decided they want to do it also. They haven't lasted very long. They should have embedded in their minds a sign that should be in every locker room, office and home. . .

Proper Preparation Prevents Poor Performance

People don't build successful businesses in a matter of weeks. People don't soar to stardom from out of nowhere, nor do they become great athletes by simply putting on a uniform. If it were that easy, everyone would do it.

Such "overnight success" type of thinking gives rise to painfully unrealistic self-expectations. Great deeds are made up of small, steady actions. You must go one step at a time.

A football team might want to win the state championship, or a national championship or the Superbowl, but each team must win that first game first, then the second, then the third. . . on the way to the ultimate goal.

A Dream Comes True

In the 1920's, Ray Kroc sold paper cups to restaurants and worked his way up the ladder to become one of his company's top salespeople.

Then, he began to dream about what could be accomplished in the restaurant business. He gave up the security of his job to go into a milk shake machine venture, selling machines that could mix several milk shakes at the same time.

Ray Kroc then focused upon a very small but popular restaurant in California and persuaded the two brothers who owned the restaurant to buy his machines, and to allow him to go into business with them. The business flourished as these new machines enabled them to make 48 milk shakes at one time on the eight multi-mixer machines.

Ray Kroc's dream became more focused as he set a goal to capture the fast-food restaurant business. He bought out the two brothers, kept their family name on the business, and built McDonald's into a billion dollar empire in 20 years.

Ray Kroc was 52 years old when, by his own definition, he became "successful." And, he started on the road to success when he chose a specific goal, embedded it in his mind and then designed plans and deadlines to make his dream come true.

Discipline

Discipline is needed in planning and carrying out your goals. For example, I discovered years ago that in order to prepare for financial security, the principle of "dollar-cost averaging" works for me. It's an investor's version of strict discipline.

Did your parents ever say to you, "You'll do it because I said so!"

Or maybe you might have heard, "We're doing this for your own good."

Dollar-cost averaging may not always be easy, nor will it always feel good, but in the long run it will be good for you - like doing push-ups, sit-ups or walking two miles daily.

The dollar-cost averaging principle of investing/saving is quite simple. It merely requires the investment of a given amount of money at regular intervals in a particular savings account, stock, stock fund, etc. The advantage of a regular system, such as is used in a mutual stock fund, is that more shares are purchased when the prices are low and fewer when the price is high. Therefore, the average cost per share is reduced.

Example Of Dollar-Cost Averaging

Let's say you invest $100 in a mutual stock fund every three months, and that the fund you have chosen is selling at $10 per share. You invest $100 and receive 10 shares.

Then, let's say the market drops and the fund goes down to five dollars a share. Your investment of $100 at five dollars per share buys you 20 shares this time.

Let's assume by the next quarter the market has returned to where it was when you started and your fund is now selling again at $10 per share. You now receive 10 shares for your $100 investment.

The results? You now own 40 shares after a total investment of $300. However, with an ending market price of $10 per share, your shares are actually worth more than you paid for them.

The average price per share over the three quarters represented here ($25 divided by three) was $8.33, but the average cost to you (300 divided by 40 shares) was $7.50. You can see what would happen over a number of years.

Discipline is all-important here. You can't chicken-out when you see the market dropping. You have to be consistent and persistent in following the dollar-cost averaging system because in the long run, that's the only way it can work.

The "dollar-cost averaging" principle will work for you in areas of life other than financial. Devising plans and deadlines, breaking things down into their smallest parts and being consistent lead to reaching goals. We begin where we are, with what we have, and go from there.

A Salesperson's Goal

A salesperson may want to make $100,000 a year, but he or she has to make $100 first. Let me show you an example of how a salesman named John reached his goal of making $40,000 a year.

John earns $210 on each sale. One out of every three people who hear his presentation buy from him. By dividing $210 by three, we learn that John earns $70 per presentation. We also learn that only one out of seven people will listen to his entire presentation. So, we divide $70 by seven and learn that John earns $10 per person he contacts.

If John works 50 weeks a year, we would divide his goal of $40,000 by 50 to find that he must make $800 a week. We then divide the $800 by five days; John must make $160 a day.

We know that John earns $10 per contact. So, we divide $160 a day by 10 to arrive at the number of contacts John must make each day - 16 contacts. If John makes 16 contacts each day, five days a week, 50 weeks a year, he's going to earn $40,000.

If we wanted even more specific information, we could say that John needs to make two contacts an hour. Now, if I said, "John, in order to earn $40,000 this year, you need to make 4,000 contacts," that would sound overwhelming. But what if I said, "John, to make $40,000 this year, you need to make two contacts an hour;" that would sound very attainable, wouldn't it? Using smaller steps, we can move from where we are to where we want to be.

I can't stress enough how important this concept is. It's so simple and, yet, dividing large goals into smaller, attainable ones is absolutely essential!

Step Four: Develop A Sincere Desire

Let's face it, we can have all types of plans for goal-setting and attainment, but the big question is: **HOW MUCH DO YOU WANT IT?** Just kind of hoping to do something won't get the job done. A burning desire to achieve something is the greatest motivator of every human action.

Strong desires create strong habits. Strong habits create success.

Human desire is a powerful force to contend with. How much you want to win in sports, in school, in family and in business plays a vital role in reaching the goals you set.

I'm the type of person who likes to "try things," and I have tried much. And, I have discovered time and again that the people who have laughed at some of my attempts, or scoffed behind my back, have later congratulated me upon my success. When people have doubted my ability to accomplish certain things, this has spurred me on and has instilled within me a greater desire.

Such "spurring" helped me to become a successful professional writer, speaker and consultant.

When I left a very stable, well-paying, good-benefits position to become a free-lance writer/speaker, some people told me (and more people told other people) that I was crazy - or at least not very smart. I was determined to make it. My desire to do what I am doing today was so great that I was willing to risk humiliation and financial disaster to make it happen.

It Hasn't Been Easy

It hasn't been easy. Early on, Carl II came home from school with the question, "Dad, are we poor?"

This caught me by surprise! "Why do you ask?" I responded.

"Greg (one of his friends) said we are."

Nine years later, Carl II came home with the question, "Dad, are we rich?"

This caught me by surprise! "Why do you ask?" I responded.

"Dean (one of his friends) said we are."

Perceptions are in the minds of the perceivers!

I've been truthful with you up to this point and I plan to be truthful with you beyond this point, so I had better 'fess up and be truthful now: In the early days, even though my desire was great, I considered giving it up. But the support from my wife Jean benefited me greatly - and I wanted it so much, I knew that even though I did consider throwing in the towel, I would never really do it. In chapter six, I wrote of values and of the power that man receives from God. In my personal struggle with failure and success, these values were vital.

A great boost to my career occurred when I made a presentation at a "speakers showcase." Meeting planners from across the nation attended; speakers and would-be speakers presented our wares to these decision- makers.

On the morning that I spoke, an older, more experienced speaker pointed to a man and told me that he was the most important prospect present. "He has influence," I was told, "and if he likes you, your content and style, it can lead to some bookings." I kept my eye on him!

I was standing in the rear of the ballroom, listening to the speaker who was on prior to my presentation. One eye on the speaker and one eye still on the important decision-maker. The speaker concluded. The important prospect stood up and headed for the exit. My heart fell!

I wanted him to hear me speak so badly that even though it was time for me to go down front and onto the stage, I headed for the same exit he was using and met him in the hall.

I walked up to him, looked him in the eyes and said, "I'm Carl Mays. I'm speaking next, and I would appreciate it very much if you would stay and listen to me."

He looked at me, nodded his head, turned around and went back in. I took my place on stage.

The man booked me for a state-wide meeting, which led to similar meetings in three other states, which led to a national meeting, which has led to well over a hundred meetings in 44 states!

When you really want something, you go for it.

A Lesson From Socrates

The Greek philosopher Socrates would take his students to the countryside or the mountains and talk about life. One day, a young man asked him, "How can I obtain great wisdom?"

Socrates casually led the young man into the water, then grabbed him by the throat and pulled him under the surface. The young man fought with all his strength and pushed to the top. Amazed and bewildered, not to mention soaked and scared, the student said, "What's the matter with you? I asked you how to acquire wisdom and you tried to kill me!"

Socrates said to him, "When you want wisdom as much as you wanted air, you will acquire it."

Simply put, if you want to realize your potential, if you want to become what you can become, if you want to gain the joy and satisfaction that can be yours, you have to give it your best. And the stronger your desire, the more likely you will give it your best.

In setting, planning and working to reach a goal, you must be on the lookout for side issues which might detract from your primary purpose. You must avoid superfluous diversions which may be fleetingly pleasant but not lastingly worthwhile.

It has been said that success is a process of selection and elimination. That is, to have sufficient time for things that count, you must cut out things that do not count. And, if you really want something, with a deep, burning, unquenchable desire, then you will do what needs to be done to get it.

In sports, you often hear a losing coach make the statement: "I guess they just wanted it more than we did."

In families, you often hear parents say: "I just can't do anything with those kids."

In marriages that become divorces, you often hear one of the partners say: "There's no way we can work things out."

In communities, you often hear citizens say: "It's all just political, there's nothing we can do about it."

In businesses, you often hear owners or managers say: "We just can't make a go of it anymore."

How much do you really want what you say you want?

They Just Work Here

As my wife and I travel around the nation, staying at various hotels, eating in numerous restaurants, shopping in different stores and flying available airlines, we have come up with the phrase: "You can tell he/she just works here."

What we mean by that is, it is usually easy to determine if someone has a vested interest or ownership in something or if someone is "just there." The desire to please the customer is usually in direct proportion to the interest in the business.

I have dealt with straight-salary salespeople who make it very evident they don't care whether or not I purchase something.

Some hotel desk clerks would rather you would not check-in while they are on duty.

In a future book based upon some of my talks and seminars, I will share ideas on how leaders - managers - coaches - can motivate people to act "as if they own the place," or at least have a vested interest.

Let's face it, you are never going to become all you can be if you allow yourself to do less than you are capable of doing. And, to do your best, you must want to do your best.

Do you merely "wish" for something or do you have a great desire for it? Do you "hope" it will happen or do you know you can make it happen?

The World's Best Residential Real Estate Salesman

Nicholas Barsan, a Romanian immigrant living in Queens, New York, was labeled "the world's greatest real estate salesman" in 1987 by *Success* magazine. In 1986, he earned $1.1 million by closing 90 deals worth $27 million.

When asked about his success, Barsan, who had been selling houses only four years, said, "To me, nothing is impossible. . . Attitude is number one with me. It affects my life, the way I look at everything. . . The important thing is not the number of hours you put in; it's how you plan your time, what you do with it. . . and how much desire you have. . ."

To his colleagues, Barsan is a legend, a model of self-initiative. The $1.1 million he earned in 1986 did not even count the many calls he made to help out his associates at Metalios Real Estate, whose 70 salespeople pulled in $7.5 million in commissions.

When describing Barsan's skills, his colleagues point out such traits as geniality, authority, perseverance, discipline, persuasiveness and *desire*.

Two Keys In Winning

I've often talked to athletes about the two keys in winning a ballgame or winning in anything: (1) the emotion that we take into the contest and (2) the way we "match-up" with what opposes us.

197

The first key determines the intensity, excitement and enthusiasm we have in a situation. The second key determines the way we use our strengths to overcome the strengths and to exploit the weaknesses of the opposition. The first key is triggered by desire. The second key is dependent upon how wisely we channel that desire.

Dance Every Dance

Sam Rutigliano, former head coach of the NFL's Cleveland Browns, once described defensive player Lyle Alzado as someone who "danced every dance."

"He was like a communicable disease," Rutigliano said. "He spread his desire and excitement in all directions within the team. That's what morale is all about. It can be good or bad, but it'll spread throughout your team, either way."

The game of football may be a perfect miniature representation of the game of life. And, according to Rutigliano, ". . . football is a very emotional game, and it's played from the neck up. It's an emotional game played in the real estate between your ears. People talk about the physical aspects of football, but emotion is what it's all about."

Emotion in football or in life depends upon desire. When focused intelligently, desire leads to victory.

Step Number Five: Don't Take Your Eyes Off Your Goals.

The Sharks' Teeth Parable

Not long ago, I had a speaking engagement at Litchfield Beach, South Carolina. My wife and I spent three nights there and had a wonderful week-end. The conference went well, the weather was perfect, but in order to make it 100% successful, we needed to walk the beach and find some sharks' teeth for my wife. We'd been on a number of beaches, but we'd never found the sharks' teeth that she so badly wanted.

So, we walked down to the beach. She began walking in one direction and I in the other as we combed the beach. In about an hour and a half, I returned empty-handed. She returned with over a dozen sharks' teeth.

"What did you do?" I asked her. "Did you catch a shark and pull the sucker's teeth out?"

She then told me, "You know, every now and then, I listen to you."

"Good," I replied, "but what does that have to do with sharks' teeth?"

"I focused," she answered. "You know how you're always talking about the power of focus."

I nodded.

"Well," she continued, "I began to focus upon only those things dark and triangular - like sharks' teeth. I may have missed some beautiful shells, or maybe, some gold coins. But the sharks' teeth seemed to jump out at me."

The power of focus - of keeping your eyes on your goals - does wonders.

Never Lose Sight

Florence Chadwick wanted to be the first woman ever to swim the English Channel. For years, she trained to reach her goal, disciplining herself to keep going long after her body cried out for relief.

Finally, the big day arrived. She set out for her goal, full of hope, surrounded by the press and well-wishers.

Things went well, but as she neared the coast of England, a heavy fog settled in and the waters became increasingly cold and choppy.

"Come on, Florence!" her mother encouraged her from a nearby boat as she handed food to her. "You can make it! It's only a few more miles!"

Then, not realizing she was within just a few hundred yards from the goal, Florence Chadwick became completely exhausted and asked to be pulled into the boat. She was defeated and heart broken, especially when she discovered how close she had been to reaching her goal.

She told news reporters, "I'm not offering excuses, but I think I could have made it if I had been able to see my goal."

Later, like a true winner, she bounced back from her temporary failure. She tried again. And, this time, she concentrated on developing a mental image of the England coastline. She memorized every feature of the distant coast and held it clearly in mind.

The big day arrived. Again, she ran into the fog and the cold, choppy waters. This time, however, she reached her goal. She became the first woman in history to swim the English Channel.

She accomplished what she had set out to do because she never lost sight of her goal. Even when physically she could not see a thing, her goal was always in focus in her mind's eye.

Potential With No Direction

I know a very talented, very intelligent young man who could choose any number of areas in which he could be successful. However, Ted (let's call him Ted) doesn't stick with any one thing long enough. Do you know someone like Ted? Someone who gets side-tracked easily? Someone who bounces from one thing to another?

Or, maybe you know someone like Judy. She is attractive, eager and talented. Life excites her and she has a way of exciting people around her. But she has no focus. She becomes involved in one cause, then leaves it behind and picks up another.

Judy may or may not keep an appointment or live up to a commitment she's made. She has all the potential in the world, but the potential has no direction, no focus.

A Lesson From Archie Griffin

Several years ago, it was my privilege to share the speaking platform with Archie Griffin, two-time Heisman Trophy winner who played his college ball at Ohio State before going to the pros. That evening when he spoke, Archie talked about his own brand of focus.

"People have asked me, 'Archie, what is it that spurs you on, that makes you the runner you are?' "

Archie then paused before he continued, "I tell these people that every time I go back in that huddle and my number is called,

200

I say to myself, 'Archie, this may be it. This may be the last time you'll ever run the ball. You may may go down with a knee injury, you may break your neck. . . you don't know what will happen.'

"Then I ask myself, 'Archie, if this is it, how do you want to go out? If this is your last run, do you want to be remembered giving it your best shot - or do you forever want to remember it as the time you gave less than your best?' "

Such a focus led Archie Griffin to those two Heisman Trophies, an award presented annually to the person chosen as the best college football player in America.

Are you keeping your eyes on your goals?

Keep Your Eyes On The Ball

Former tennis champion Billie Jean King recommends that tennis players set aside 15 minutes a week and do nothing but stare at a tennis ball. "If you can stay interested in the tennis ball by doing nothing else but staring at it for 15 minutes," King said, "it will make it that much easier to stay interested in the ball and pay attention to it more in a match. And if you can pay enough attention to a ball in a match, distractions will become less of a problem for you."

Setting goals means little if we allow ourselves to get off course. We have to stay aware of where we're heading and stay determined to keep on track.

Step Number Six: Concentrate On The Task At Hand.

In other words, do the things you need to do in order to reach the goals you need to reach. And do them now!

Develop a strong determination to follow through on your plans regardless of obstacles, criticism, circumstances, weather or what people might say or do.

Set priorities. Inspect your priorities. Are you actually doing the things right now you need to do in order to go where you need to go? It's a simple question and your answer will reveal to you whether there's a strong possibility you will reach your goals and become the person you want to become.

201

My belief has been, if we take care of the little things, the big things will take care of themselves. If we concentrate on the day-by-day small details which go into making something perfect, then big things will happen.

Pay Attention To Details

I recently had the opportunity to hear former UCLA basketball coach John Wooden speak. As coach at UCLA, he won an almost unbelievable 10 NCAA championships. Coach Wooden told us, "Over the years, I became convinced that every detail is important and that success usually accompanies attention to little details. It is my judgement that it makes the difference between the champion and the near champion."

I mentioned earlier that a sign in my office reads, *Proper Preparation Prevents Poor Performance*. That's more than just a tongue twister. Let's face it. If we're ready for something, when the time arrives, it makes all the difference in the world if we're prepared. If we prepare to meet the little details, then few surprises will be sprung on us.

Behind The Scenes

When speaking, I may present pretty much the same ideas 75-100 times a year. I may use the same stories and examples over and over again, adapting them to various groups. However, I never make a presentation unless I take time to write down an outline and then go over the ideas, stories and examples.

In working with hundreds of meeting planners through the years, I can certainly appreciate the ones who pay attention to the little details that make a meeting run smoothly.

In the letter of agreement sent out from my office, we pay attention to the type of microphone to be used, other audio-visual needs, height of platform or risers, arrangement of chairs and/or tables, the room temperature, etc.

Attention to detail and concentration on the task at hand, such as how a football team stands during the playing of the national anthem, and which hand the players hold their helmets in, leads to winning.

Recently, I checked-in at a very expensive hotel where I was going to speak. I had a mini-suite with a large balcony with tables and chairs overlooking the city. The furniture in the room was of high quality - the king bed, sofa, chairs and tables were impressive. But the details betrayed the room.

Water marks and a sticky substance were on the beautiful marble top leisure table, even though a basket of fruit and a bottle of wine had been placed on the table. The facial tissue dispenser in the bathroom was empty and the roll of toilet tissue was about empty with no spare in sight.

Details. Concentration on the task at hand.

The late Dr. R. G. Lee, former pastor of one of the largest churches in the Southern Baptist Convention, Bellevue Baptist, Memphis, Tennessee, was greatly respected and admired by thousands of ministers and young ministers-to-be. Once in a question and answer session at a seminary, he was asked, "What is the last thing you do before you walk out to the pulpit?"

The students sat on the edge of their seats, pencils in hand, awaiting his reply.

His answer: "I check the zipper on my pants."

Details. Concentration on the task at hand.

Step Number Seven: Don't Set Your Goals Too Low - Or Too High

The better you know your strengths and weaknesses, your likes and dislikes - the better you know where you have been, where you want to go and what it will take to get you there - the better you can set your goals at just the right height.

There is an art to goal-setting, not only in setting your ultimate goals but your short-range goals along the way. As I have mentioned previously, if you set your goals too low, there is not enough challenge. If you set them too high, you can become frustrated and give up.

Dream Forward - Work Backward

As you set your goals, keep in mind that people usually overestimate what they can accomplish in a short period of time and usually underestimate what they can do in a longer period of time.

To overcome this problem, you should set goals far enough ahead so that the vision of what you can accomplish won't be muddied by the present. Using the goal chart that I presented earlier, dream big dreams, projecting as far into the future as possible. Then, work your way backward as you build your stairway to the top.

There are not many things you could not accomplish if you give yourself five, 10 or 15 years in which to do it. And, you won't grow impatient along the way if you are constantly reaching smaller goals, yearly, monthly, weekly and daily.

Self-Imposed Limitations

Remember, most of our limitations are self-imposed. We often put caps on our talents and abilities and, thus, our dreams.

As two big football rivals prepared for an upcoming game of extreme importance, everyone, including the players on both teams, expected it to be a close game, to be decided by a touchdown, or maybe a field goal or extra point.

In speaking to one of the teams prior to the game, I told the players, "This game doesn't have to be close, unless you allow it to be. Don't let the expectations of fans, sports writers and the players on the other team cause you to expect less of yourself."

I went on to tell the team, "You should not go into the game expecting it to be close. You should beat this team 30-0."

The final score was 35-6, our favor.

Stay Hungry

I'm sure you're familiar with the *Rocky* movies. In *Rocky I*, Rocky Balboa had the goal to go 15 rounds. He didn't win the fight, but he reached his goal. In *Rocky II*, he grew and his goal grew. His goal was now to win the world championship. He won. In *Rocky III*, he lost his crown because he lost sight of his goal. He forgot his priorities. He got accustomed to the good life. He wasn't hungry anymore.

That's when Apollo Creed, his one time foe, challenged him to find the *eye of the tiger*. He took him back to his beginnings. He took him back to the sweaty, dirty, cramped gym. Rocky found the eye of the tiger, he got hungry again and regained his world championship.

The advice here is, "stay hungry." Winners never become self-satisfied. A winner is always aware of what he or she doesn't know and works to improve. A winner says, "I was great this time but I'm going to be greater next time."

A winner lives with the eye of the tiger.

And, to find the eye of the tiger, use "visualization," as described in chapter eight. . .

Chapter 8

VISUALIZE

The television commentator spoke in a soft, hushed tone as the golfer approached the ball. "He's getting ready to putt," the announcer said. "Usually a good putter, he seems to be having trouble with his long putts today. However, he's had no trouble dropping his shorts."

There was a moment of embarrassed silence, then the station broke away for a commercial.

We've all had embarrassing moments. We've all said things we did not mean to say. We've all done things incorrectly or fallen short of our expectations. And, many of us have endured some embarrassing times on the golf course.

I once read this rule from a country club's beginner's manual: "If you have taken 15 strokes on one hole and have missed the ball three times, you are allowed to pick it up and throw it!" To have to take advantage of that rule would be embarrassing! Sometimes it's not much fun being an amateur golfer. Those balls have a way of landing on fairways other than your own.

Difference Between Novice And Champion

But one way that we can improve our performance in golf or anything else is visualization. The principle of visualization will assist us tremendously in any endeavor. As I've mentioned, one difference between the novice and the champion is that the novice thinks, "I hope it gets on the green." The champion actually sees the flight of the ball and where it lands on the green before he or she ever hits it.

The difference between the novice salesperson and the champion is that the novice thinks, "I hope I can make this sale." Meanwhile, the champion actually sees the sale in progress, knows what the prospect's objections or questions will be, knows how to respond and sees the sale coming to a successful conclusion before the presentation is ever begun.

Jack Nicklaus, champion golfer, says that before he putts, he visualizes the putter moving forward, feels the impact as the putter meets the ball, watches it roll to the cup and feels the success of the ball's dropping into the cup. "Then," he says, "I'm ready to putt."

Similarly, a champion salesperson experiences a "mind rehearsal" prior to making a presentation. He or she vividly visualizes the situation, sees the changing expressions on the client's face, sees the interest rise and gains an even greater feeling of confidence as the client is persuaded. Finally, the champion hears the client say, "Yes, I want to go with that." The champion then visualizes the contract being signed and later sees himself or herself celebrating. After visualizing all of this, the salesperson is ready to make the presentation.

Seeing Things Happen Before They Happen

Visualization is seeing things happen before they actually happen, then doing the things that need to be done to make them happen. Simply put, visualization is making pictures in your mind.

Throughout **A Strategy For Winning**, I've emphasized the tremendous power of the subconscious mind. When you visualize, you form vivid pictures in your conscious mind. Then, you continue to keep these pictures of your goals or objectives alive until they sink into your subconscious mind. When they reach your subconscious mind, untapped energies are released to help visualized pictures become reality.

207

Let me give you a personal example of exactly what I'm talking about:

The Story Of The Luxury Car

Several years ago, I wanted to buy a luxury car. I cut a picture of the car from a magazine, the color and style I wanted, and framed it on a wall in my office. Wanting to obtain the best deal possible, I typed a script of what I was going to say and do when I went to make the purchase.

Prior to going to the dealership, I rehearsed the event in my mind. I visualized it. I talked aloud as if it were actually occurring.

In my mind, I saw myself arriving at the dealership and saw a salesman approaching me as soon as I got out of my car. The salesman was about 5'10", with light brown hair and a pretty sharp dresser.

I took the initiative, introducing myself to him before he could tell me his name was John. I then said, "John, there's something I would like for you to do - something that would benefit both of us."

"What's that?" he asked.

"I would like for you to introduce me to your General Manager. I need to talk to him about something."

You see, I knew that with the deal I wanted, things would eventually wind up where I would have to talk with the General Manager anyway. Still visualizing, I was introduced to the General Manager. I then handed him an outline of my proposal and discussed it with him, point by point.

I had done my homework, researching the mark-up percentage on various cars, the average profit dealers made on various styles and then focusing on the car I wanted.

We bickered and dickered for a while, as I knew we would do. Then I received the deal that I knew I would receive. Then the General Manager, admiring my style, presence and presentation, invited me back to speak to his staff as I knew he would.

After having visualized this several times and then vividly getting into it on the 40 mile trip to the dealership on the day of the event, I arrived at the dealership, parked my car, got out and was immediately approached by a salesman - about 5'10", light brown hair, sharp dresser.

I quickly introduced myself and he responded, "My name is John." I'll have to admit this surprised even me, but at that moment I also knew I was in like Flynn!

I received the deal. The General Manager invited me to speak to his sales force the next week and told me to tell his secretary to write me a check for my fee, whatever it was. He never even asked.

I've spoken to his staff several times since then. And, I still tell his secretary how much to make out the check for!

Mental Engineering

A defensive lineman I worked with in football came to me after a game and told me that he and a teammate had visualized knocking the ball out of a runner's hand and his catching the ball and running 50 yards for a touchdown.

I asked him if he was successful. He said, "Well, in the game they had the ball about mid-field, third down, two yards to go. Kevin (the teammate) hit their fullback, the ball popped out, came my way, I grabbed it in mid-air and started running. But I got caught at about the five yard line." Of course, he was smiling ear to ear.

"That's great," I replied, "but next time, visualize yourself running a step faster."

Visualization can help you improve and keep improving. Remember, it begins in the conscious mind, seeps down into the subconscious mind and brings forth mysterious power that helps us to do what we really want to do. It is "mental engineering" at its best.

Carl's Discovery

When I first ran across the principle of visualization quite a number of years ago, it really caught my attention. I had been using it ever since I was a kid, especially in sports, but I never knew what it was called or how to use it scientifically, most effectively.

I initially read about the scientific approach to visualization (sometimes called "imaging," derived from "imagination") in a report involving three basketball teams used in an experiment. Team One was asked to shoot 100 free throws a day for three weeks. Team Two was asked not to shoot any free throws for three weeks. Team Three was asked to visualize perfectly shooting and perfectly making 100 free throws a day, without physically shooting a basket.

The results: Team Two came in last; Team One came in second; and Team Three, who visualized shooting free throws, came in first when the teams competed at the end of the three weeks.

When I finished reading about scientific visualization, I decided to try it out firsthand, even though I had not shot a basketball in quite a while. So, I went over to my sofa and lay down, closed my eyes, relaxed and began shooting free throws in my mind.

I could feel the grainy texture of the basketball. I could hear the sound and feel the impact as I bounced the ball a couple of times and then adjusted it in my hands. In my visualization, I looked up and saw the orange rim and white net with the backboard in the background. I felt comfortable and focused my eyes on the front of the rim.

As I began to shoot I could feel the slight bending of my legs, the perfect release and the follow-through with my eyes still on the front of the rim. I watched the ball barely pass over and drop through. Swish! Nothing but net. I hit 100 out of 100.

As soon as I finished this procedure, I arose, took a ball from my son's room and went outside to the basketball goal. It was the first time I'd had a basketball in my hands in months. Without taking a practice shot, I shot 10 free throws and made eight. As I shot, I felt like I had already been hitting them time and time again. I had. I had made 100 in a row in my mind.

We Fool Our Subconscious Mind

The bottom line is this: When we correctly use visualization, we fool our subconscious mind, for our subconscious mind makes no distinction in what is real and what is vividly imagined or visualized. For all practical purposes, my subconscious mind thought I had physically made 100 straight free throws! The rhythm, the feel, the coordination will all be implanted in the subconscious mind.

Most Beneficial Principle

Does it sound amazing? That's because it is. That's one reason a sports team can turn around its losing record. That's why losers in any area of life can become winners. I have often asked groups with whom I've worked on a continuing basis, "Which principle in **A Strategy For Winning** have you benefited from the most?" The majority responds, "Visualization."

Let me share with you how a young lady named Michelle used visualization.

Michelle's Story

Michelle worked in the sales department of a large convention hotel. She didn't actually get involved in front-line selling, but she did contribute to the success of conventions and meetings running smoothly. Michelle felt she had been unfairly overlooked in the department's last salary raises. She thought she deserved a raise. And, she thought she had every right to resent the fact that two employees who had been with the department for less time than she had and - in her mind - contributed less than she had - received raises.

For several weeks, Michelle didn't share her thoughts with anyone. One day, however, after I had led in a seminar at the hotel, she told me of her feelings. We discussed the situation for quite a while that day and I made it a point to meet with Michelle when I had occasion to visit the hotel.

Michelle and I discussed her positive qualities and the areas in which she was important to her department. We also talked about how she could make the department head become more aware of her value. Then, we compared the way she looked to the appearance of others in the department. We decided that in order for the department head to treat her more "professionally," she needed to look more "professional," like the front-line salespeople and others who had received raises.

With a more professional look, involving her clothes, hair and demeanor, Michelle began to visualize herself as a true professional. We talked about how to ask for a raise in a professional manner. She began to visualize herself confidently asking the boss for a raise by carefully explaining why she deserved it.

As Michelle visualized herself becoming more professional, she lost any resentment she had over the raises of others. She began to realize why she had been overlooked. She saw herself as she had been, as she currently was and as she was becoming.

When Michelle and I talked, I emphasized the importance of positive visualization. For example, if she visualized obtaining a certain position, she should not visualize the individual above her being fired. Rather, Michelle should visualize this person as moving on to better things . That way, everyone wins. It's a matter of seeing our potentials realized while not seeing another's destroyed.

Michelle did not approach her boss about a raise until she had lived with her positive visualization for several weeks. Her confidence grew and she knew she would receive the raise when she eventually asked for it.

She made an appointment to talk with her boss and the big day arrived. She was prepared. As rehearsed many times, she professionally explained her value to the department. She told of her loyalty and willingness to go the extra mile.

Not only did Michelle receive the raise she had visualized, but she also heard her boss say, "I have had my eye on you for the past several weeks. With your background and knowledge of the behind-the-scenes work here, I believe you would be an excellent sales representative."

Then Michelle heard the boss say, "I don't know why I had not seen this before."

Michelle knew that the reason the boss had not seen it before was because *she* had not "seen it" before.

Mind Tells Body What To Do

When Sebastian Coe of England set the world record for running the mile, he was asked how much more he could reduce the time. He replied, "It's all in my head. Whatever it's going to be, it's going to be my mind telling my body what I can do."

See The Invisible - Do The Impossible

George Bernard Shaw said, "Some men see things as they are and say, 'Why?' I dream things that never were and say 'Why not?'"

For years, I have had printed on the back of my business cards:

Those who can see the invisible can do the impossible.

The football team I have worked with on a continuing basis accepts "making pictures" in their minds as much a part of game preparation as anything else they do. To them, visualization is a vital part of the game.

Perfect Practice Makes Perfect

It's extremely important, however, that we use visualization correctly. Set your goals, make your plans, visualize your success; then, do the things you need to do to accomplish what you want to accomplish. Never sit back and wait for things to happen. A thread that runs through all the principles of winning and holds them together is work. Practice, Practice, Practice.

And how we practice makes all the difference in the world. I was once a starting guard on a basketball team that went through the pre-season, the regular season and the post-season undefeated. The thing I remember most about our coach is his statement: "Practice doesn't make perfect. Perfect practice makes perfect."

A successful individual athlete or a sports team that has it together mentally and physically is a powerful adversary. Their secret to success is their successful practice and hard work: lifting the weights, running the killer sprints, watching their diets, proper rest and playing the game in their minds before they ever take the field.

Things don't just happen. We make them happen. And visualization plays an important part in this. There's nothing quite like winning, and there's nothing quite like visualization to help you win.

You're Going To Make A Difference

Because of my speaking schedule, I don't get to attend all the games involving the team I've been working with for nine years. Last year, however, I was able to attend a championship game. Both teams were undefeated. We were the visitors. The stadium was filled. Emotions were high.

I spoke briefly to the team before the game. Then as they prepared to go out onto the field, I called one young man aside, a defensive end named Lee. He didn't have a lot of size, strength or speed, but with his determination and desire, I would put him up against anybody. I said, "Tonight's your night. You're going to make the difference in this game. Picture yourself getting to the quarterback."

I told Lee that, because I knew we had to put pressure on their fine quarterback and I honestly believed he could do what needed to be done.

The game began. We went ahead by seven points, then 14 points. In the second quarter, the opponent scored, then we scored again. Right before the half ended, the opponent put together a nice drive and took the ball into the end zone. Time ran out and the score now stood at 21-14, our favor.

Although we were still ahead, the other team left the field elated, giving each other high fives, low fives and fives in-between. Our players walked off the field dejected

In the locker room, the defensive and offensive coordinators talked about some adjustments. I knew that the biggest adjustment needed was one of attitude. As I've said earlier, I firmly believe that more games are lost than they are won. Other teams do not beat a team as much as a team beats itself. Many games are won in the mind, not by ability alone.

I asked the coach if I could say something to the team before they went back out onto the field. The coach asked everyone else to leave the dressing room, leaving only the players and me.

There was silence for a few seconds and then I said, "Why are you down? You're ahead 21 to 14." There was silence.

Then one player said, "Because they're happy." He hit it right on the head.

I said, "I can't believe you're letting them beat you at your own game. I can't believe you're allowing them to be mentally tougher than you are."

I talked about mental toughness, as described earlier in this book. I talked about how no one can change our winning attitudes unless we allow them to. "We should beat this team by 21 points," I said. "It shouldn't even be close and it will not be close unless you allow it to be."

I knew that we would be kicking off to them and said, "This is great. We have an opportunity to stop them and put them out of their misery early. We have a chance on the very first series of the second half to show them that they are not in control."

I paused and looked around the room. "Picture in your minds the scoreboard at the end of the game. See yourselves 21 points ahead." I paused and looked around the room again. I let them think about the scoreboard. "Now," I continued, "picture in your minds what you have to do to win by 21 points."

There was silence as I let them think about what they had to do, individually and as a group.

"Twenty-one points," I repeated. "We ought to beat this team by 21 points."

The team erupted out of the locker room.

As we were leaving, I called Lee over one more time. "You can turn it around," I said. "Make a picture of what you need to do, how you are going to do it and then get in there and make it happen. The quarterback is yours."

We kicked off. They weren't able to move the ball and punted. We weren't able to move the ball and punted. Then they started taking it down the field. It was another strong drive, similar to the one with which they ended the first half. Their fans were standing. Their team was up. Our defensive coordinator called a time-out. I was on the sidelines and caught Lee's eye. "Lee, this is it. Do it!" Time in.

It was third down and four yards to go. They were inside our 30 yard line. Their quarterback dropped back to pass. Lee shot through their pass protection and sacked the quarterback for a 12 yard loss.

The final score: 35-14. Twenty-one points.

We Make Things Happen

As I've said before, things don't just happen. We make them happen, and visualization plays more than just a small part in this. Winners expect to win in advance, and they work to do the things that need to be done in order to make it happen. Life becomes a self-fulfilling prophecy.

Sam Walton's Vision

At the writing of this book, Sam Moore Walton was named the wealthiest man in America by *Forbes* magazine. But the Bentonville, Arkansas, resident, now in his 70's, wasn't born the billionaire that he is today. He paid his way through college by operating a paper route. After college, he began his retail career selling shirts for J. C. Penney.

In 1962, Walton opened his first Wal-Mart discount store. Today, the chain has approximately 1,000 outlets spread across the nation. Analysts who have tracked Walton for years to determine why he has been so successful have consistently come up with what is considered to be his key strength.

From the beginning, Walton pictured Wal-Mart as an efficient, low-cost retail outlet that offers value to its customers. While other retailers may brag about their ability to get better mark-ups or to alter their mix of merchandise, that kind of talk has never come from Walton.

Walton has constantly focused on the steps Wal-Mart can take to contain costs. That way, the chain can continue to enjoy the lowest operating costs of any major retailer in the country. Walton's focus has always been: People don't want cheap items; they want value. We all want to get the best quality at the lowest price.

While Wal-Mart's headquarters are still in the same spartan Bentonville building in which they have been for years, Walton is no penny pincher when it comes to his employees. From the beginning, Walton has pictured employees as "associates," who share in the business with him. As a result of financial incentives, some store managers earn over $100,000 annually. Hourly employees have profit-sharing and stock-purchase plans. Scholarships are also available.

Walton is known as a great motivator. He visualized and brought into existence his dream. Now, he helps others to catch hold of the vision and grow with it. Wal-Mart's annual meetings have been described as resembling everything from religious revivals to high school pep rallies. And Walton, the man who had the vision, is always head cheerleader.

Can Visualization Help You?

Maybe you want to use visualization on the golf course, or to design a new product, or to purchase a luxury automobile, or to improve your performance as a football player, or to look and act more professional in your career. Maybe you want to use it to help in family relationships, or to do better in school, or to polish your professional sales presentation, or to hit free throws when the basketball game is on the line.

Whatever you wish to use visualization for, you must be willing to do your homework - to do the things you must do to help the pictures come true!

Know What's Happening

One day a man saw his insurance agent driving an expensive car. "Boy, you must be the world's best life insurance salesman!" he said.

"No," the agent replied. "I just tried to sell a policy to the world's best automobile salesman."

The lesson here? Know what's going on. Know what you're up against. And prepare to meet those challenges by visualizing what you're going to do. But never visualize what you are not going to do.

Avoid "Don't Do It" Visualization

Negative visualization, or what I call "don't do it" visualization, has a way of backfiring.

Just ask a certain football coach I know. His team was leading in a championship game. The opponent had the ball with not much time left on the clock. It was fourth down and they were backed up deep in their own territory. The coach knew all his team had to do was safely field the punt and pick up a first down to run out the clock. But then, right before the snap, he yelled to the player back to receive the punt, "Don't fumble! Whatever you do, don't fumble!"

Guess what happened? He fumbled. And the other team recovered and won. Visualization means visualizing what you are going to do. Never visualize what you don't want to happen.

Make It Positive

If a free throw can win a close basketball game, never tell the shooter, "Don't miss!" Rather, tell the player to "Make it!"

In baseball, rather than saying, "Don't strike out!" say "Make contact!"

What are we programming a salesperson to do if we say such things as, "Don't blow it!" "Don't foul up!" "Don't get your tongue twisted!" "Don't get your figures wrong!"?

The bottom line: Tell the person what positive action is needed and avoid implanting a negative visualization. I maintain that people dominated by negative thoughts and negative visualizations can't change things. Things change them. When you fear a possible outcome, you're setting yourself up to achieve that outcome.

Like the golfer I described earlier who hooked a ball into the woods and said, "I knew I was going to do that," or like the tennis player who double faults and says, "I knew that was going to happen," some people program themselves to lose.

Maybe you have said one of the following:

I knew I wouldn't get that promotion.
I knew I would flunk that test.
I knew that company wouldn't hire me.
I knew I wouldn't make that sale.
I knew we would lose.

Or, maybe one of the following statements has been yours:

With my luck, they'll choose someone else.
With my luck, I'll study the wrong thing.
With my luck, there won't be any tickets left.
With my luck, the flight will be cancelled.
With my luck, the ball will bounce their way.

Remember, your subconscious mind reacts to what you think and foresee - to what you visualize. Picture yourself as a winner, not a loser. I've said it before, but I repeat: Winning isn't everything, but wanting to win, planning to win and knowing how to win is.

Carl's Visualization

Let me share my personal strategy for visualization prior to a speaking engagement. I get alone. Then I tell myself, "Carl, you are terrific. You are the Number One motivational speaker in America. And you are so fortunate because today you are speaking to a terrific group, a group that appreciates you as much as you appreciate them."

I get excited about my opportunity to share. I have things down inside of me that are so great that I can't wait to release them. You almost have to put a leash around me to hold me back. It may not show on the outside, but it's bubbling on the inside, because I know I am going to say some things that will turn losers into winners and will encourage winners to reach even higher. It causes me to appreciate myself more, to appreciate and love my neighbor as myself and to appreciate and love God for making this exhilarating experience possible.

No Strike-Outs

I may not hit a home run every time I speak, but I'll tell you this: I will never strike out. It may be a triple; it may be a double. Every now and then, it may be a single, but I guarantee that I am not going to strike out as a speaker. My self-esteem, my attitude, my creativity, my visualization is not going to allow me to strike out.

What About You?

What about you? Are you now using visualization as you should? If you are not using it effectively or not at all, are you anxious to learn how? I hope so. Let me share with you six steps that will assist you as you "make pictures" in your mind.

Step One: Determine Exactly What You Want To Visualize.

As in goal-setting, make sure your visualization is specific rather than vague. Remember in the championship football game how I kept emphasizing "21 points," rather than using such terms as "a lot" or "three or four touchdowns."

As you determine exactly what you want to visualize, make sure the desire is *your* desire and not what someone else wants for you. It gets back to the question, "How much do you really want it?" If it's just a "take it or leave it" situation, you're off to a bad start. However, if you want it so badly you can almost taste it, you'll be able to see it clearly as you visualize.

Step Two: Believe That What You're About To Visualize Will Make A Tremendous Difference In Your Life.

Believe that you're going to take more control of your life. You're going to make things happen.

But be realistic. If you visualize that you're going to win *Star Search* as a vocalist this month, but haven't practiced singing and don't even know the words to a complete song, you're daydreaming rather than scientifically visualizing.

Remember Michelle who works with the convention hotel. Recall how she visualized herself being more professional. With visualization, you cannot only take more control of your own life, you can also take control of situations. You can make things happen.

Step Three: Relax.

Creativity can't be forced. Good visualization can't be coerced. Anytime your subconscious mind is involved, relaxation pays big dividends. When possible, recline. Close your eyes. Let your mind go blank. Then, as if you turn on a projector, let your visualization play on the screen of your mind. Be receptive. If your mind wanders, refocus.

Even though I want to raise my energy level prior to speaking, I still start my visualization of the event in a relaxed state of mind. That way, I can get into the proper focus.

Often, you can't lie down or even close your eyes, but you can relax. I sometimes relax and visualize as I'm driving a car. Salespeople can do this on the way to an appointment.

At other times, I have become extremely relaxed while sitting in a waiting room prior to an appointment. With eyes wide open, sitting straight up, with both feet on the floor, I have visualized what is going to take place in just a few minutes.

On an airplane or a bus on the way to a game is a perfect time for athletes to relax and visualize. In a quiet locker room prior to a game, relaxing for visualization helps prepare the athlete both mentally and physically.

Step Four: Experience The Visualization With As Many Of The Five Senses As Possible.

Remember when I told of visualizing John the salesman? I saw him as standing 5' 10", with light brown hair and being a sharp dresser. When I visualized shooting 100 free throws, I felt the grainy texture of the basketball and focused on the front of the rim.

You might smell the perfume or cologne of the client as you visualize your sales presentation. Or, maybe you can smell the autumn football scent that is in the air as you visualize the upcoming game.

You might taste and smell the chlorine in the water as you visualize your swimming race. Or, as you prepare to shoot a free throw in basketball, maybe you feel the sweat rolling from your forehead and then taste its salty taste as it trickles to the corner of your mouth. Feel the sting as it drips into your eye and you reach up to wipe it away, leaving your vision blurred for a few seconds.

Maybe you can hear the client clear his throat. Maybe you can see the smile break forth on the face of another customer as she nods her head and agrees to your terms.

Step Five: Be Enthusiastic.

There is nothing quite like enthusiasm. It brings hope where hope did not exist before. It turns on a light in the middle of darkness. It turns losers into winners.

One of the greatest qualities of a leader is the enthusiasm that he or she has in reaching a goal or objective. When a person is excited about something, the excitement is catching and it turns-on other people with whom the person comes in contact.

As a matter of fact, when I receive speaking fees, I am paid for the knowledge I share and the professional manner in which I share it. I am paid for the research, study and experience that I have organized into a definite form. But to no small degree, I am paid for the energy I share, for the enthusiasm and commitment I bring to the group.

You need to bring this same commitment and enthusiasm to your visualization. Get into it physically and emotionally. Sometimes I may visualize something so strongly that I may suddenly smile or laugh aloud or come out with, "Alright!" When I was on my way to purchase that first luxury car to which I referred earlier, I carried on a conversation. It's a good thing I was alone. A companion would have thought, "He's really lost it this time!"

The bottom line here: Visualization infused with emotion makes it powerful. You cease being a spectator and become a participant.

Step Six: Visualize As Often As You Can.

I visualize constantly and I think that successful people in various areas of life do also. My visualization may not always be as scientific as I have described it, and sometimes I get into it before I even realize what I am doing.

For example, as I'm approaching a place of business, an auditorium, a hotel, a stadium, a restaurant or a theater, I may visualize a parking place. Usually, I actually expect a good parking place to be available for me. You would probably be surprised at the number of good parking places I find.

This is not to say that I have control over inanimate objects. I don't profess to be a magician or sorcerer. However, I do know from experience that I usually find what I'm looking for if I really expect to find it.

For example, I recently had a speaking engagement in Birmingham, Alabama, scheduled to begin at 7:30 p.m. My flight out of Knoxville, Tennessee, was supposed to depart at 3:00, connect through Atlanta, and arrive in Birmingham at 4:55. That flight was cancelled after I arrived at the airport. I was rescheduled to depart at 4:00 and arrive in Birmingham at 6:05. Then, at about 20 minutes prior to departure, that flight was scratched.

Another flight was due to leave at 5:00 and would get me to Birmingham at 7:00, but it was already overbooked. The airline representative said he could get me on an 8:20 departure that would arrive in Birmingham at 10:05 p.m. Too late, of course.

Using the power of visualization, I knew I would make it to my engagement on time. There was no doubt in my mind. Here's what I visualized: I would get booked on the 8:20 flight, then rush to the gate of the 5:00 p.m. departure and get someone to swap tickets with me. No problem.

Here's what happened. At 4:35 I arrived at the gate. I stepped into the center of the waiting area and announced, "May I have your attention please!" I spoke as one with authority. Everyone looked toward me. I continued my spiel: "Who in here has Atlanta as your final destination?" I looked at them as if they were supposed to respond. About a dozen passengers raised their hands.

I looked at the dozen. "How many of you have no checked luggage?" Five raised their hands. "May I see you over here, please?" It helped that I had on a blue suit, similar to those of the airline representatives.

I explained to the five that I had to be in Birmingham for a speaking engagement. Then, I gave them brochures advertising my five-tape video series of **A Strategy For Winning**, and followed with the proposition: "If one of you will swap your 5:00

ticket for my 8:20 ticket, I will send you a complimentary set of the tapes."

A regional sales manager based in Atlanta took me up on the offer. I arrived in Birmingham at 7:10, arrived at the near-by convention hotel at 7:25, and spoke at 7:30. I had notified my business manager of the situation and she had notified the client, so stress was not too excessive on anyone's part. When I began my presentation at 7:30, I told the group of my experience and they rose to give me a standing ovation. The remainder of the presentation was a delightful piece of cake!

A few days ago, I booked an engagement with the regional sales manager who had received the tapes!

Those who can see the invisible can do the impossible.

You may also use visualization to some degree without even being aware of it. You may visualize how you will look in certain clothes. When buying jewelry as a gift, you may visualize how it will look on the recipient. You may visualize how someone is going to respond to a question you ask or a statement you make.

Special Times

However, there are special times when scientific, overt visualization should be very consciously used.

(1) Goal-Setting. I wrote about goal-setting in quite some detail in the previous chapter. As you look over that chapter again and consider the various steps involved in goal-setting, please realize that visualization will be a great asset each step of the way.

In chapter seven, I also emphasized the importance of setting *specific* goals. Visualization will help you to hone in on the specifics. As in the example I used of the athlete wanting to run faster, if he sets his goal to run the 40 yard dash in 4.5 seconds, he can use visualization to solidify it in his mind. He can see himself getting a terrific start and increasing his speed from start to finish. He can observe his perfect form and technique and see the stopwatch hands hit 4.5 as he crosses the line.

As you put your goal in writing and develop a plan and deadline to reach it, visualization will help you to crystalize what you put on paper. The fourth step in goal-setting is to develop a sincere desire, and visualization will certainly help you to do that. The better you visualize what you want, the stronger the desire will become. And, the stronger the desire, the more enthusiastic you will become as you visualize.

I suggested in step five that you should never take your eyes off your goal and I used the story of the sharks' teeth to point out the importance of "focus." How better could you possibly focus than with visualization?

Then as you concentrate on the task at hand, visualization will support your concentration. And, through the power of visualization you can set your goal at the correct height. Visualization will help you to make the right choices.

(2) Decision-Making. In an earlier chapter, I wrote about "choices." I told of how a character in my musical drama, *The Clown*, stepped forward, addressed the audience and then said: "Choices. That's what life is all about."

The evening that I received the *National Faith and Freedom Award* in October, 1987, is a memorable evening. And one thing that makes it so memorable is the fact that W. Clement Stone placed around my neck the silver medallion attached to the red, white and blue ribbon .

W. Clement Stone - founder and chairman of the six billion dollar Combined International Corporation, author of *The Success System That Never Fails*, founding publisher of *Success* magazine, co-author with Napoleon Hill of *Success Through A Positive Mental Attitude*, director of Alberto-Culver Company and chairman of the board of Religious Heritage of America - says that we humans have five great powers.

Mr. Stone lists these powers as the power to think, the power to be creative, the power to choose, the power to pray and the power to act.

I'm led to say that the greatest human power is the power to choose. We can choose to win, we can choose to lose. We can choose to succeed, we can choose to fail. We can choose happiness, we can choose sadness. We can choose abundance, we can choose poverty.

And we choose by the way we see ourselves, our situations, our lives. We choose by the way we visualize. By the way we visualize, we program ourselves. By the way we program ourselves, we set our goals. By the way we set our goals, we make our plans. By the way we make our plans, we do our work. By the way we do our work, we live our lives.

When the time comes for you to make various decisions, visualize the outcomes before you choose. Look into your future. Make your list of "pros" and "cons." Choose from the outcomes you see, then vividly visualize to make the chosen outcomes a reality.

Whatever the visualization, it is especially good to visualize at night, just before going to sleep, or in the morning right after you wake up. At these times, the conscious mind is not as open and the subconscious mind is more open. Therefore, you're more susceptible to impressions.

Visualize often. When Neil Armstrong stepped out onto the moon and then returned to earth, a reporter asked him, "What did it feel like?"

"It felt like I had been there 1,000 times before," Armstrong replied. He had done it so many times in his mind, that when it actually happened, it wasn't new. You can have the same feeling when your visualizations come true.

In Summary

Daniel Burnham wrote, "Make no little plans; they have no magic to stir men's blood and probably themselves will not be realized. Make big plans; aim high in hope and work, remembering that a noble, logical diagram, once recorded, will not die."

Everything begins with an idea. The light bulb in your room, the shoes you wear, the automobile you drive, the books you read, the television you watch - they all began with visualizations and were developed through desire, dedication, discipline and plain old hard work. Should you expect any less from yourself as you make your visualizations come true?

Visualized thoughts are like blueprints. They create a mental picture which "magnetizes" and guides the physical energy around us to flow into the form set by the blueprint. That's why the Bible tells us, "As you sow, so shall ye reap."

The Bible also tells us that in the beginning, God created. . . And now, Carl is creating; Bill is creating; Nancy, Jean, Steve, Jeff, Mark, Deanna, Carol, Tom and Cindy are creating. *You* are creating. We are creating day-in and day-out as we visualize and work to make these visualizations come true.

We are all in it together; that's why it is so very vital to enjoy, like and appreciate other people - a subject that is covered in chapter nine. . .

Chapter 9

ENJOY, LIKE AND APPRECIATE OTHERS

In a *Peanuts* cartoon, Lucy walks up to Charlie Brown and says, "Charlie Brown, I'm going to be a doctor."

"You can't be a doctor," Charlie Brown replies. "You don't even like the human race."

"I love the human race," Lucy says. "It's the people I can't stand."

Lucy may be concerned about the poor in India, the unfortunate in the New York ghettos, the indigent in Mexico, but please deliver her from those turkey people she has to associate with everyday! Yes, she loves "the human race," it's the people that drive her up the wall.

Through the years, I've noticed that so many corporations, sports teams and communities with talented individuals have never become winning groups because they can't live together, work together or win together. They're like the members of the committee that wanted to plan a New Year's Eve party, but couldn't agree on the date.

Couldn't Get Along

In my work in the hotel industry, I recently saw a convention hotel lose approximately one million dollars a year in room revenue because of conflict between departments within the hotel. One million dollars a year in lost revenue because of personal conflicts. One million dollars a year gone down the drain because four or five people "couldn't get along." Remember what I've said throughout the book? More teams beat themselves than are beat by others. More games are lost than won.

John D. Rockefeller once said, "I will pay more for the ability to deal with people than for any other ability under the sun."

Superstar Loser

A while back, I was presenting an after-breakfast talk to a group of association executives. Sitting at a table with several of the men and women present, I couldn't help but notice one woman who was very attractive, well-dressed and appeared to be extremely intelligent. I also noticed, however, that the other people at the table just didn't seem to let her into the group. And, to be honest with you, there was something about her - I didn't really know what - that seemed to turn me off, also.

Following my presentation, I stayed around to speak to some of the executives. The woman at my table exchanged a few comments with me, expressed how much she enjoyed my address, then excused herself. As she walked away, a man standing with me shook his head and said, "I sure hope she really listened to what you said today when you talked about reaching excellence through other people."

I looked at the man but didn't say anything. With my facial expression, though, I indicated, "Please continue."

"She's sharp," he did continue, "and very perceptive about most things. But when it comes to working with people..." He cut himself off and shook his head again. "It seems like she knows she's sharp, and she lets other people know that she knows."

It's not always easy being a superstar who appears to have everything. The woman was a superstar, but not a team player. She could get a lot from herself, but she couldn't get much out of other people.

Leadership

Clarence B. Randall, when board chairman of Inland Steel Company, said:

> Leadership, like everything else in life that is vital, finds its source in understanding. To be worthy of management responsibility, you must have insight into the human heart. Unless you have an awareness of human problems, a sensitivity toward the hopes and aspirations of those you supervise, and a capacity for analysis of the emotional forces that motivate their conduct, the projects entrusted to you will not get ahead - no matter how often wages are raised.

We must never lose sight of the fact that people are the principal asset of any business group, sports team, community or any type of organization. Put the people first and other things will follow. Nothing moves until people make it move.

Winning Combination

In the 1980 Olympics, U.S. hockey coach Herb Brooks wanted adaptable players who could work together. Rather than trying to assemble superstars, he sought team players who could respond effectively to pressure.

The U.S. team was ranked seventh in the eight team field and drew the toughest schedule. With the deck apparently stacked against them, they accepted the dare. First, they upset Sweden. The next victim was Norway. With each game, the U.S. seemed to gain new strength and more confidence.

Czechoslovakia fell. So did Rumania and West Germany. The U.S. team appeared to draw from some hidden reservoir to win. And the win always came with a scoring blast in the final period. The team grew closer under pressure and as a group attacked the individual weaknesses of the opponents.

And then came the big match. Standing between the Americans and a gold medal was Russia. The contest was compared to having a football game between a small college team and the Superbowl Champions of the NFL.

But the impossible happened. U.S. 4 - Russia 3. One of the greatest upsets in all sports history. There were 20 young men on the American team. As individuals they were good - as a team, they were the best in the world in 1980.

Two-Headed Snake

With great interest I read a recent newspaper report with the headline: TWO-HEADED SNAKE FIGHTS SELF FOR FOOD.

The report told of a black snake that researchers at the University of Tennessee have been studying. The part of the report that intrigued me was that if one head gets a good grip on the tail of a mouse and the second head grips the other end, they will fight and pull against one another for hours unless someone steps in to stop them.

The two heads are fighting for the privilege of swallowing the mouse, even though the food winds up in the same stomach. And the fact is, the snake could possibly starve to death or die from exhaustion unless someone intervenes to make one of the heads let go.

How much like that two-headed snake some groups are!

Whether the group is a sports team, business, family, community or some other type of organization, to succeed the group must work in unison. Like an orchestra, the best efforts of all the members must complement each other if the goal is to be reached.

Cooperation

Cooperation is what we're talking about here. And, I've heard cooperativeness described as:

"Not so much learning how to get along with others as taking the kinks out of yourself so that others can get along with you."

Take a long, hard look at the people with whom you associate. Then, choose what you consider to be their best attributes and praise them for it. Major on their positive points. This will help them to increase their self-esteem and they will appreciate you for making them glad of who they are.

If someone can truly feel, "I like me when I'm with you; you make me glad I'm me," then you and this person are going to do well together.

As stated in the very first chapter of this book, not too many of us are living up to the best we can do. Remember the farmer who told the young assistant county agent, "I ain't farming now half as well as I know how!" Therefore, we can help people greatly as we recognize their positive points and draw these attributes from them.

Performance improvement is apparent when people are encouraged to think well of themselves rather than constantly being reminded of their weak points. You are attracted to someone who contributes to your positive self-image. You feel a bond with this person. You want to be involved with this person, to work with this person. You grow to love this person.

The Strongest Point

Last year, the father of the starting quarterback on the football team with which I've been working on a weekly basis for nine seasons, told me he had asked his son what the team had done in one of my meetings. His son, Jake, told him we had talked about strengths and weaknesses. Then the father asked Jake what he listed as the team's strongest point. The father said he was surprised, make that "floored," when Jake told him that the team's strongest point was their love for each other.

The father said he thought back to when he played football and couldn't conceive of anyone on his team writing down something like that. He said everyone was too macho. He went on to say that his team also never had an 83 and seven record and had never posted four undefeated seasons. What Jake wrote down was the feeling of the team. They cared for one another and played as a well-oiled machine. There was no jealousy among them. They didn't care who received the recognition.

Working With Stinkers

Of course, you'll come across people in life whom you may not like very well. Some, you will strongly dislike. Some of these people may even be in your own organization or on your own team.

Winners, however, do not base cooperativeness upon likes and dislikes. That would be selfish. That would be placing yourself first and the organization second. A winner wants to like everybody. A winner wants to love everybody. At the same time, a winner doesn't base how well he or she can work with someone on how much he or she likes or loves that someone.

Somewhere along the line I ran across this advice: "No rewards are handed out for cooperating merely with the people we like. It's cooperating with the stinkers that counts."

You are going to deal with some "stinkers" in your life. Just keep in mind that if the world consisted only of perfect, likeable, loveable people, there would be no problems. And, in an earlier chapter, I revealed that it is the problems - opportunities, I like to call them - that make life challenging. Problems bring out our creativity, keep things interesting and help us to grow.

A Stinker I Know

Seventy-five to 80% of my speaking engagements are now by referral or recommendation by previous clients. It hasn't always been this way. When I first began as a professional speaker, I often had to struggle to obtain engagements. And, even though my fees were very reasonable (they still are, for what I provide), I often had to defend them to people who were "tight" with their budgets.

One meeting planner in particular, contacted me on a regular basis through his secretary, requesting outlines, sample handout materials, tapes, fee structures, etc. But we never got together for an engagement.

Later, I learned that he was using some of my material in his organization's newsletter without giving me credit. Also, it came to my attention that he lifted material from some of my tapes and used it as if it were his own in some of his meetings.

As requests for current materials, fee structures and such continued to come from his secretary, I treated these requests as I did the other 99% of meeting planners who are very honorable.

Then, this meeting planner was replaced. But his secretary remained in her position when the new meeting planner came on board. The new meeting planner discussed an upcoming conference with the secretary and she suggested that he obtain my services. I have done numerous presentations for this group since that time.

You never know, do you?

Obviously, the first meeting planner was a "stinker." Maybe the quarterback on your football team is a stinker. Or, maybe it's someone in your office, on your committee or even in your family. But, recall the chapter that asked the question: "Do you act or react?"

A Lesson From Robert E. Lee

Someone once asked the great Confederate leader, Robert E. Lee, what he thought of a certain individual.

"I think he is a very fine gentleman," Lee replied.

"He goes around saying some very uncomplimentary things about you," the other man responded. "What do you think of that?"

"You didn't ask me what he thought of me," Lee answered calmly. "You asked me what I thought of him."

Whether you have to deal with stinkers within your organization or outside, keep in mind that an organization's success is usually determined by how well the members work together. No organization can be fully successful if there is constant internal dissension and bickering; too much energy that should go into constructive purposes is wasted on negative or destructive activities.

Unity Leads To Championships

UCLA Basketball Coach John Wooden said, "The best players don't necessarily make the best team. . . Unselfishness, discipline and unity lead to championships."

It's interesting to note that in the history of NCAA basketball, only one national championship team has had on it the national individual scoring champion. That was way back in 1952 when Clyde Lovellette played for Kansas. The championship team usually has more balanced scoring.

As you watch winning football teams, notice how offensive linemen react when their running back or quarterback is tackled a little rougher than they think necessary. You'll see the linemen pull off the defensive men and then help up their players. At the same time, smart backs take up for their linemen and show them appreciation.

I strongly believe that lack of team unity causes more defeats than lack of talent does. And when I speak to a sports team or business group, I challenge the organization to concentrate on two things:

(1) They must improve as individuals.

(2) They must improve relationships with teammates.

They must erase cliques, play no favorites and not ridicule or make fun of others in the organization. They must be like an ideal family where everyone is important and everyone feels important.

No one is ever unimportant. You're either contributing in a positive way or detracting in a negative way. No one is just there. It's like the old saying, "If you're not part of the solution, you're part of the problem."

We Find What We Look For

And some people are a problem. They always find the bad in a situation or in other people. You may be saying, "Yeah, well you don't know the people I have to work with."

Let me share a parable with you. A man was standing outside a village one day when a traveler approached him and asked, "What type of people live in your town?"

"What type of people live in the town you came from?" the man responded.

"They're terrible, backbiting gossips," the traveler said. "Nobody could get along with them."

"I'm sorry," the man from the village said. "You'll find the same type of people here." So the traveler moved on.

Pretty soon, another traveler came by. He stopped and asked the man outside the village, "What type of people live in your town?"

"What type of people live in the town you came from?" the man responded.

The traveler replied, "Good people. They'd do anything for you. Positive, uplifting citizens."

The man from the village said, "Come on in. You'll find the same type of people here."

We usually find what we're looking for.

A man walked into a room and saw a dog playing poker with three men. He was amazed to see how good the dog was. When he commented on this, the dog's owner said in disgust, "He's not so smart. Every time he gets a good hand, he wags his tail." Some people are never satisfied.

Teamwork

A poster I've shared with groups for years is titled, "Teamwork." In Scene One, two mules are tied to one another by a rope. They're facing in opposite directions, sniffing different stacks of hay. In Scene Two, they begin to try to reach their goals but have no luck. The rope is too short and they're pulling against one another. In Scene Three, it seems the harder they pull, the harder it is to reach their goals.

In Scene Four, they have turned around, sitting down now and looking at one another, probably thinking, "Hey! If we can just get our acts together instead of pulling against one another, something good could happen." Then in Scene Five, they eat one stack of hay together and in Scene Six, they accomplish the second goal as they eat the other haystack together.

The sad thing is, there are so many groups living in Scene Three, pulling against each other and it seems the harder they work, the harder it is to reach their goals.

Knute Rockne, sometimes called the greatest football coach who ever lived, said: "A football team is like a fine watch - all

TEAMWORK!

precisioned. If one small part is not working in harmony, the watch fails to function properly."

Rockne's statement can be applied to any type of organization.

Sniffing Different Stacks Of Hay

In the business world, a recent report reveals that it costs an organization six times as much to attract a new customer as it costs to keep one. Yet, daily, businesses have to work to replace customers they lose.

And, here's the sad part: Two-thirds of the customers who stop patronizing a business are turned off by inefficient service. Relocation, changed buying habits and death, all together, account for only a third of lost customers.

On the one hand, you have part of the organization spending a great deal of time and money to attract customers. On the other hand, you have part of the organization communicating to the customer, "I don't care if you do business with us or not." A perfect example of the two mules facing two different directions, sniffing different stacks of hay.

In all areas of life, with so many teams not uniting as teams and playing as one, a united group is almost assured of a win. It's amazing what can happen to a group of people who are committed to a task and committed to one another.

United We Stand

I like the Biblical story of the young man, Gideon. When called to lead his country Israel against the enemy, he replied, "I can't do it. I am the least thought of member of the least thought of family in the least thought of tribe in all of Israel. But the emphasis to Gideon was: *Believe.*

Gideon began to believe and as his faith grew, others began to follow him. His army reached 32,000, but he was fighting an enemy army of 135,000! The odds were rather heavy against Gideon. They didn't get any better when Gideon sent 22,000 home because they didn't have winning attitudes, leaving him with 10,000 men. Then these 10,000 were reduced to only those

who were 100% committed, 100% united, 100% believers in the cause. Only 300 were left. That's 300 vs. 135,000 if you're keeping count.

But Gideon led them to victory because the enemy, in the end, beat themselves. They became confused, lost their heads and dispersed while Gideon's band fought as one well-oiled machine. As I have said before, most teams don't lose to other teams. Most teams beat themselves. It's amazing, however, what can be accomplished when a person or player has self-confidence, group-confidence and commitment to the cause.

Unbeatable Strength

A few years ago, at a conference in which I was speaking, a man asked, "Mr. Mays, what is the number one thing I can do as a leader to bring my group together?"

I replied immediately, "Believe in them, and let them know you believe in them. Help each individual to believe in himself or herself and help them to believe in each other. Help them to see their potentials are multiplied tremendously when everyone in the group joins together."

Individually, just about anything or anyone can be defeated. If I'm working with a group that has a number of "stars," I will take several small sticks, tie them together to form one large stick and ask each member of the group to attempt to break the bundle. No one can. It's too strong. Then I take a knife, cut the cord and hand a stick to each person. I then ask the individuals if they can break the sticks. No problem.

Individually, just about anything or anyone can be broken. But together, the individuals have a strength that is unbeatable, unbreakable. What seems to be an impossible task becomes very possible when each member of the group works together.

Working Together

WORKING TOGETHER FOR A BETTER SCHOOL was the headline above a story in our local newspaper. The story described how a few concerned parents formed a support group to assist a high school to achieve excellence. When the group formed, the school was inadequately equipped. And, it was not accredited by the Southern Association of Colleges and Schools.

The local school system claimed it did not have the money to supply items needed and could not pursue accreditation. The support group set some goals, devised some plans and worked the plans. Four years later, the group had raised over $100,000 to purchase library books, typewriters, computers, file cabinets, window shades, a public address system, science department equipment, athletic department gear and other items that were needed.

And, after a hard-fought battle, the school received accreditation from SACS. It was the first school in the county to be accredited, but set the pace for ten others to follow.

I know the story well, because I was charter president of the support group and remained in that position for four years. Then, for the next four years, I was school board chairman. When we had first begun, many people shrugged their shoulders and said that not much could be done. "That's just the way things are," people would say. Well, I've got news for you - nothing has to be the way it is. If a few dedicated, committed people can get together on something, anything can be changed.

Because of some lobbying and some resulting legislative action being passed, the first year I was school board chairman we had an additional $300,000 to disperse to the two schools in one city. Similar amounts are still coming in annually.

Get Turned-On

You have heard it said in different ways: The whole is larger than the sum of its parts. In sports, the great team is much better than its individual players. The great corporation is much better than its individual workers. The great community is much better than its individual citizens.

When members of a team, organization or group "get turned-on" to what they are involved in, they outperform themselves. Being a part of something that is bigger than you are, helps you to reach beyond yourself. There's nothing quite like getting turned-on. You become an active participant in something that appears to be a winning cause, whether you win or not. I've said it before: Winning isn't everything, but wanting to win, planning to win and knowing how to win is.

Don't ever get into the rut of believing that you weren't meant to win or that your organization wasn't meant to win. Don't let anybody smother the hopes and dreams that you have or once had. Don't be afraid to challenge yourself and your associates to become all you have the potential to become.

If you are willing to work to develop the unique abilities that you have; if you are willing to help your associates, team members or co-workers to get the best from themselves; if you can develop an exciting, enthusiastic burning desire to excel; and if you can get others turned-on with your own sparks, you will be a champion among champions. You will be a winner among winners.

Winners Create Winners

Winners work together. Winners support one another and believe in one another. Winners are interested in getting the job done together.

And winners don't keep winning to themselves. They share with other groups outside their own. They are not selfish. They create other winners. As Walt Disney said, "People look at you and me to see what they are supposed to be. And, if we don't disappoint them, then maybe, just maybe, they won't disappoint us."

An elderly man was planting a small apple tree. A younger man said, "Why are you planting that tree? You'll be dead before it bears fruit."

The elderly man answered, "Son, everything is not just for ourselves."

In chapter three I told of Wallene Dockery who said, "I can't pay back. I can only pay forward." You can never fully repay those who have helped you along the way. The best form of repayment is to help someone else.

The Essence Of Competition

Reggie White is known as the "Minister of Defense" in the NFL where he has been voted the league's Most Valuable Player and has become an All-Pro Defensive End. He gained the title "Minister of Defense" while a student at the University of Tennessee because he became an ordained minister, playing football on Saturday and preaching on Sunday.

In one game, late in the fourth quarter, after beating his blocker and sacking the opposing quarterback three times in a row, Reggie helped up the blocker and said, "I love you. God loves you. But brother, you've got to learn how to block!"

I think that's the essence of competition in sports, in business, in life. Let people know that we're not trying to kill them. Let people know we like them, that we actually love them as brothers or sisters. But tell them we're going to do our homework and we're going to be ready and if they haven't done their homework and are not prepared, they're going to be in big trouble.

Competition can be very positive and uplifting. But, there can be an evil side to competition. Sometimes in very strong competition, we have performers in sports, business or communities who are seeking to win so badly that they lose sight of their moral values and will do anything to win. When this happens, even if they should win, they lose and become losers.

A report recently came across the news wire, telling of how 42 cars in a small town had been vandalized. The local police were puzzled, left without a clue, until a teenage boy finally confessed. "I slashed the tires," he admitted, "but Mr. Smith paid me." Mr. Smith owned a local tire store.

Mr. Smith is like the athlete who cheats to win a medal, like the student who cheats to pass the test or like the politician who uses the office for personal gain.

But positive competition with positive participants builds character, confidence and discipline. It challenges us to reach our potentials. It challenges our dedication, desire, discipline and determination. And it challenges our opponent. We both have a chance to grow. We want to win. But we want to win with dignity and preserve the dignity of the one who loses.

In business, we strive to out-sell, out-produce or out-hustle, not out-kill. Communities battle one another for prestige, but they don't throw hand grenades.

Win With Class

I've prepared a sign to be hung in locker rooms, offices, homes and communities. The sign is entitled *CLASS*. I'd like to share it with you.

CLASS

Practice with...

"Attitudes First,

Results Second."

Commitment
Loyalty
Aggressiveness
Sincerity
Self-awareness

Play with...

"It happens in the

mind before it

happens in

the muscles."

Certainty
Leadership
Abandon
Sharpness
Self-confidence

Win with...

"Those who can see

the invisible can

do the impossible."

Creativity
Love
Authority
Smartness
Self-control

The Magic Of J.B.

Several years ago, I wrote the book, *The Magic of J. B.* A 10 year-old girl who is the fastest runner in her school, J.B. does seem to be magic. For example, she took in a sick, frail parakeet that never made a sound and through J. B.'s care, the parakeet became healthy and very noisy. Later she found a skinny, little stray kitten. She took the kitten home, talked her mother into letting her keep it and soon the little kitten became a healthy, fat cat.

Next, J. B. saw a dog get hit by a car. The dog's leg was broken and it looked like he had not been cared for in ages. J. B. took him in and he became a champion. Finally, J. B. came to the aid of a boy in her class . Other kids laughed at him, teased him or ignored him. J. B. simply became his friend. Toward the end of the book, when it was very evident that J. B. had a very positive effect on the parakeet, the kitten, the dog and the boy, some of the kids say, "She must be magic!" Then someone says, "Her magic is the love and concern she has." That's the magic we all need. That's the magic we all can have.

Believe In Me

Do people like being around you? Do you help bring out the best in people? Louisiana State University basketball coach Dale Brown is a great motivator. No matter where his teams wind up in the regular season standings, they always seem ready to play the tournament games. A few years ago, when LSU upset every team they played in the NCAA post season tournament to reach the Final Four, a sports writer asked one of the players, Derrick Taylor, "Your coach is known as a great motivator. What is it that he does that gets you ready to play?"

Derrick answered, "Well, I guess the main thing is, Coach believes in us. And, you know, when a coach believes in you, it helps you to believe in yourself."

Another basketball player, Danny Ainge, was asked how he accounted for his great turnaround in professional basketball. When Ainge first went to the Boston Celtics, he barely made the team and only later became a vital part of a championship group for several years. Ainge answered, "At first, I felt like none of the coaches or players had confidence in me and I began to lose confidence in myself. But then things began to change when they began to indicate I had potential. When they began to believe in me, it helped me to believe in myself. I became a better player and we became a better team."

Providing that type of support and concern is a skill that we all can develop. How? By simply treating others the way you want and need to be treated: Pay compliments. Express encouragement. Show you care. Take time to listen. Be thoughtful. You'll be amazed and delighted with others' reaction. Be the friend you want to have!

Three Steps To Success

In talking about people working together and winning together, let me mention three things that have been inherent in this book and should be brought into a clear focus at this point. In order to truly succeed, these three things will be of tremendous benefit:

(1) Find the thing you love to do, then do it. Success comes in loving what you do and having a burning desire to do it well.

(2) Specialize in some particular area of what it is that you love to do. Through study and experience, become an expert in that particular area.

(3) And, importantly, be sure that the thing you do doesn't lead to your success only. Your desires and goals must not be selfish. Selfish people are very rarely real winners.

Real winners concentrate upon *Win-Win* situations. There is plenty of "success" to go around. You don't have to horde it.

Bill Cates, a songwriter friend who lives in Nashville, penned a song entitled *After Morning Rain* that illustrates the *Win-Win* concept beautifully. The chorus of the song says:

> *Giving's not subtracting,*
> *it's adding, don't you see;*
> *what you lose becomes another's gain.*

Sharing's not dividing,
it's multiplying life,
like the flowers after morning rain.

I personally believe that the more opportunities I have, the more responsibilities I have to other people. And the more responsibilities I have to other people, the more opportunities will open up to me. It's another positive circle.

A Tragic Lesson From Jerry Lee Lewis

Maybe you have seen the movie about Jerry Lee Lewis, *Great Balls Of Fire!* Or, maybe you know the story of how he plummeted from the top of the entertainment world to the bottom because he ignored the views of others.

Jerry Lee was the hottest thing going in the world of Rock 'n Roll. He was positioned to reign as *King.* But then, he unwisely married his 13 year-old cousin. That was the beginning of the end of the career that might have been.

People warned him of the consequences. He was advised to quietly have the marriage annulled and back-out gracefully. He was warned to at least downplay the marriage, keep it secret if he would not dissolve it.

But Jerry Lee Lewis thought he was above reproach. He believed that his talent was so great and his showmanship so tremendous that he could do anything he pleased. He was wrong.

His fans and admirers turned against him. Record sales took a nose-dive. Major concert offers ceased.

At his height, Jerry Lee was making at least $10,000 per appearance. In the late '50s and early '60s, this was a lot of money. After the fall, he was lucky to get $500 per appearance for his band and himself.

Earlier, when I mentioned my brief Rock 'n Roll career, I told of my experience with Elvis. Well, I was on some programs with Jerry Lee Lewis - and on some programs in which he was *supposed* to appear, but was a no-show.

In '60-'61, I had taken a leave from college to promote my first record, *Daddy Rabbit* on one side and *The Locket* on the other. During this period, I lived in Memphis and traveled across the country for concerts, TV shows and dances. As you might imagine, I grew to know quite a lot about the inner-workings of the music entertainment business. I also got to meet and associated with numerous entertainers and industry personnel.

Knowing of my contacts, the fraternity of which I was a member at Murray State University (KY) asked me if I could get a "big name" entertainer for their annual dance. I booked Jerry Lee for $300. They were ecstatic! But I calmed them down by saying he might show and he might not. They took a chance that he would.

More tickets were sold for that concert/dance than had been sold for any event in the history of the campus. It became so big that my fraternity brothers just about developed ulcers, wondering whether or not he would show.

Thirty minutes prior to curtain time, Jerry Lee Lewis and his entourage appeared. It was a dynamite event and everyone got much more than bargained for. A resounding success.

And Jerry Lee Lewis, a great talent, a tremendous showman, received $300 for himself and his band. A man who could have had it all was struggling to have anything at all. A man who had played to packed, giant concert halls was now featured at a relatively small fraternity dance. And, this was only one of the many tragedies that befell him.

Why? Jerry Lee Lewis had not learned and applied the lesson: *No One Is An Island*.

No One Wins Alone

No one wins alone. Even athletes in single-player sports credit parents, coaches and others with helping them along the way.

If you are a winner, you will love yourself, but you will love other people as well. You will develop your abilities, but you will also develop the abilities of those around you.

Ralph Waldo Emerson said, "Nothing great was ever achieved without enthusiasm." Let me add to that by saying:

There is nothing as powerful and contagious as positive, uplifting enthusiasm that is handled wisely by a group of people who love one another and contribute their individual talents and abilities, coming together as one united force to reach one common cause, goal or dream!

Such is **A Strategy For Winning.**

Take advantage of this strategy today. Hesitation on your part can ruin everything. See why this is true as you read about procrastination, covered in chapter ten. . .

Chapter 10

DO IT NOW!

Claim It!

Have you ever received some clothes for Christmas and you knew exactly what you were getting before you opened the gift? Before Christmas, someone wanted you to try on the clothes at the store, to make sure they fit. Then after they're tried on and they fit and you like them, they're wrapped up and placed under the tree.

You know what you're going to receive, but you have to wait until it's time to open the gift. It's there. You know what it is. You know it belongs to you and when the right time comes along, all you have to do is claim it.

That's the way it is with **A Strategy For Winning:**

(1) You have developed self-worth, appreciating who you are.

(2) You have a positive, winning attitude.

(3) You're creative.

(4) You don't fear failure.

(5) You have clarified your values; you act rather than react.

(6) You have set goals.

(7) You have visualized.

(8) You enjoy, like and appreciate other people.

Now it's time to reach out and claim your victory.

Don't procrastinate. Claim it. Do it now!

From Ancient Greece To Rita Coolidge

An ancient Greek proverb says, "The beginning is half of your action," and many things never get accomplished simply because they are never begun. Or, maybe they are begun too late. Jumping from ancient Greeks to contemporary country music, singer Rita Coolidge claims, "Too often, the opportunity knocks, but by the time you push back the chain, push back the bolt, unhook the two locks, and shut off the burglar alarm, it's too late."

I recently told a young lady who works with me that I would give her the day off - a beautiful day in May - if she would spend the entire day with her three and one-half year-old son. "Go out and make some memories," I told her. "Grab hold of the day and do some things together. Make it count. Don't waste it." I submit the same challenge to you: Go for it!

Get On The Offensive

Look at the playbooks of football teams. Every offensive play in the playbook will show the ball carrier quickly heading straight down the field toward the goal. The X's and O's and the dotted lines with slanted blocking symbols show a touchdown being scored on every play. That's the result of being on the offensive. That's the way you put points on the scoreboard.

To reach your goals in life, you have to take the offensive. You can't sit back and wait for things to happen. You have to make them happen.

In business, you can't let your competition lead the way, causing you to constantly have to defend against them. You take the offensive with new ideas, new services, new products, new markets, new strategies for winning. You may not score a touchdown with every new effort, but at least you're going for it! You have a winning attitude and you're thinking touchdown on every play. And, importantly, you're initiating the action.

A-C-T-I-O-N

In working with sports teams, business groups and associations, I have designed a poster with the acronym, A-C-T-I-O-N.

"A" stands for attack. You don't wait for the other person, team or group to make the first move. You take the initiative.

You attack the problems or obstacles that stand between you and your goal. My football team with the 83-7 record is known for an attacking, "offensive" defense. This team, when on defense, takes the offensive away from the other team that is supposed to be on offense.

For years, McDonald's has been known for their "attack" on the fast-food business. Surging ahead with new ideas and items on their menu, a "Mc-this" and a "Mc-that," they have forced other chains to defend their markets with new items also.

A parent shouldn't wait until a child has a huge problem before stepping in to try to do something about it. The "attack" upon the problem needs to be made when early signs signal a warning.

A father came to me for counseling a while back and here's the sad story he shared: He was almost 100% sure his son was involved with drugs at the age of 12. He had planned to talk with his son about the matter and had set aside in his mind some plans to discuss the problem with him one Sunday afternoon. But, in his words, "The Dallas Cowboys were playing the Washington Redskins on TV, so I decided to wait until that night."

The father "didn't get around to" talking with his son that Sunday evening, so he planned to talk with the boy Monday - which became Tuesday, then next week, then next month. . . "That was seven years ago," the father went on to say. And now, the young man is serving time in prison as a result of his drug involvement.

Molehills are easier to conquer than mountains.

"C" stands for create opportunities. And this is exactly what you do when you attack. Waiting for the opportunities to come to you just won't get the job done. An ancient Chinese proverb says: "One who waits for roast duck to fly into mouth must wait very, very long time."

Some people spend their lives waiting for opportunities to come to them. Then, when the opportunities don't come, these people rationalize that they just weren't "meant" to succeed or to be winners. You can't afford to sit back and wait for the opportunities if you want to develop the potential that is within you.

Remember the Parable of the Talents as recorded in the New Testament of the Bible? A man called three servants before him and gave them talents. Then, he went on a journey, leaving the servants to do with their talents as they would. The first and second servants invested their talents, doubling their shares. But the third servant was afraid to use his gift and buried it in the ground. When the master returned, he was pleased to hear what the first two men had done with their gifts and he rewarded them with greater responsibility. However, he admonished the third man for hiding his talent and having nothing to show for it. The master then took from the third man the talent he had not used.

What does this parable tell us? Use it or Lose it! Create the opportunities that are inherent where you are, using what you have, or the opportunities will never exist. Actively seeking opportunities versus passively waiting for opportunities are miles apart and make miles of difference.

Success Breeds Success

You have heard the saying, "Success breeds Success." This is true, because opportunities open up for people who work to succeed. In football, a good block opens up an opportunity for a touchdown. In your career, a good track record in your endeavors opens up an opportunity for advancement. In your family, good early parenting opens up an opportunity for positive parent-child relationships during the teen years.

I've said it before, I say it now and I'll probably say it again: Nothing just happens. We make it happen.

Being In The Right Place At The Right Time

Another saying you are familiar with deals with the importance of "being in the right place at the right time." Don't attribute this to luck. Rather, attribute it to "doing something." In football, some defensive players seem to "have a nose" for the ball and wind up getting in on an unbelievable number of tackles or make numerous pass interceptions. The fact is, these players have done their homework, studied films, planned strategically and created the opportunities.

We can do the same in all of life. To be in the right place at the right time, we do our homework, study the game plan, map our strategies - and then move!

As mentioned in an earlier chapter, winners don't accept temporary failure as total defeat. Winners sometimes make the wrong moves or choices, trying to be in the right place at the right time. When some moves don't work out, alternative maps can be used.

In a behavior-test among second grade students, it was discovered that successful students try several approaches to a given problem and, if none of them work, they move on to tackle the next problem. The average student, in contrast, tries one approach over and over again, until defeated by the self-imposed label of "failure." Being in the right place at the right time often means "keeping on keeping on."

And remember, if you want to be a winner, do the best you can do at what you are currently doing, no matter what it is. If you fall into that category of people who do mediocre work where they are with intentions of doing great work when they get to where they want to be, you may discover you never will be in the right place at the right time. *Wherever you are, truly be there.*

Create Connections

A third saying that is often heard is, "it's *who* you know, not *what* you know." This saying is often used by losers who think winners become winners by knowing the right people.

Let's look at the saying in a positive light, however, and emphasize that it is very important to know people who are involved in what you want to be involved in. And, if you are prepared to take your next step in your endeavors, don't be afraid to seek help along the way.

Think and Grow Rich by Napoleon Hill is one of the most influential books of all time in pointing the way to personal achievement. And this book places a special importance upon associating with the right people. From being an apprentice while learning and sharpening your talents, to forming a Master Mind group to help you stay on the top when you get there, Hill emphasized the importance of influence. More than once, he said that the most common weakness of all human beings is the habit of leaving our minds open to the negative influence of other people. Thus, he stressed the importance of positive influence.

Step out and make contacts. You never know what will happen.

For example, I was flying to a speaking engagement in Orlando, Florida, but missed my connecting flight at the Atlanta airport. Quickly flipping through my pocket flight schedule directory, I saw where another airline had a flight departing for Orlando in 20 minutes. I rushed to the appropriate concourse and got on the plane with three minutes to spare!

I struck up a conversation with a gentleman seated next to me, telling him of my close experience and good fortune. The conversation led to our sharing descriptions of our occupations, which led to my booking a speaking engagement with his corporation. He had liked my attitude and the way I had handled myself under adverse conditions.

There is nothing quite like making good contacts, if you are prepared to produce when the contacts open doors. In the previous chapter, I said that approximately 75% to 80% of my speaking engagements now come from referrals or recommendations of satisfied clients.

Several years ago, I spoke at a national convention involving associations from the various states. Since then, I have spoken to the related associations in 46 states. That's how contacts work. You should take action to create opportunities and then take good advantage of the opportunities.

You can begin making contacts anywhere. I have made contacts on airplanes, in hotels, while standing in a line at a supermarket or theater and have picked up a speaking engagement in an elevator. At least, the contact was made in an elevator. The follow-up was later. The bottom line here is, create connections; keep your antennae up. Don't pass up chances to meet people, to connect with people, to network with people. Making contacts with people is a skill within itself. It is a skill that can be developed and when developed can reap great rewards.

"T" in A-C-T-I-O-N stands for team-up for togetherness. I covered the concept of teamwork in the previous chapter. Remember the example of the bundle of sticks tied together? Remember how a group of good players on the 1980 U.S. Hockey Team achieved a great accomplishment? Remember how I emphasized that the total of an outstanding team is greater than the sum of its individual parts?

"I" stands for instill an overpowering desire. The vital necessity for desire has been discussed throughout this book. Especially was it spotlighted in the chapter dealing with goals. I have stated it in various ways but let me say again: Success in business, in families, in sports, in school and in all of life is not reserved for the people who are the most talented. It's not reserved for the ones who are graded to have the highest I Q's. It's not reserved for the people who have the greatest gifts at birth. It's not reserved for the people with the best physical appearance or mental equipment. *Success is almost totally dependent on desire, drive and persistence.*

"O" stands for overcome adversity. Again, this subject has been covered throughout the book, but it cannot be over-emphasized. When you overcome adversity, you do not remain at status quo, you become stronger. This is something I constantly tell sports teams.

In football, for example, if my team fumbles the ball inside our own 20 yard line and the other team recovers, we have a chance to grow stronger or weaker. If they go on to score, then we lose from the adversity. However, if we keep them from scoring, we gain from the adversity and they lose. When they don't take advantage of their opportunity it builds us up and tears them down.

The writer/philosopher Horace said, "Adversity has the effect of eliciting talents which in prosperous circumstances would have lain dormant." Winners have to overcome adversity. There is no "if," "and" or "but" about it. You cannot become a true winner unless you can overcome adversity.

"N" stands for Now. Do It Now.

Don't be like the 16 year-old girl who was in her bedroom one evening. She walked by a full-length mirror, saw herself in a certain light and said, "I have got to lose some weight! I couldn't get in my swim suit if I used grease!" So she decided to go on a diet "tomorrow." All of a sudden, she felt great - as if a huge burden had been lifted from her shoulders.

That evening, she had one last splurge - ice cream, cookies, candy. . . When the next morning came, she awoke to the smell of bacon and eggs coming from the kitchen, along with some sweet rolls. So, she decided to postpone her diet until lunch. She never liked what they had in the school cafeteria anyway. Lunch time rolled around, and, lo and behold, they had something she liked - for the first time in three years! So, she decided to postpone her diet, rationalizing, "It's better to start a diet in my own home, anyway." That evening when she walked through the front door, she discovered her mother prepared her very favorite meal plus a chocolate pie with a delicious, high meringue topping! The girl said to herself, "The best time to start my diet would be *tomorrow*."

"Tomorrow"

Tomorrow, the greatest labor-saving device ever invented.

Many goals are never achieved; many dreams never come true; many wins never happen because of "tomorrow." Procrastination - simply putting things off until tomorrow. . .

> which becomes. . . next week,
> which becomes. . . next month,
> which becomes. . . next year,
> which becomes. . . never.

Jump On The Problem

Whenever you have any type of problem, the sooner you attack it with as much energy as possible, the more likely that problem is going to be eliminated. However, the longer you let the problem linger, the more likely the problem is going to grow and get out of hand.

The problem may be a conflict in your office. It could be a certain assignment in school. It may be a sales proposal. It could be an end of the year report. It might be a family problem. Or, it could be another team standing between you and a win.

Keep in mind, when a favored team is playing an underdog, the favored team needs to put the game away as soon as possible. Why? Because the longer the underdog hangs in, the stronger the underdog becomes and the weaker the favored team.

For example, in football, if the score is close at the end of the first quarter, the underdog begins to think, "Hey, they're not so great. We can beat them." Meanwhile, the favored team begins to have some doubts and begins to see the other team as being stronger than they originally thought. The favored team creates a problem for itself, and the longer they wait to take command, the better the chances for an upset.

If you are favored, you need to put the game away in the first quarter. Don't procrastinate. By the time you get around to doing what you should, it may be too late.

On the other hand, if you are the underdog, attack, attack, attack! Do everything in your power to keep the favorites from getting untracked. Keep them off balance. Surprise them. Do what you can do to stall them from playing up to their potential. That's how upsets happen. You can use their procrastination for your good.

Procrastination will destroy teams. Procrastination will destroy businesses. Procrastination will destroy families. Procrastination will keep you from winning!

Why is procrastination almost a chronic disease in our society? Why did a survey taken among 25,000 men and women reveal that procrastination is one of the major causes of failure? Why do people procrastinate? More importantly, why do *you* procrastinate?

Why You Procrastinate

(1) You are not prepared. Maybe you are not prepared mentally, physically, emotionally or spiritually to do what needs to be done. A lack of preparation causes you to doubt what you should do and when you should do it. You may even get the feeling that you are incapable of doing what needs to be done, so you continue to put it off.

(2) You see something as being unpleasant, difficult or boring. You want to push it aside and take care of it later. It just doesn't interest you at the present time. You don't want to fool with it or maybe you want to avoid it altogether. You go out of your way to find something else to do. This is why students spend all night finishing term papers or cramming for exams. This is one reason why salespeople "put off" making calls. This is why so many Americans mail in their income tax returns just before midnight on April 15.

(3) You don't feel the problem is squeaking loudly enough yet. You may see other things that require your immediate attention so you put this one farther down the list. You say, "I've got plenty of time to do this later." People run out of gas using that philosophy. And rather than observing a maintenance program by checking the oil before the squeaking begins, you get into a crisis management program which applies oil to the squeaks. Too late. The damage is done.

(4) You don't have enough time to do it now. So you decide to put it off until you have a larger block of time with which to work. You don't consider doing a little here and a little there, using 15 minutes here and 20 minutes there. You tell yourself, "I'm going to put that aside until when I have a whole afternoon to work on it." Or, "I don't have enough time to really get into it this afternoon, so I'll make plans to do it Saturday morning."

(5) You allow other people to talk you into procrastinating. Perhaps you hope they will talk you out of doing what you want to put off anyway. You allow them to rationalize for you, combining their reasons with yours for why something doesn't need to be done right now. This allows them to help you in setting your goals, making your plans and working your plans. This allows others to determine if you will be a winner or a loser.

These are five major reasons why you may be currently procrastinating. Now, let's look at some techniques to help you overcome such obstacles.

How To Quit Procrastinating

(1) Plan ahead. Make sure you do your homework and are truly prepared for something before you have to face it. From your previous reading in this book, you know that I believe that not being prepared is one of the major causes of failure in any endeavor. The will to win is of little value unless you have the will to prepare. Years ago, Louis Pasteur said, "Chance favors the prepared mind." That is still so very true today. For example, the number one fear in America is caused by lack of preparation. The fear? Public speaking. I frequently hear, "Carl, how can you get up and speak like that? You look like you're really enjoying it. I would be scared to death!"

Well, it's natural to experience some stage fright when speaking. But undue fright usually results when preparation is poor. Knowing you are unprepared and are about to humiliate yourself is enough to give anyone stage fright. Speakers should outline their thoughts, rehearse and practice to the extent that they know every point, every example, every anecdote and every story frontwards and backwards.

A salesperson should know his or her product well and know the competition's products well. Know all about your client and your client's needs. Know essentially the questions the client will have and the objections the client will bring forth. Be prepared to answer the questions and field the objections.

If you are an athlete, know what you are going to do, what your opponent is going to do, and then know what both of you are going to do when you both do what you originally do. (Think about this for a while!)

(2) Make things creative or fun. When things are basically unpleasant, difficult or boring, use your imagination. Remember, attitudes are more important than facts. You might also remember what Roger Staubach said after leading the Dallas Cowboys to the Superbowl Championship: "In business or in football, it takes a lot of unspectacular preparation to produce spectacular results."

At a recent speaking engagement at a large hotel, I went to inspect the ballroom where I was going to speak. I asked the set-up personnel to add a riser to the platform and then I left the room for a few minutes. Upon my return, the riser was in place. And one of the guys was up on it, dancing, while the others clapped in rhythm. Kidding with the dancer, I said, "Hey! It looks like you're having too much fun."

"Man," he replied, "sometimes it gets so boring, we gotta make it fun."

Let's look at some things that could fall into the category of being unpleasant, difficult or boring: (1) mowing the grass, (2) researching a report, (3) lifting weights, (4) paying bills, (5) correcting a child, (6) dealing with an embezzler, (7) walking daily, (8) studying for a test, (9) bathing your dog, (10) preparing a sales graph. You can add additional tasks I'm sure. Whatever the task, though, before you push it aside, consider the consequences of not getting it done.

Before leaving this point, I must say that the way you look at your occupation has much to do with the way you perform your work. If you see a job as a dull chore, it is a dull chore.

I participated in a program in which Dr. Norman Vincent Peale spoke on the subject of enthusiasm. He told how an employer was going to fire a man and Dr. Peale suggested to the employer that he should fire the man *into* the business rather than *out!*

This meant, of course, that the employer should get the man to try enthusiasm. He did, and the employee became an important person in the business. He was fired alright, but it was not *out*. Enthusiasm fired him on to new participation. He became a new personality - successful, happy, creative.

You may say, "My job is dull and has no future." But it could be that you have a dull attitude toward it. Try enthusiasm and watch it change. And see how you change with it.

Enthusiasm changes a job because it changes the job holder. When you apply enthusiasm to the job, the job comes alive with exciting new possibilities. So if you wish for a new job, try to apply enthusiasm to your present one; that will make it new.

(3) Don't wait for the squeak. Look ahead. Make something happen before it happens to you. Write down the things you need to accomplish and the dates by which they need to be accomplished. Then, examine the "hang-on" tasks that have been hanging over your head and making you uncomfortable. Make a list of these "hang-on" tasks.

Compare the two lists you now have. Do you see any over-lapping? Do you see anything that can be eliminated and never really missed? Rearrange the two lists into one, arranging the tasks in order of priority. Set your goals on completing your tasks, determine what you are going to do by certain dates, then get to work. Mix up your tasks according to length when possible. Rather than spending too much time on one thing, arrange to take care of some short-term tasks along with one that requires a greater amount of time. And, this leads us to the fourth suggestion:

(4) Take advantage of small bits of time. Don't concentrate only upon the large segments of time available to you. Look for 15 minutes here and there. Look for longer portions that seem to be wasted. For example, I know that I am able to accomplish a lot of writing, reading, studying and preparing while on airplanes, in airports, in doctors and dentists' offices or anyplace else I have to wait.

A Strategy For Winning was written in Gatlinburg and Memphis, Tennessee; Portland, Oregon; Las Vegas, Nevada; Detroit, Michigan; Dallas, Texas; Columbus, Ohio; New York City, NY; Steamboat Springs, Colorado; Scottsdale, Arizona; Portland, Maine; Tulsa, Oklahoma; Miami, Florida; Washington, D.C.; Atlanta, Georgia; Chicago, Illinois; Olive Branch, Mississippi and various other places around and in-between.

Not long ago, I spoke to a national sales group about time and territory management. Their salespeople seemed to always be behind, playing catch-up. The sales force claimed they just did not have enough time to do all that needed to be done. The real problem, however, was that the salespeople were not using their time wisely.

The salespeople concentrated too heavily upon looking for large portions of time and overlooked blocks of 15 to 20 minutes made available to them. Doing a little at a time, here and there, adds up. An opportunity to set aside an entire afternoon to accomplish something may be quite a while in coming. Waiting for such an opportunity may not allow you to do what needs to be done by the time you need to do it.

Look ahead. Be aware of the amount of time that you are going to have on certain occasions and plan accordingly. Reducing activities to blocks of 15 to 20 minutes allows you to accomplish a large task in small manageable units. Remember, "It's a cinch by the inch."

A common misconception is that time can be saved. But time can only be spent. The problem is spending it wisely, whether it's an hour or five minutes, like spending a dollar or a nickel.

And, we spend time wisely as we spend money wisely, by using a budget. When you budget your money, you may discover you can't buy everything you want right now. When you budget your time, you may discover you can't do everything you want to do right now. So, in both cases, you set priorities. A person who says, " I don't have enough time," is actually saying, "I am spending or budgeting my time poorly."

(5) Be decisive. Practice discipline. There will always be people around who will try to talk you into putting things off. But it is you who have to live with the consequences. View your time with regard, high esteem and value. When necessary, tactfully let people know that you are in command of your time and your decisions.

A customer entered Benjamin Franklin's store once to buy a book. Thinking he could get a better price on the book by speaking to the owner, he insisted on seeing Franklin. Noticing that the price of the book was a dollar and hearing the reason for being interrupted, Franklin quoted the price at $1.25. The surprised customer objected, "Why the clerk said it was just a dollar!"

"True," said Franklin. "And I could better afforded to take a dollar than to have been taken out of my office."

Thinking this was a joke, the customer repeated his inquiry for a cheaper price.

Franklin's reply this time was $1.50.

Franklin was saying what we all should say, "My time is valuable and the more you waste, the more it will cost." It is no wonder that Franklin said, "Do you love life? Then don't squander time, for that is the stuff life is made of."

Don't let people steal your time. Don't let them steal your hopes, dreams and aspirations.

If you need to study for an examination, if you need to go on a diet, if you need to prepare for a presentation, if you need to rest or exercise, if you want to change careers, if you want to spend time with your family, if you want to set higher goals in life, or if you have some other personal decision to make, don't let other people keep you from it.

Expert Advice On Procrastination

In chapter seven, I responded to the question, "What exactly do you do?" by saying that among other things I'm a professional writer, speaker, motivator and leadership consultant. I could have also answered, "I'm an expert on procrastination."

I have been involved in much, have spread myself thin and have procrastinated much. How else do you think I could write so in-depth about the topic? Through experience, study and trial and error, I have fought determinedly not to procrastinate.

In my study and observation, as well as personal experience, I know that many people's lives consist of a bunch of loose ends. They get involved in too much and wind up doing too little in any one area. They have good intentions, but just don't follow through. They procrastinate in getting started, then when finally started, they procrastinate ending or completing the task.

Following are some additional suggestions, some "how-to" hints that have worked for me. These ideas, combined with the previous guidelines I shared with you, should set you well on your way to winning in any endeavor... without delay.

(1) Forgive yourself for all your past failings. Start over right now with a clean slate. Think about what you're going to do rather than what you haven't done.

(2) Promise yourself that you'll give five minutes to something you have been putting off. Getting started on a project is usually the hardest part of it. After you become involved, you will probably spend more than five minutes on it.

(3) Meet your rationalizations head on. Challenge all the reasons you have for not doing something. For example, if you say, "I can't start my diet today because I didn't sleep well last night," then challenge yourself by asking, "What does sleep have to do with a diet?" Meeting your excuses head on will make you realize how flimsy they are.

(4) Set a reward for yourself - maybe a gift or meal or trip to the theater - to be received when you take care of the task you have been putting off. Make sure you follow through on your reward and don't let yourself talk yourself out of it. Always give yourself credit for what you accomplish. This will boost your self-esteem and help you to accomplish more.

(5) Tell some supporting, positive associates about your undertakings. You're more likely to get started on a long, time-consuming project if you share your desire with others. Later, you are more likely to complete it if people ask, "How's it coming?" Tell them about your progress or show them how you're doing and you'll get gratification along the way. Caution: Don't share your goals with negative people or cynics. Share only with those who will support you and affirm you. You don't need discouragement and cynicism.

(6) Don't try to do too much at one time. If you don't allow enough time to complete something, you will have a tendency to stress-out and to run out of patience. Also, be sure you have everything you need in order to do what you need to do. If you have to stop in the middle of something because an essential item is missing, you'll lose your momentum. Get rid of all visible stumbling blocks beforehand.

(7) Project into your future. Consider the consequences if you don't do what needs to be done. Then, imagine the pleasure of the finished project. You can get started and keep yourself going by thinking of the triumph you will experience at the end. See all the benefits that will come your way.

(8) As I have mentioned in previous chapters and already in this chapter, look at the little pieces of the big picture. Procrastinators tend to blow things out of proportion to a point where the task seems unconquerable. Tackle bits and pieces of the task rather than seeing the task as one huge foe you must defeat immediately.

What Are You Waiting For?

Don't be like the man planning to drive his family from New York to California. The car was all packed, everyone was ready, but the man sat motionless behind the wheel. His wife asked, "What are you waiting for?"

He answered, "I'm waiting for all the traffic lights between New York and California to turn green."

Well, you can't wait for all the lights to turn green. You can't wait until all the doors are opened to you. The conditions will never be perfect to do anything. But if you take obstacles one at a time, if you go step by step, light by light, door by door, you will find yourself accomplishing tasks that once seemed impossible.

Henry David Thoreau said:

If one advances confidently in the direction of his dreams, and endeavors to live the life which he has imagined, he will meet with a success unexpected in common hours. . .

If you have built castles in the air, your work need not be lost; that is where they should be. Now put the foundations under them.

To put foundations under your dreams, you must begin. Then, you must continue to study, to grow, to perfect - to become more and more what you have the potential to become.

Closing Thoughts

That great American writer Henry Wadsworth Longfellow left much food for thought for future generations to consume. And one of my favorite morsels from the man is . . .

Great is the art of beginning, but greater is the art of ending.

In other words:

Get into it. . .

Get with it. . .

And get it handled!

Don't mess around with beginning and don't mess around with ending. So many people waste their time and their lives by postponing something and then by dilly-dallying around once they finally *do* begin.

Another great American, champion golfer Sam Sneed, said:

Prayer works, if you know how to putt.

You can't fake it. If you really want to succeed in something, make sure you put in the time and effort needed in order to become a master of what you want to do. The nine principles covered in this book will lead you to the winner's circle if you do your homework to become the best you can become at what you want to accomplish.

YOU CAN BE A WINNER

If you know what you are doing, if you do your homework, if you're prepared. . .

If you believe in what you're doing, if you have a strong commitment, and match your skills, your interests and your desires. . .

If you practice, practice, practice, with both your mind and body, and visualize how you are going to perform. . .

If you relax and quit worrying, and control your emotions instead of letting your emotions control you. . .

If you create opportunities instead of waiting for things to happen. . .

If you will act, take that first step, and never, never, never, never, never give up. . .

You can be a winner!

– CM

INDEX

INDEX

INDEX